To Col.

Thank you for your many years in the Army—

Louis S. Salvers

2006

MARAUDER

MARAUDER

Memoir of a B-26 Pilot in Europe in World War II

Louis S. Rehr

with Carleton R. Rehr

and with a foreword by Trevor J. Allen

McFarland & Company, Inc., Publishers

Jefferson, North Carolina, and London

LIBRARY OF CONGRESS CATALOGUING-IN-PUBLICATION DATA

Rehr, Louis S.
Marauder : memoir of a B-26 pilot in Europe
in World War II / Louis S. Rehr with Carleton R. Rehr ;
and with a foreword by Trevor J. Allen.
p.   cm.
Includes index.

ISBN 0-7864-1664-5 (illustrated case binding : 50# alkaline paper)

1. Rehr, Louis S.   2. Bomber pilots—United States—Biography.
3. Marauder (Bomber)   4. World War, 1939–1945—Aerial operations, American.
5. World War, 1939–1945—Personal narratives, American.
6. United States. Army Air Forces. Bombardment Group, 323rd.
I. Rehr, Carleton R.   II. Title.
D790.R446   2004   940.54'4973'092—dc22   2003018525

British Library cataloguing data are available

Cover photograph: Marauders from the
386th Bomber Group *(National Archives)*

Manufactured in the United States of America

*McFarland & Company, Inc., Publishers
Box 611, Jefferson, North Carolina 28640
www.mcfarlandpub.com*

To those whose efforts have kept alive the heroism,
sacrifices and spirit of the Marauder Men and their aircraft.
Their work stands as a perpetual reminder of the role these men and
their beloved bombers played in liberating the world from tyranny.

Acknowledgments

Lt. Col. Ross E. Harlan. For meticulously preserving in text and photographs the history of the 323rd Bombardment Group and the 456th Bombardment Squadron. In the spirit of the corps, he generously contributed memories and rare photographs of the three years he served with the group and especially the five months he worked alongside me as the squadron's ground executive officer.

Maj. Gen. John O. Moench. For compiling the history of the 323rd Bombardment Group in his book *Marauder Men: An Account of the Martin B-26 Marauder.* His detailed and extensive research enabled me to maintain historical accuracy in this narrative.

Lt. Frank Burgmeier. For his devotion to keeping a war diary during his tour of duty and sharing this invaluable resource with me. His dated entries illuminate details that could have been lost in history or forgotten in memory.

Trevor J. Allen, B-26 historian. For his tireless research on behalf of all of us who seek the truth about the Martin B-26 Marauder at war, the crews who flew these bombers, and the fate of those who never returned.

Jacques Evrard. For friendship that springs from his deep appreciation for all that the men of the 323rd sacrificed while flying missions from Laon-Athies airbase.

Jean-Claude and Beatrice Tassot. For friendship and making it possible for me to sit once more in the left seat of a Martin B-26 Marauder, the beautiful restoration at the Paris Air and Space Museum.

Mark Gatlin, editor. For remembering what it is like to write a first book and caring enough to offer advice.

The Maui Writers Retreat, August 2000. For the writers who provided guidance and encouragement to Carleton during the writing of this book: David Fryxell, editor/

instructor. Jim Alter, Rosemary Dimoff, Nigel Hey, Wanda Lee, Georgina Lindsey, Chris Loos, Arlynn Nellhaus, Marilyn Ribble, Pamela Shandel, Patricia Walters.

Mike Smith. For establishing his website, B26.com, which is dedicated to all B-26 Marauder crews. It has evolved into the leading forum for those seeking information about the men and their aircraft.

Leilani Ng at Colorprints, Inc., Honolulu. For extraordinary professionalism in caring for and reproducing our priceless negatives.

Robert "Sandy" Rehr. For his love and support.

Ernie Pyle. For inspiration.

Lt. Col. William and Col. Kathleen Ingwersen. For the ideal writers' retreat— their beautiful Makaha home.

Contents

PART III : GERMANY

Foreword

by Trevor J. Allen

Growing up in England during World War II, my friends and I saw our skies full of airplanes of all shapes and sizes. Naturally, we each had a favorite. Mine was the Martin B-26 Marauder—perhaps because its superb, streamlined shape seemed so much more beautiful than the others. Since that time, I have spent over 40 years researching the combat history of the B-26 Marauder, including the role this bomber, its crews and ground support played in the winning of, perhaps, the greatest war this world has experienced to date.

In the late 1930's, the United States Army Air Corps recognized that any forthcoming air war would have to be fought both strategically and tactically. The strategic offensive would target vital armament, transportation and oil manufacturing installations deep in enemy territory. Strategic bombers would have to fly long distances and carry the maximum bomb load. The Army Air Corps selected two major aircraft types to carry out these campaigns: the Boeing B-17 and the Consolidated B-24.

To provide support to the armies in the field with the least cost in men and materiel, the tactical campaign focused on closer targets. Preventing the enemy from transporting supplies and reinforcements to the battlefield was essential. The role of the tactical aircraft would be to destroy bridges, railroad yards and tracks, and enemy units on the move. Another important objective was to deny the enemy air superiority by destroying its airfields, radar installations and communications. To carry out this offensive, the Army Air Corps selected three aircraft: the Douglas A-20, the North American B-25, and the Martin B-26 Marauder.

With the attack on Pearl Harbor on December 7, 1941, the only fully equipped and operational Martin B-26 Marauder Group was the 22nd Bombardment Group based at Langley Field, Virginia. All personnel were immediately recalled to base, and the group flew to Hamilton Field, California, where their aircraft were dismantled and loaded on ships headed for the island of Oahu, Hawaii.

1

The crews of the 22nd then island-hopped their reassembled Marauders westward to the Brisbane area of Australia where their squadrons were distributed across several airfields. At the time, no one seemed to know how to use the B-26. Nevertheless, in April 1942, they flew their first combat mission, staging from Australia through Port Moresby on New Guinea. The facilities were poor, and the squadron commanders and pilots were forced to work out their tactics on each succeeding mission until they found the method of approach and attack that favored them.

November 1942 saw the Allied invasion of North Africa with the United States and British armies landing in Morocco and Tunisia. Again the Marauder was called upon to give tactical support to the invading armies by bombing enemy airfields, troop concentrations, supplies and communications.

During November and December of 1942, two other Marauder bombardment groups, the 319th and the 17th, were deployed to North Africa. Their crews ferried the Marauders by way of the South Atlantic route—from South Florida to Brazil to Ascension Island and up the coast of Africa—and were immediately thrown into the battle. The facilities were almost nonexistent, and crews were forced to locate targets using only Michelin tourist maps. Again, as in the South Pacific, these Marauder men were forced to learn tactics through experience. Flying at low altitudes, the 319th and 17th Bomb Groups suffered unacceptable losses. Only when Marauders were allowed to attack their targets at the medium altitudes, between 10,000 and 12,000 feet, did the losses begin to diminish.

With the build up of the strength of the U.S.'s Eighth Air Force in England, several more B-26 Marauder groups were sent to the European Theatre of Operation. In early 1943, the 322nd Bombardment Group arrived and settled into bases at Rougham, Bury St. Edmunds, and Rattlesden. However, the military thinking of the Eighth Air Force planners was that its organization should be a strategic air force equipped solely with the Boeing B-17 and Consolidated B-24 heavy bombers.

The B-26 did not fit into this policy envelope and was placed with 8th Army Air Force Support Command. In spite of command knowing that the B-26s of the North African Air Force were now operating at medium altitudes, the 322nd was ordered to fly its first two missions at low level. The first mission on May 14, 1943, was flown against the heavily defended area of Ijmuiden in Holland. Flying so low that enemy flak gunners were firing down on them, they dropped their bombs. While no planes were lost on this first attempt, many were damaged, and several crewmembers were wounded. Unfortunately, there was no damage to the primary target. Three days later, a second, low level mission to the same target ended in tragedy when 10 out of 11 Marauders were lost to flak and fighters.

The Marauders flew no more missions from England until July of 1943, when the "White Tailed Marauders" of the 323rd Bombardment Group, flying at medium altitude, proved that the Marauder could survive in the hostile environment that enveloped Europe's skies. Finally in October 1943, the four B-26 groups stationed in England—the 322nd, 323rd, 386th and 387th—were transferred to the tactical Ninth Air Force.

With the turn of the year 1943 to 1944, the Marauder had almost vanished from the embattled skies of the South Pacific. Replacing it was the North American B-25

Mitchell, which was deemed more suitable for the needs of that area. However, in the Mediterranean and European Theatres of Operation, the B-26 Marauder had at last achieved recognition as a effective combat weapon, able to attack its targets accurately in spite of intense flak. Operating whenever weather permitted, Marauder crews flew once or even twice daily to hammer targets such as bridges, airfields, V-1 bomb launching sites, radar installations and communications vital to the enemy.

Its rugged construction enabled many pilots to bring their crews home safely, despite severe damage to the aircraft. More often than not, Marauders that belly-landed at home bases were quickly repaired and returned to the fray. However, as the tempo of operations increased, so did the casualties. But even those occurred at a lower rate than the planners predicted, resulting in the lowest casualty loss rate per sortie of any U.S. Army Air Corps aircraft.

Nevertheless, their combat-weary crews suffered. In those early months of 1944, replacements were well below what was required. Airmen had their tours of duty extended from 40 to 65 missions before they had any hope of returning home. An increasing number of men suffered combat fatigue as they continued to fly day after day in the deadly skies over Italy and Europe. The result was the inevitable increase in the losses of experienced men. There was now a desperate need for replacement crews, who finally began to arrive in the combat areas during the spring and summer of 1944.

One of those replacements was an experienced B-26 Marauder pilot, Capt. Louis S. Rehr, who for two years dogged his commanders for a transfer from the training command to combat. In May 1944, he arrived in England after piloting his Marauder along the same 10,000-mile South Atlantic route flown by his predecessors. He and his five-man crew were assigned to the 323rd Bombardment Group, the unit whose leadership proved the Marauder could be a formidable weapon when used as a medium bomber.

The Rehr crew was about to enter into the fiercest battleground ever fought by opposing air forces—a deadly war of attrition and stress fought day after day with crews aware that there was no option of turning back until they completed their full combat tour of 65 missions or the enemy laid down its arms in defeat.

Part I

ENGLAND

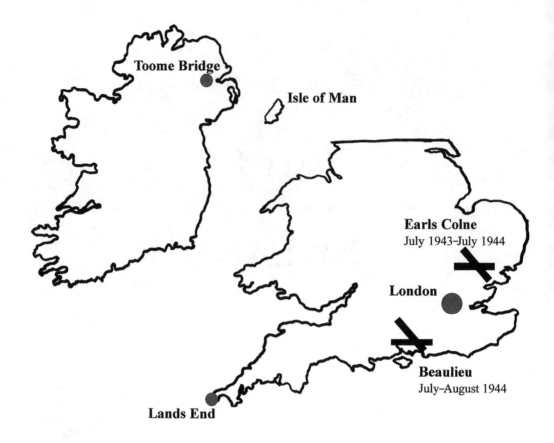

Toome Bridge

Isle of Man

Earls Colne
July 1943–July 1944

London

Beaulieu
July–August 1944

Lands End

Bases in England occupied by the 323rd Bombardment Group, July 1943–August 1944.

1

D-Day and the
White Tailed Marauders

They spent the morning killing the enemy. Their bombing target was a defended area on the French coast south of Calais. This was no railroad bridge or marshalling yard, but a German stronghold—enemy troops dug in behind guns that pointed west across the English Channel. There was no way of telling how many dead and wounded lay beneath the billowing smoke over the target. But the bombs from the B-26 Marauders had walked right through their pillboxes, bunkers and artillery.

At least a dozen 88mm guns protected the area. Nothing unusual these days. For months, the Germans had been stiffening their positions in anticipation of an allied invasion. Fortunately, on this mission, the B-26 Marauders had help from their little friends—strafing P-47s that drove the flak gunners into their holes before the bomb run. By late morning, all 36 Marauders returned to their base in England with only minor flak damage.

That afternoon, June 5, 1944, a few young men from the 323rd Bombardment Group assembled in the situation room. They were lead crews mostly—the pilots, bombardiers and navigators who led formations of bombers to the targets. Some had been up since 0430 hours for that earlier mission to Ambleteuse, which was delayed three hours by stormy weather. Their talk was about the unusual activity in the English Channel. Many more ships floated and steamed off England's coast. Some towed huge, strange floating objects, barges maybe.

As soon as this small group realized that they were the only ones called to the situation room, they knew something big was up. The briefing officer told them that soon—maybe tomorrow—54 Marauders from the 323rd would join streams of aircraft in the skies over England in support of the invasion of France. Their role, along with hundreds of other Marauders from five other groups stationed in England, was to knock hell out of the German coastal defense positions along the Cherbourg Peninsula, just behind a place code-named Utah Beach. Destroy minefields, tank barriers, barbed wire, guns, bunkers and personnel. There wasn't much time to do the job right. They would be among the last bombers in before low flying attack bombers, the A-20s, laid a smoke screen on the beach to protect thousands of Americans coming ashore. Bombs away had to be between 0605 and 0624 hours. At 0630, the landing craft would hit the beach. Leave big holes in the ground so that those guys have a place to duck as they battle their way inland.

In the meantime, the young men in that afternoon briefing were removed from flying status. They were a privileged few sharing one of the greatest secrets of the century. They knew *where* the long awaited invasion would take place. A crash landing or bailout would lead to interrogation by German intelligence. The last order was to go to bed early every night to be fully prepared for the call.

When the briefing was over, no one left the room. So the bombing that morning at Ambleteuse, far north of the invasion beaches, was a distraction. Make the Germans think that when the Allies finally mounted an invasion, they'd be crossing the channel at its narrowest point. For the past few months the group's bombers had been hitting targets up and down the French coast and even further inland near Paris—airfields, ports, bridges, rail yards, and the most difficult targets of all, camouflaged sites from which the Germans planned on launching flying bombs against England. As far as these Marauder men were concerned, this invasion was long overdue.

This would be a story to pass on to their kids and the generations to follow. But the responsibility weighed heavily on them. Thousands of American lives depended on their skill as pilots, bombardiers, and navigators. They spent the rest of the afternoon reviewing flight plans and studying the detailed maps depicting gun emplacements—thick concrete bunkers, mostly buried in the earth within yards of the beach. Here the enemy hunkered down with powerful guns ready to massacre any who dared approach from the sea.

For 1st Lt. Frank Burgmeier, an experienced navigator for the 456th Bombardment Squadron, this mission would be his 39th. His job was to guide a Marauder formation, which could be as many as 54 aircraft, to the target and keep everybody out of harm's way. He rode up front where a copilot usually sat. For him and the crews he flew with, every mission carried extra risk. Flak gunners and enemy fighters targeted lead aircraft. Blow a leader out of the sky, and the followers lost their bombing accuracy.

Burgmeier's focus that afternoon was on the areas where they could expect the heaviest concentrations of antiaircraft fire. He also reviewed enemy airfields near the target where the Germans would launch their fighters. What worried him most was every navigator's nightmare: getting lost and leading the formation through a barrage of flak. It happened a few months ago to a classmate of his. This navigator mistakenly directed his ships over Boulogne, a heavily defended area on the French coast. Three crews in three aircraft never came back. Paralyzed with anguish, he was unable to fly again. Shortly after, they sent him home.

It could happen to anyone. The lousy European weather and the frequent course changes every 15 to 20 seconds to evade the flak complicated the task of navigating with precision. Usually Burgmeier shed his flak jacket and helmet so that he had more mobility to check his flight plans, maps and the terrain below.

With him in the situation room that afternoon were his pilot and his bombardier, both good friends. Capt. J.B. Stirling, the son of a Navy admiral, loved partying as much as flying. In the evenings, he and Burgmeier often headed to a local pub or a movie together. Their bombardier, 1st Lt. William "Hutch" Hutchens, was Burgmeier's singing partner after they'd downed a few scotches at the officers' club.

Outside the situation room, the ground crews worked quickly to paint the black and white stripes on the wings and fuselage of every Marauder. For easy identification, the 323rd's Marauders already sported a wide, white stripe on the tail, which gave them the nickname, "white tailed marauders." The added zebra look was to help the Americans on the ground in France sort out friend from foe.

At 2000 hours, Burgmeier tried to go to sleep. His usual routine was to hit the sack between 2200 hours and midnight after he'd written letters home—most of them to Tedi, his bride of 10 months. They spent only a couple of nights together before he shipped out. How he missed her! But tonight he lay on his cot thinking about his next mission. For the past two weeks, he'd flown 13 box or group leads, sometimes two in one day. All that target bashing was reaching a climax. "Let's get it over with," he thought. The invasion meant the beginning of the end of a dragged out affair that kept him—kept all of them—from their homeland, homes and loved ones.

It might have been 2230 hours when he dozed off. At midnight the wake-up call came. Burgmeier dodged heavy rain and deep puddles to join the hundreds of other men in a smoke-filled Quonset hut. Suddenly the sound of "a-ten-hut" stilled the voices and brought the men to their feet. Col. Wilson R. Wood, the popular base commander from Chico, Texas, made his way down the long aisle to the front. The time was 0115 hours.

With a wide grin, he announced in his Texas drawl. "Boys, this is it."

Months of anticipation erupted into deafening cheers, whistles and applause.

Only six years before, Col. Wood had been a private in the U.S. Army. He joined the Air Corps in 1940, and after earning his wings, quickly rose through the ranks. At 25, this handsome colonel had the respect and trust of enlisted men and officers alike. He had a way of making all of them feel important. "Chico" or the "Old Man" as his men affectionately called him, had flown the first mission of the group in July 1943 and had led many others. Now he was full colonel, a hands-on commander, who watched from the tower as his men returned from their missions. Once he even wielded an axe to free one of his men trapped in a crashed Marauder.

After Col. Wood uncovered the map showing the targets of the day, the weather briefer subdued the crowd by reporting low clouds over the target areas. Then the colonel spoke the words nobody wanted to hear. "For our men to come ashore, these defenses must be knocked out," he said pointing once again to areas with pretty sounding names like Beau Guillot and Madeleine. "We are to go in at any altitude necessary to strike the targets visually and effectively. I repeat, any altitude necessary."

Silent fear washed over the group. Nobody had to say the unpronounceable: Ijmuiden. A year ago, 11 Marauders from another group, the 322nd had orders to

Formations of White Tailed Marauders approaching the coast of France months before D-Day. Note no boat traffic in the Channel (courtesy Ross E. Harlan).

hit a generating plant at Ijmuiden, Holland. They were supposed to come in real low—50 feet off the ground if necessary.

The Marauder was a fast airplane, 250 mph with a 4,000-pound bomb load. But at those altitudes, a fully loaded bomber couldn't maneuver quickly. Nevertheless, on May 17, 1943, 11 Marauders left England headed for Ijmuiden. They had no fighter protection. Heading toward the target, one Marauder developed electrical problems. Its crew dropped out of the formation and headed home. The other 10 ships, all doomed, attempted the ground-hugging mission in the face of concentrated and accurate antiaircraft fire. Explosions from ack-ack severed flight controls and killed the crews. Crash landings behind enemy lines and in the sea killed more crews. Climbing and dropping to evade enemy fire, two aircraft collided then exploded. How a couple of tail gunners survived is a mystery. German fighters—like hawks diving on wounded prey—finished off a disabled aircraft or two. How an engineer and tail gunner escaped seconds before their Marauder disappeared under the waves, then found a life raft floating nearby, is another mystery. Other survivors became prisoners of war.

Ijmuiden, a place of infamy. Word of the disaster even reached the training centers at Del Rio, Dodge City, and Shreveport. Once again, there was talk of ending the use of the B-26 in combat altogether. Since then, the brass figured out that the Marauder was better suited to bomb at altitudes between 10,000 and 12,000 feet. But sometimes it didn't work out that way. Well at least today they could expect fighter protection.

After momentarily revisiting Ijmuiden in their minds, the men in that D-Day briefing came back to the present. To stay there robbed them of the focus they needed for what could be the most important mission of their young lives.

Col. Wood emphasized that thousands of aircraft would be headed for France. "Don't screw up times, make turns or sightsee," he said. Then he added, "Let's kick the hell out of everything Nazi that's left!"

Outside, rain still penetrated the darkness. Under any other circumstances, this would have been a scrubbed mission. Burgmeier piled into a crowded jeep and headed to the line where he joined Stirling and Hutchens and their three gunners. A seventh man, an Army Air Corps photographer, also climbed aboard and joined the gunner in the open waist position at the rear of the plane.

The sky was lightening just a little when the Marauders following Sterling lined up behind his aircraft. Sitting in the right seat, Burgmeier always felt this mixture of fear and pride as he scanned the long line of Marauders following their lead.

As rain pelted the windscreen and streamed off the wings, Stirling pushed the throttles full forward. The time was 0430. At 500 feet, he entered a cloudbank and relied on his instruments to break out of the gloom. Instinctively, Burgmeier tensed. Suddenly they emerged into an opening between the thick layers. There, less than 100 feet away at the eleven o'clock position, a yellow-tailed Marauder from the 386th crossed their path. There had to be others following, significantly raising the odds of a midair collision.

"We're going to die up here," he thought as he tried to slow his breathing. As quickly as the sky opened up, it closed around them. Burgmeier strained his eyes looking for ghostly shapes passing in the fog. They had to be all around. But there was no escape. Nothing to do but keep climbing. A bad start to such an important mission. Then came the blessed breakout.

What glorious chaos surrounded them! Planes, planes, and more planes everywhere. Formation after formation, above, below, beyond. Off in the distance, clouds of dots headed east. Above, contrails streamed across the heavens. Stirling slowly circled looking for the other 11 Marauders in his formation. They were wasting precious time and fuel. At some point, ten planes fell into place behind his Marauder, three from other groups.

As they joined the swarms of aircraft headed over the channel, Stirling led his Marauders lower and lower to stay beneath the cloud cover. He leveled off at 4,000 feet as they neared the Cherbourg Peninsula, where Navy destroyers belched fire from their giant guns at the shore defenses. In response, the Germans fired away from their positions making bombardier Hutchen's job a lot easier.

Never before had Burgmeier flown a mission "on the deck" and been chased by "light flak," intended to destroy low flying invaders. As they neared the target, green and yellow streaks climbed into their path then veered off at the last moment. For

D-Day bombing of Utah Beach by 323rd Bomb Group Marauders (courtesy Ross E. Harlan).

Burgmeier, they were scary and distracting, and he wondered how Hutch kept his concentration up there in the nose as he guided Stirling along the bomb run.

Never before and never again would Burgmeier have a box seat on such a spectacle unfolding beneath him. As they held steady on the bomb run, low level attack planes, the A-20s, laid parallel smoke screens that obscured the white sand beaches and dark, churning waters lapping the shore. Beyond 23,000 men in countless landing craft drew inescapably closer to the shoreline. Over the intercom, tight-throated crew uttered, "God bless 'em!" "God bless 'em!"

Then "bombs away" and the crew experienced another first. As Stirling pulled away, turbulence rocked the Marauder tossing it around like a toy. Concussions from their own bomb blasts violated their airspace. Clearing the target area and heading westward over the Cherbourg Peninsula, Burgmeier checked his watch. 0630 hours. Contracting chicken skin sent a chill through his body.

Over the channel, Hutch crawled out of his compartment in the nose to assure them their bombs walked right through the target. The crew reveled in their success until Stirling told them to hold the applause until they reached the base. They'd been airborne nearly four hours—their longest mission yet—and they were almost out of fuel.

Back at the base, the returning crews were jubilant. Everyone landed safely. There'd been no emergencies calling for red and orange flares. The official debriefing turned into hundreds of informal debriefings as crews shared their experiences. The bombing was good. The troops had landed. No way could the Nazi bastards hold their positions after today. Piece of cake. Burgmeier and the others agreed that the broken gliders and different colored parachutes sprawled over the landscape just meant our troops were everywhere. The enemy was surrounded. The men of the 323rd couldn't wait for the next mission!

The celebrations that day at Earls Colne near Colchester, northeast of London, reflected the group's own limited view. Their efforts had spared the lives of thousands of men landing at Utah Beach that morning. Of the 23,000 who came ashore that day, there were fewer than 200 casualties. But to the east, at a beach called Omaha, a different story unfolded: hundreds of bodies lay dead on the beachhead and floated in the Channel. American casualties numbered 3,000. Something had gone terribly wrong there. But only the generals saw the whole picture, and they were not talking.

2

Fugitive from a Training Center Arrives in England

May 1944

As the Martin B-26 Marauder neared Lands End, the southwestern tip of Great Britain, the sun rose bright orange behind bands of gray clouds. I'd been flying all night after lifting off from Marrakech, Morocco. Most bombers destined for the war in Europe left Marrakech in daylight. Streams of them. I preferred to fly alone.

Below, breaks in the overcast assured me that we were still over the dark waters of the Atlantic. Easing back on the throttles, I descended to 2,000 feet and leveled out directly over a convoy of battleships and destroyer escorts cutting a path through the washboard surface of the sea.

Suddenly the destroyers on both sides peeled off, positioning to fire on our aircraft. Immediately, I lowered the landing gear—the universal signal indicating I intended no harm.

Welcome to England and the war.

My crew—a bombardier, a copilot, three enlisted men—and I were nearing the end of a two-week, 10,000-mile flight that started at Morrison Field, near Palm Beach, Florida, on April 30, 1944. Shortly we'd be touching down at a British airbase on the Cornwall coast. Seated on my right was a navigator I picked up in Marrakech. He just wanted out of that dismal city with its bad liquor and swarming flies. Using the stars to navigate, he kept me tracking along the 10th Meridian— well west of Portugal and Spain, where German fighters could launch an attack. We flew unarmed. Instead of the twelve .50-caliber machine guns used in combat, this Marauder carried long-range fuel tanks stored in the bomb bay.

During the flight, we ran into heavy thunderstorms somewhere off the coast of Portugal. A weather briefer back at Marrakech warned me of the possibility. But the way I figured it, the storms would keep the enemy on the ground.

My crew and I with the bomber I named *Fugitive from a Training Center* wait at Waller Field, Trinidad, for weather to clear at British Guiana, our next stop. Our final destination is Lands End, England. *Left to right:* Capt. Louis Rehr, pilot; Lt. Joseph Searle, copilot; Lt. Victor Jacobs, bombardier/navigator; Sgt. Richard Bailey, engineer/gunner; Staff Sgt. James Alexander, radio/gunner; Sgt. Charles Allen, armorer/gunner.

For a good hour, crescendos of rain pelted the Marauder's skin. During surging updrafts, I throttled back, keeping the speed below 180 mph. A couple of times we climbed so rapidly, that I lowered the landing gear to increase the drag. The Marauder was a rugged aircraft built for combat. But just like any other airplane, it could tear itself apart in the violence of a thunderstorm. I battled downdrafts with more power from the Marauder's 2,000 horsepower engines. Flying in Texas, I'd bumped into enough thunderstorms to know you have to figure them out, get comfortable with their shapes, and then keep the aircraft level.

During this Atlantic storm, bursts of jagged lightning charged the air, creating the mysterious "ball lightning," an orange and blue glow that appeared to roll through the fuselage. This might leave a couple of pinholes in the fuselage, but nothing serious.

After clearing the storms, we saw the lights of coastal villages off to our right, which meant that we had drifted too far east. But the navigator knew his stars and guided us back on course, where we eventually turned right for a direct heading to England's coast.

Within half an hour of leaving the convoy behind, rugged cliffs appeared on the horizon. "Hey look, Lands End!" I called back to the crew in case anybody was still sleeping. Six hours after lifting off from Marrakech, the wheels of the Marauder touched down in England.

I'd been up all night and much of the day before, so I was dead tired when I entered the base headquarters to pick up my orders. I still had one more leg to fly to some Royal Air Force base well north of London. Apparently things were jammed up at bases south of the city. Permanent assignment to a Marauder bombardment group and squadron would come later.

While the Brits arranged for one of their navigators to ride along, I stepped outside and saw ground personnel boarding our plane.

"What's going on?" I asked my copilot, 2nd Lt. Joe Searle.

"They've got orders to take our food," he said.

On board were cans of chicken, beef and fish for emergencies. The flight to England, via the South Atlantic route, carried us thousands of miles over water, South American jungles, African deserts and mountains. An emergency or mechanical problem could leave a crew stranded for weeks.

Only once did we come close to breaking out the canned goods. My bombardier, 1st Lt. Victor "Jake" Jacobs, dared me to make an unauthorized stop at Tindouf, Algeria, during the 1,300-mile leg between Dakkar, Senegal, and Marrakech, Morocco. There was a gravel strip at Tindouf, but orders were to use it only for emergencies. Jake was all fired up about visiting a French Foreign Legion outpost that he had seen in the movie *Beau Geste*. He was sure we'd find Arab women there performing a candle dance. But nobody was quite sure what that was. I imagined us sitting in a dark bar surrounded by strange smells and sounds.

"Ok, we'll stop," I said. "Just remember those slides we saw back in Florida." Guys heading overseas were required to sit through pictures showing various stages of gonorrhea, syphilis and elephantiasis.

The Tindouf airfield was dismal. A run-down hangar that served as a repair shop sat adjacent to small wooden operations building. There was nothing else around but desert. After landing and parking by an abandoned B-24 stripped of its four propellers, I entered operations and asked the base captain for transportation to town and back again.

"The only vehicle around here is that half-track," he said pointing to an armored personnel carrier near the operations building. "It's for my use only. If you're planning on parking for long, there is no place to stay."

From his chilly reception, it was obvious he didn't want to be bothered with us. "We'll skip the entertainment," I said turning to Jake.

"Searle, crank her up." We still had the formidable Atlas Mountains to cross, and I wasn't going to hang around here anymore. By the time everybody was back on board, copilot Searle had the left engine fired up and running smoothly. But when he attempted to engage the right starter, the engine wouldn't budge.

"It's a problem with the electric starter," said Searle, who had been an aircraft mechanic before entering cadet training. A replacement part could take days to reach us. We were going to be stuck in this miserable desert outpost sleeping in the aircraft and living off the canned goods.

Fortunately, a sergeant came out of the repair shop carrying a long rope, which he wrapped around the hub of the propeller. He then attached the other end to the half-track. By stepping on the accelerator and pulling the rope, he spun the 2,000-hp engine so fast, it turned over immediately, like starting an outboard motor. I had the feeling the good sergeant had done this before. Stuck out here, I guess you had

During the winter months, pilots ferried military aircraft to North Africa and Europe via the South Atlantic route. Leaving Morrison Field in West Palm Beach on April 30, 1944, I flew my Marauder *Fugitive from a Training Center* over water, jungles, mountains and deserts before reaching Lands End, England. My brief stop in Tindouf, Algeria, was unauthorized.

to be creative. Cheering and waving our goodbyes and thanks, we roared down the gravel strip, stirring up a great cloud of dust before lifting off and heading north.

Now that we made it to England, the Brits were welcome to our food. There were severe food shortages, and our canned stuff tasted better than the usual staple—stringy, dried "bully beef." Not until later did I discover the plane's binoculars were missing. I didn't see how they'd be useful anyway.

At mid-morning we left Lands End. On instructions from an R.A.F. naviga-tor sitting in the right seat, I leveled off at 3,000 feet. After nearly three years of looking down on the dusty landscapes in Texas and Kansas, I had forgotten how many shades and patterns of green the natural world offered—clumps of dark woods and groves, emerald pastures dotted with cattle, yellow green fields with their per-fect rows of sprouting crops. On such a day, it was easy to forget there was a war. But not for long.

Below, formations of military gliders—with wings nearly as long as the C-47 tugs they flew behind—practiced landings. For a few seconds after release, these gawky birds appeared to hang motionless before aiming for some ubiquitous triangle of an airfield. Long lines of olive drab military jeeps, armored personnel carriers, and trucks—mainly heading south toward the English Channel—motored along the roadways. There was little other traffic. As we neared London, giant, gray balloons swayed in the breeze. Beneath these barrage balloons hung heavy cables intended to snare low-flying enemy aircraft that threatened strategic facilities.

The R.A.F. base where our journey ended had many British and American warplanes scattered around. But the four-engined British bomber, the Lancaster, dominated the scene. Come nightfall, their crews boarded these snub-nosed giants and headed for bombing missions deep into France and Germany. They were the heavies, flying at frigid altitudes above 20,000 feet. In contrast, the Marauder, with its torpedo-shaped fuselage and shorter wings, was a medium bomber—a sleek, mean looking warplane intended for shorter and lower bombing runs.

Back in the states, the B-26 Marauder turned heads, partly because of its rep-utation as a "widow maker" and "winged coffin." It was a fast, unforgiving bomber that required experienced pilots at the controls. But shortly after it rolled off the production line, too many low-time instructors and trainees—some with no twin-engined experience—ended up crashing and dying in the Marauder. At Macdill Field in Tampa, Florida, a base where crews trained together before heading over-seas, the Marauder crashed an average of once a week. Yet it gained a reputation for "one a day in Tampa Bay," and many pilots refused to fly it. Adding to the training problems were design flaws and poorly trained mechanics—byproducts of the rush to keep up with wartime needs. In 1942, a powerful senator named Harry Truman called for its permanent grounding. But the combat pilots, supported by Brig. Gen. Jimmy Doolittle, stood by this bomber, praising its maneuverability, significant firepower, and ability to carry heavy bomb loads.

I volunteered to instruct in the Marauder in February 1943. More than any-thing else, I wanted to be a combat pilot. Flying a real warplane like the Marauder brought me one step closer to receiving an assignment to a combat unit overseas—a chance to escape the training command, where I'd been stuck since earning my wings from Kelly Field, San Antonio, Texas, exactly one year before.

When the United States entered the war against Germany and Japan in Decem-ber 1941, I was in the second phase of Army Air Corps cadet training. Earning our pilot's wings took on even more importance because most of us wanted to be heroes for our country, families and friends. Encouraging us was the genuine patriotism among Americans. As I drove my Mercury convertible along the dusty four-lane streets of West Texas towns, enthusiastic citizens cheered and waved at the sight of my uniform. I felt proud to be a part of the war effort.

But the Army Air Corps had other ideas about how the majority of my cadet class should serve: as instructors in training commands scattered throughout the country. At graduation, only about a third of the class received assignments to single-engine pursuit planes, fighter aircraft such as the P-39 and P-40, a sure ticket into combat. This group included my two best friends, former classmates at Washington and Lee University.

Bill Dabney from Lynchburg, Virginia, with his sandy blond hair and blue eyes, could have been a poster boy for the Army Air Corps. When we frequented bars around our training bases, he was the one the women noticed first. But outside of flying, there was only one love in his life, a Lynchburg, Virginia, girl named Kitty Spruce, whom he married on April 4, 1942, shortly before shipping overseas.

Bob Boyce, from Chillicothe, Ohio, was a natural leader. At Washington and Lee University, where the Army Air Corps recruited the three of us, he was captain of the swim team and president of the Sigma Alpha Epsilon fraternity. Boyce was a serious guy in manner and speech, somebody you could trust to do the job right the first time. At the university, the three of us knew each other only casually. But the camaraderie of cadet training and a few raucous off-base parties cemented our friendships.

Their orders were to report to Orlando Air Base for checkout in the P-40. I remained behind, stuck there at Kelly Field as an advanced flight instructor. I could barely hide my disappointment as we said our good lucks and good-byes. But there was no arguing with the Army Air Corps. Their attitude was, "You guys are all pilots. You've got your wings, and you can fly anything we assign."

My love of airplanes and flying overcame the frustration, and I made the most of training advanced cadets in the BC-1 and AT-6 aircraft. After a day of formation flying and rat-racing among the cloud canyons, the other instructors and I played golf at Fort Sam Houston and mingled with restless wartime women in San Antonio's bars. Late into the evening we argued endlessly over the translation and real meaning of Antoine de Saint-Exupéry's *Night Flight* and *Flight to Arras*. The world of fiction was more engaging than the distant battles in the Pacific and Europe.

But not for long. Within two months of graduation, word arrived that Boyce had been killed in a training accident. Somebody in Florida sent me an article headlined "Pursuit Ship, Bomber Hit: Seven Killed." Flying a P-40, Boyce collided with the B-17 bomber during strafing exercises. The burning bomber dropped into a Florida orange grove. Boyce's charred fighter ended up two miles away. Seven lives incinerated in one violent moment. Shocked, my first reaction was to blame him. My friend, a pilot with fewer than 300 hours, must have miscalculated or lost control. But he was a good pilot. How could he let this happen? Laying blame on someone was how I coped. Public weeping didn't happen. This was war. Killed in training, killed in action, missing in action—casualties happened every day. Those of us who remembered 2nd Lt. Robert Boyce gathered for a long evening of drinking. With moist eyes, we cursed the war then carried on.

After six months in San Antonio, I transferred to the farmland of Waco, Texas, to give advanced students twin engine training in AT-9s and AT-10s. At that time, I received a letter from Bill Dabney, my other Washington & Lee friend. He ended up in England flying Spitfires with the 308th Fighter Squadron, 31st Fighter Group. Dabney was one of those guys who was not afraid to share his feelings. He began by thanking me for the wedding gift I had sent to him and Kitty. He wished to hell that I could be there with him flying those "damned fine Spitifires." He said he was gaining confidence in his flying and even participated in a demonstration for the king and queen of England.

But the odds against his survival as a fighter pilot in Europe's hostile skies must have weighed on his mind. "So much has happened since we were last together that I'd sure like to get around the old beer table and thrash it all out," he wrote. "And if and when I get back, that's what we'll do. I miss the bunch a hell of a lot and sure wish we were together." He asked me to look up Joe Bankhead, his instructor at Kelly. "Tell him I'll come back there some time and just rat race the fool out of him. If a Jerry doesn't get me first," he wrote. He ended with "sincere hopes we can get together some day." His postscript was an emphatic, "Be sure and write by damn. Willie."

At the time, I probably did not focus on the ominous "ifs" and "sincere hopes" but rather the memories of "the old beer table" and rat racing in the Texas skies. Shortly after, I knew his "some day" would never come. Within a month of writing that letter, on August 19, 1942, his Spitfire was one of 107 British aircraft lost during the land, sea and air assault at Dieppe, France. I had difficulty imagining and accepting his death until Kitty sent me his obituary. The Lynchburg paper included a photo taken at Kelly Field as he stood proudly in front of an AT-6, the advanced trainer.

Privately, I reviewed more personal photos of a weekend of partying that I spent with Dabney, Boyce and a few other cadets before the war started. This was during basic training at San Angelo, Texas. A whole crew of us piled into cars and headed for a Mexican border town, Piedras Negras. There, the Silver Dollar saloon served some vile red whiskey the Mexicans called bourbon. After dinner and a lot of drinking, we rolled back over the border to the Eagle Pass Hotel, where Dabney and I started a drinking contest, which I had the dubious distinction of winning. We were just kids—cocksure Army Air Corps cadets, who within weeks would be studying a map of the Pacific trying to locate a place called Pearl Harbor.

Briefly, I wondered if I had the guts to take on the enemy in aerial combat. But guts had little to do with Boyce's and Dabney's deaths. I blamed the Army Air Corps for sending them into something much bigger than anything they'd trained for. I was the lucky one, given the chance to develop my flying skills through instructing. But it took me a while to accept that truth.

The deaths of my two good friends did not discourage me from keeping an eye open for opportunities to join a combat unit. One day, I saw a notice asking for five volunteers to instruct in the Marauder at a base in Del Rio, Texas. Several of us Waco instructors—but not all, especially those with wives—jumped at the opportunity.

We were seasoned instructors with at least 1,000 hours of flying time in both single and twin-engine aircraft. That experience paid off as we quickly mastered flying the Marauder with its faster landing speeds and higher stall speeds. Skilled instructors taught us, including Captain Vincent "Squeek" Burnett, a former air show and military test pilot. Burnett was Brig. Gen. Doolittle's trusted technical advisor, hand-picked by his boss to demonstrate to transition instructors and new pilots those maneuvers that rumor said could not be done in a Marauder: low level turns, single engine operations, including turning into the dead engine, and recovery from unusual attitudes. To look at his slight frame, you would not think he was such a hot shot. His shoulders sloped a good 45 degrees, pulled south by extraordinarily long arms. His demonstration flights and an evening spent drinking and listening to his ribald humor at Ma Crosby's Bar and Grill across the Rio Grande in Mexico made us more comfortable with teaching these techniques. But as much as we enjoyed watching him dance around the airport at low levels, we practiced these maneuvers with lots of altitude.

Still, the Marauder was an aircraft that suffered no fools. Crashes, not always fatal, occurred every week at Del Rio—sometimes because of engine problems, but more often because trainees approached the runway too slowly, that is less than 140 mph. After one of these crashes, a wing panel split open on impact. There, painted on the right spar was the prophecy of some factory worker, "In this plane 5 men will die." Fortunately, that didn't happen—this time anyway. Then there was the wag who found a sign along a Texas highway and planted it at the end of a runway. It said, "Barbecue ribs 1,000 feet." Black humor thrives in wartime.

Every now and then the Marauder held a few surprises even for us instructors. While at Del Rio, new longer winged models manufactured in a Martin factory in Omaha arrived at the field. This design enabled the aircraft to lift off more quickly and carry heavier loads. But the engineers forgot to lengthen the stall strips on the leading edge of the wings. Located close to the fuselage, these pencil shaped additions were intended to give pilots adequate warning of the imminent stall, especially on landing. Manufacturing screw-ups like this were not unusual. Unfortunately, a relatively inexperienced West Pointer who had been rushed into the role of Marauder instructor ended up spinning one of these new models straight into the ground from 10,000 feet taking the student and four crewmembers with him.

He was supposed to be demonstrating stall recovery, which was always done with plenty of altitude. But something had gone wrong. By playing with these longer winged Marauders, several of us instructors concluded that as a result of inadequate stall strips, stalls broke with little warning and required immediate attention. Subsequently, these models went back to the factory for a modification.

Flying the Marauder only heightened my desire to be sent overseas. Every month, I sent my commanders a letter requesting assignment to a tactical unit. After repeated denials, they transferred me to another Marauder training center at Dodge City, Kansas, and promoted me to captain.

Finally in January 1944, three instructor buddies and I received orders to head to transitional combat training at Barksdale Field in Shreveport, Louisiana, where combat crews assembled and practiced together. After a year of Marauder instruction, we all had at least 1,000 hours in this bomber. The experience couldn't guarantee survival, but it steeled us with an added measure of confidence.

SATURDAY, MARCH 4, 1944   THREE

Barksdale Bombers Plunge Deep Into Bossier Parish Fields

Training accidents took the lives of many airmen. These photographs published in the March 4, 1944, edition of *The Shreveport Times*, show the wreckage from two Marauders that collided shortly after I arrived at Barksdale Field for transitional training. It was the second midair in less than a month. Reprinted with permission of *The Shreveport Times*.

I sent my dad a Western Union telegraph dated January 19, 1944, that announced the good news: "TWO YEARS IS A LONG TIME TO WAIT BUT MY NEW ADDRESS IS THIRD AIR FORCE BARKSDALE FLD REPLACEMENT DEPOT BARKSDALE FLD LA—LOUIS."

In late February, just days before I arrived at Barksdale, there was a midair collision between two Marauders during training exercises. Twelve crewmembers perished. Shortly after on March 3, another mid-air collision left two more crushed and burning Marauders lying in fields eight miles north of Shreveport. Twelve more airmen's names were posted as killed in training. But the grieving took place far from Barksdale, where the losses were impersonal. Nobody called a halt to the training to evaluate the situation. This was wartime, and training accidents were inevitable, if not here then elsewhere.

And as luck would have it, my crew included a highly skilled bombardier-navigator, 1st Lt. Victor E. Jacobs, from Anaconda, Montana. Like me, Jake was in his mid 20's—old compared to the right-out-of-high school types we flew with. But somehow he was more mature than I was. His deep voice and strong laugh projected confidence. A trim six feet, he always appeared perfectly groomed—from his dark, wavy hair that flowed from a slight widow's peak in the center of his high forehead to his meticulously creased and tailored uniforms. Yet, beneath thick, dark eyebrows, his sensitive eyes suggested some elusive vulnerability. Before entering the service in July 1942, he'd managed an F.W. Woolworth store in Anaconda where Marie Jacobs, a single mother raised him. Careful with money, he probably sent some home in the frequent letters he wrote to his mother and a sister. I had a feeling he wanted to be a hero for his family.

He, too, was a former instructor, most recently at Kirtland Field in Albuquerque, New Mexico. Jake was an expert with the Norden bombsight, a new and highly advanced computer-like instrument developed for bombing accuracy. We respected each other immediately. During our training exercises at Barksdale, we learned to trust each other's ability to do the job with extraordinary skill and harmony. Jake and I became a team with two objectives: hit the target with precision and stay alive.

After six weeks of training together at Barksdale, Jake, copilot Searle, three enlisted men—an engineer, Sgt. Richard P. Bailey from somewhere in New England; a radio operator, Staff Sgt. James B. Alexander from Middletown, Rhode Island; and a tail gunner, Sgt. Charles M. Allen from Daly City, California—and I boarded a troop train to Savannah, Georgia. There, we picked up a brand new stripped down version of a Marauder, designated as an AT-23, which was destined for training replacement crews overseas. I was so happy to be heading to combat that I named it *Fugitive from a Training Center*. It didn't matter that it lacked the ring of other Marauder names like *Little Lulu* or *Weary Willie*. But creating the nose art for *Fugitive* really stretched the talents of the two Florida women who were hired to do the job. Oddly, they painted a picture of a pilot with angel wings and a halo. He carried a book and looked as it he were marching off to heaven. I can't explain what the picture had to do with the words that encircled it. But afterwards, the name, *Fugitive from a Training Center*, drew the attention of other pilots, who understood the joke—Marauder instructors preferred overseas duty where they didn't have to fly as often, and the aircraft were newer.

Now all of us stood on the ramp of a Lancaster base somewhere north of London. *Fugitive* ended up with the 322nd Bombardment Group, where the brass decided to use it for ferrying each other around. On July 3, some officers took off for holiday in Northern Ireland. Typical European weather—rain and poor visibility—forced them lower and lower until they hit a mountain on the Isle of Man in the Irish Sea. All perished.

Jake, Searle and I carried our duffel bags into one of the officers' barracks. Although there was a room full of metal cots, we were the only guests that night. It wouldn't have mattered because I fell asleep as soon as I lay down. Sometime during the night, Jake shook me. "Lou, you gotta see this," he said. Outside, the Lancasters with their crews of seven were returning from a night raid. You could see the muffled glow of their exhausts as their pilots guided them on the final approach. Overhead, some fired red flares to let everybody know they were shot up badly and may have had wounded on board. Orange flares requested priority landing because of some damage to the plane, but no wounded on board. Over enemy territory, these heavies were fair game, not only for the flak gunners with their 88mm cannons, but for the German night fighters. Witnessing these landings was my first taste of the real war. But frankly I was too tired to comprehend the seriousness of the situation.

The following day, we joined other newly arrived crews in a base theater to see a film called *Welcome to Britain* starring Burgess Meredith. One of the scenes featured comedian Bob Hope, who was instructing us in the coins of the realm. With the timing and phrasing of a master joke teller, he held up a large white bill worth around $20. It looked more like something you would throw away, so he concluded by reminding us "not to mistake this for toilet paper." His humor brought down the house.

The public relations folks also handed out a little booklet called *A Short Guide to Great Britain* to make sure we did not alienate our British hosts by complaining about their lukewarm beer, cold boiled potatoes, and bad tasting English cigarettes.

For the next few of days, we stayed close to the base while somebody worked out the paperwork for our transfer for more training in Northern Ireland. Jake tended to go his own way. But copilot Searle and I frequented the local pubs where we drank lukewarm beer and probably ate cold boiled potatoes. 2nd Lt. Joe Searle was a real likeable 21 year old from Vera, Oklahoma. After our arrival in England, he asked Jake to shave most of his head, except near the top where he left a shadow of growth out of which sprouted a tuft of dark hair. You might call it a modified Mohican.

Searle had been in the service longer than any of us. He joined the Army Air Corps in March 1940 right out of high school and trained as an aircraft mechanic. Eventually, he passed an equivalency test for two years of college so he could enter pilot training. When he joined my crew at Barksdale Field, he was fresh out of an advanced school in Arkansas, where he trained on twin-engine aircraft, but not Marauders. He was married to a Georgia girl from the Savannah area named Vera, who worked as a welder in a Savannah shipyard after we headed overseas.

He probably had fewer than 300 hours flying time, which was typical of the copilots the Army Air Corps rushed into combat. But he was eager to learn how to handle the Marauder, and I took advantage of every opportunity to turn him into a first rate pilot. Once during the long flight to England, I sat in the right seat so he could make the landing at Belém, Brazil, near the mouth of the Amazon River. In South America, equatorial fronts reduced the visibility and kept things wet including the runways. Hydroplaning on landing was a potential hazard that could lead to a skid and a broken plane. As soon as he touched down on the watery surface, his rudder action was too slow. Then he hit the brakes causing the nose of the plane to swing left. "No brakes!" I yelled. He responded instantly. My feet pumped the rudders, fast and hard to straighten us out. I had no brakes on my side. The last thing anyone wanted was to end up in a ditch with a bent ship, stuck for weeks in that humid jungle town.

Here in England, Searle and I enjoyed the boisterous pub scene around the base.

All types of military men crowded around smoky bars and oak tables. All the talk was about the upcoming showdown with the Germans. The long awaited invasion of the French coast was imminent. Nobody knew when or where. But everybody was certain something big was going to happen—soon. Tons of men and equipment converged on England. The joke was that if any more men and artillery arrived, the island would sink. Then there were the reporters who had been visiting bases and flying with crews all over England for the last month. Their presence was a sure sign something big was about to happen. The excitement generated camaraderie, and I felt proud to be joining the effort. My crew and I still had a couple more weeks of

"Two Haids." Lt. Joe Searle (*right*) from Vera, OK, shaved his head when he arrived in England. I check out the new cut (my nickname was "Head") as we sit atop *Weary Willie Jr.* Earls Colne, England (courtesy Joe Searle).

training in Northern Ireland before we could join a combat group. But we were here now. There would be plenty of action once the troops landed in France.

The anticipation energized everyone. Around the base, even the British enlisted men marched with extra enthusiasm as they sang,

> Cats on the rooftops
> Cats on the tiles
> Cats with syphilis
> Cats with piles
> Cats with their assholes wreathed in smiles
> As they revel in the joys of copulation.

Tail gunner S/Sgt. Kermit Pruitt (*left*) helps war correspondent Ernie Pyle into his Mae West before he flew with this crew from the 456th Bomb Group, April 1944. Pyle recalls this flight in the article "The Flying Wedge." *Continuing from left:* S/Sgt. John Siebert, Lt. Jack Arnold, Capt. William Collins, S/Sgt. Eugene Gaines (courtesy Ross E. Harlan).

For some reason, that one stuck with me.

Within a couple of days of our arrival in England, the crew and I took a train to Liverpool, where we picked up a ferry for transport across the Irish Sea to Belfast, Northern Ireland. The rough seas made the trip miserable. It was hard to sit, hard to walk, hard to stay dry. The Irish Sea was living up to its reputation as a mean stretch of water. I didn't get sick because I stayed on deck in the fresh air.

Our final destination was the 3rd Combat Crew Replacement Center at Toome Bridge, west of Belfast. There to greet me was Captain Chester "Spike" Gist. He and I'd shared the bachelors' officers quarters in Dodge City with a couple of other Marauder instructors, who like Gist and me just wanted out of the training command. Gist's passions were flying and women. When it came to flying the Marauder, he was a good as they come. But he didn't have much patience with guys who wrecked airplanes or killed themselves in training. "Cubbies, Lou, just cubbies," he'd say with no remorse. And when it came to women, he really knew how to charm them. There was something about Gist they just loved—maybe because he was always such a happy guy with laughing eyes and an easy-going style.

Dodge City Marauder instructors gather around their barracks bar. In early 1944, four of these men received orders to join a combat unit. Of the four sent overseas, only I survived. *Left to right:* me, Bob Farrell (shot down over Germany), Bob Browning (shot down over Italy), Jack Moore, Chester Gist (killed while hitching a ride home in a B-25 that crashed on an approach), and Barney Barnes.

At Dodge City, those of us who shared the BOQ drank too much, shot pool and frequently entertained women. At one end of our BOQ, we built a bar out of sturdy 2 × 8s and hung trophies like propeller pieces behind it. Signatures of friends and a few drawings adorned the front, which was painted white. Here we drank mostly beer and sang songs about the Marauder with lyrics like

> Oh it was sad
> Yes it was sad
> It was sad when that 26 went down
> Many instructors lost their lives
> Many students burned alive.
> It was sad when that 26 went down.

Another favorite went like this.

The Marauder's a very fine aircraft
Constructed of rivets and tin,
Top speed well over three hundred
Especially when you're in a spin
Oh, why did I join the Air Corps?
Mother, dear Mother knew best.
Here I lie 'neath the wreckage,
Marauder all over my chest.

When the drinking light was on, the women showed up. Gist brought around the local talent. But mainly our female visitors were five of the 12 Women's Air Service Pilots or WASP who were training at Dodge City. These particular women were tall and strongly built. When they completed their training, their primary jobs were to ferry aircraft across the country and tow targets for antiaircraft trainees firing artillery from the ground. These WASP trained to fly every ship in the fleet, and their presence really cheered things up.

The last time Gist and I were together was in the officers club at Borinquén Field, a large military base in western Puerto Rico, where we relaxed over rum and coke and talked about our final destinations. Like all other bomber crews leaving Florida, we weren't allowed to open the secret orders until an hour out of Morrison Field, somewhere over the Caribbean. They could have sent us to North Africa, but with the imminent invasion of France, they needed more crews in England.

I don't know how Gist arrived at Toome Bridge ahead of me, but we were happy to see each other. He couldn't wait to tell me the news. "Hey Lou, we're headed for the 323rd," he said. The 323rd Bombardment Group was the second oldest Marauder group in England. They were based at Earls Colne, northeast of London, and according to Gist had a lot of high mission men who just wanted to go home.

It happened that Gist was good friends with the base commander here at Toome Bridge. This guy was responsible for assigning crews to different bombardment groups around England. If we'd been placed with a newer unit populated with West Pointers, we might have remained captains for the rest of the war and never be given lead positions. Now that we were overseas, our goal was to move up in rank and lead missions. The truth was that every group was short handed at the time. Experienced new talent was welcome everywhere.

Training at Toome Bridge focused on survival techniques in case we were shot down over France, Holland, Belgium or Germany. Survival meant evading the enemy and escaping. Our instructors issued us an elaborate silk scarf, really a map, to carry on missions. Printed on one side were Holland, Belgium, northeast France, west and central Germany. On the other side were the borders of southeast France, southwest Germany, Switzerland, and Belgium. Roads, railways, canals, former and present frontiers, woods, orchards, forts, churches—they were all there, folded into a neat square. I carried it in my chest pocket on every mission. I never knew anyone who actually used it. But I appreciated having it just in case.

We were even taught some French idioms such as "Où est la frontière espagnole?" I don't know what would have happened if we ended up in the hands of the Spanish. But apparently our chances of survival were better than if we remained in German

These five Women Air Service Pilots (WASP) trained to fly the Marauder at Dodge City. They were good bar friends, who could fly everything in the fleet. *Left to right:* Martha Smith, Shirley Slade, Sandy Sanford, Lyn Fletcher, Lib Gardner.

occupied France. Then they gave us a fake passport with our photo taken in civilian clothes—the same outfit for everybody. It didn't take a bright German to figure out that scheme.

We had lectures on protecting ourselves against poisonous gases. One morning while walking through a ravine to get the mess hall, we found ourselves surrounded by noxious clouds of something resembling mustard gas, an early form of napalm that burned and scared the skin and lungs. They probably didn't use the real stuff, but we had to hold our breath to run up the other side. Apparently intelligence reports indicated that the Germans were preparing to use gas as they did in World War I, especially on invasion forces. If they carried out the threat, the U.S. had its own supply of mustard gas bombs ready.

We had classes in recognizing plastic explosives with barometric triggers that could be planted in airplanes by spies. Ground crews were to look for these during preflights. One afternoon, they even had some trigger happy officer—who seemed to take great pleasure in firing different weapons over our heads—teach us to recognize guns by their sounds.

We did a lot of flying too, and I continued to train Searle. One day, I sat in the right seat so he could practice taking off. The taxiways at Toome Bridge were narrow, with soft shoulders on either side. While taxing, he began some gentle S turns. I figured he knew he did not have much room. But he didn't. Before I could yell, "Stop!" the left wheel was in the mud. It would take a while for ground crews to jack this one up and free it. Behind us a whole line of Marauders had to wait because there was no place for them to turn around.

Searle was apologetic, but I told him not to worry about it. In wartime, my philosophy was "It's nobody's money," which I said to make him feel better. It took at least half an hour to get things moving again.

A couple of days into the training, Gist ended up in a local hospital with something he'd picked up in Shreveport. Like a lot of guys headed off to war, he got carried away during those final weeks in the states. Shreveport was a party town. The bars were always crowded with young men testing their life force and women living on the edge.

Gist wasn't missing much while he was in the hospital. It seemed like we had lots of free time, so Jake and I bought bicycles. Bikes were readily available in Northern Ireland, unlike England, where they were a scarce commodity because so many were needed by the military for getting around the bases. Ours had skinny tires on a simple metal frame and an open chain that snagged the right pant leg if we did not roll it up. The handlebars came equipped with handbrakes and a ringer.

Jake and I enjoyed peddling around the Irish countryside. We visited Gist in the hospital, but mainly, we were looking for something that tasted like real food. Not the powdered eggs and oatmeal served in the mess. We stopped at some of the timbered and stone farmhouses and offered to exchange American dollars for a steak and eggs breakfast. I don't know if they were allowed to take our currency, but no one ever turned us down. This way, we enjoyed wonderful farmstyle meals seated at large kitchen tables. One strict order we did not violate was getting close to the border of the Republic of Ireland, just south of us. This country had declared itself neutral and was off limits to all military.

One Tuesday in early June, I was flying the Marauder over the Irish Sea so my gunners could practice shooting at floating targets. We were probably at 500 feet over the waves. There was another pilot up front with me. I asked him to take over while I tried my hand at firing the .50-caliber gun from the waist gunner's position. I'd done this before back at Shreveport, but I just wanted to play the game.

I was still firing away while the pilot flew low circles around the target—closer than I wanted to be to the water—when the word came over the intercom. At 0930 hours, the base radioed the news. The invasion of France was on! "Son of a bitch, we missed it," I said returning to the cockpit. I wanted to get back to the base at Toome Bridge immediately. Once on the ground, everyone around us cheered and waited for more news over the radio. According to monitored German broadcasts, troops came ashore between Cherbourg and Le Havre on France's northern coast. Well, what a surprise for Hitler! That was a long stretch of water. There was no news about casualties from either side. I knew terrible things had to be going on, but we might as well have been back in the states for all the information we got that day. Everybody wanted to stay tuned, so training flights were cancelled on that day, June 6, 1944.

While everyone stood around waiting for news, I told my crew to pack up their things, including the bikes, and be ready to move out quickly. Then I headed straight to operations to make sure the Rehr crew was at the top of the list of men to be sent back to England. If we could get to Earls Colne, we'd know more. For sure those guys must have had a piece of the action.

3

D-Day Plus 24,
Earls Colne, England

June 1944

On June 6, I hoped to get out of Toome Bridge immediately. But my crew and I had to wait around one more day for transport to Earls Colne. The invasion had jammed up the system. With so much equipment needed in England, it was difficult to coordinate the logistics. But I was impatient. I kept thinking Jake and I are going to miss this. Our troops will blast right through, and the war in Europe will end. We won't have a chance to prove ourselves.

Finally on June 8, the Rehr crew climbed aboard a C-47 cargo plane headed for Earls Colne. When we entered England's airspace, a British fighter, a Hawker Hurricane, escorted us through the drizzle and low clouds. Showing off, he even entertained us with a victory roll—a little premature as it turned out.

Although the men in operations greeted us warmly, they were frustrated by the weather. The bomber crews were stuck on the ground by rain and fog, the same stuff I'd just flown through. Low clouds hampered their efforts to knock out targets, mainly bridges and marshalling yards. They managed to bomb a highway and railroad, but bombing altitude was a ground hugging 1,500 feet. These guys had spirit. Whatever it took, they were determined help those troops who'd come ashore. Rumor had it that the going had been rough for everybody who landed over there.

Jake, Searle and I settled into a dome-shaped, steel hut surrounded by a grove of elms and old growth chestnut trees. Called Nissen huts, these shelters and the larger Quonset huts—both of which looked like soup cans cut in half and laid on their sides—were the primary structures on bases throughout England. These huts and every other building, like the low concrete barracks, on this sprawling base were painted green. Our living quarters already housed three other officers. It was obvious they wanted nothing to do with bright eyed, new crews, so they ignored us. I later heard these guys had flown as many as 75 missions, far more than the usual 60 or

65 before a tour ended. If these crews weren't the survivors of bailouts and crash landings, they knew plenty of guys who were. More than likely they'd limped across the English Channel a few times with control surfaces and hydraulics shot out—perhaps with wounded or dead on board. Surely they had been witnesses to the final seconds of life for a Marauder crew whose aircraft spiraled to earth in flames or exploded in a single violent instant. We shared a tent, but that was all. When it came to experience, they were old men, who no longer possessed a sense of invulnerability. Perhaps if we'd arrived a month earlier, they'd have been more cordial. We could have been their tickets back to the states. Now, the invasion of France curtailed most transfers home.

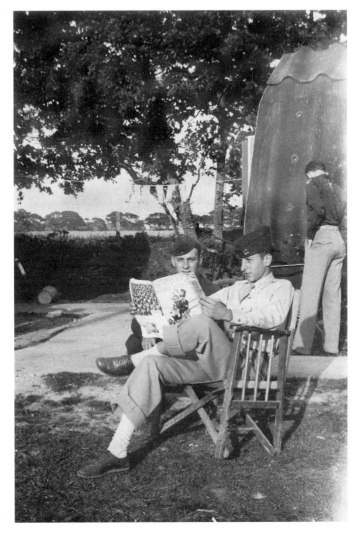

In between missions, copilot Searle (*left*) and I relax with a copy of *Esquire* magazine in front of our Nissen hut at Earls Colne, England.

What the men of the 323rd began long before D-Day, I helped bring to an end 11 months later as the squadron commander of the 456th Bombardment Squadron. But for now, I was a replacement pilot—required to fly two missions in the right seat to learn formation procedures.

Sunday June 11, I awoke at 0430 hours for my first briefing at 0530. Skipping breakfast, I arrived early in a large room, which looked like a movie theater. A center aisle separated rows of benches on either side. I took a seat near the back. On a table in the center aisle sat a projector pointed to the front, where there hung a large, brightly-lit chart depicting England, the channel, and Normandy.

The room filled with crews sharing small talk about movies, bike rides, card games—off duty stuff that kept them from frustration and boredom. I introduced myself to those sitting near me. They greeted me cordially as they would any new-comers to the group. But I was outside their circle of camaraderie. Many of these men had been together since May 1943, when the group first arrived in England. I just listened and watched.

Conversations ceased when several officers carrying photographs and trans-parent maps made their way up front. Among them was Col. Wilson R. Wood. Everyone stood at attention. "Rest, men," he said. I liked his style immediately. This guy was real Texas. Broad shouldered and tall—over six feet even without the spit polished cowboy boots. I'd heard he was "a bend any rule" commander if that's what it took to show loyalty to his men. In turn, he expected absolute support, and he got it. Today, he welcomed new crews. He congratulated everybody else for doing such a damn fine job since D-Day, despite the piss poor weather. He announced— to cheers and applause—that Lt. Harry Brown and crew were OK after crash land-ing behind British lines the day before. Everybody assumed they were MIA, missing in action. While he spoke, others pinned the transparent maps depicting the day's course over the chart of England and France.

Next we focused our attention on a briefing officer and the chart. Thirty-six Marauders, two "boxes," each with 18 planes flying in formation, were going to bomb a railroad junction at Torigny-sur-Vire south of St. Lô, a German stronghold. Hit the target and interrupt the flow of men and supplies to the area. Take-off would be at 0720 hours. With his pointer, he traced an imaginary line across the English Channel to the beach now known as Omaha. Cross the beach and head inland to the target. At the moment, clouds were right down on the ground over there. The exact altitude for bombing was up to the leaders. Although I wouldn't be doing much more than observing on this flight, he had my full attention. I did not want to end up asking any dumb questions of the men I'd be flying with on my first mis-sion.

When he finished, the group navigator provided the course readings for each leg of the trip. Then about half the men rose and quickly left the room—the navi-gators to mark the courses on their own maps, the gunners and radiomen to check their equipment.

Next, the group bombardier darkened the room and projected photos of the target area on a large pull down screen. He noted three separate areas in the tangle of rails that converged where the bombs should hit. When the lights came up, he answered a few questions about bomb loads and weights before the bombardiers left the room and headed for their aircraft.

With only the pilots left, the briefing officer reviewed the course once again. He updated us on the weather. No improvement, but by the time we got there, maybe. Expect heavy antiaircraft fire. Finally someone else outlined the logistics of the takeoffs, and emphasized the importance of sticking to the plan to avoid con-fusion or worse, an accident. He concluded with, "Good luck, men."

I'd sat in the back of the room with the idea that I wanted to get to my aircraft early.

In an adjoining room, I picked up a Mae West life jacket, a parachute, a steel flak helmet and a heavy flak jacket that was slipped over the head and worn like a bulletproof vest. Outside, under lightening skies, jeeps and trucks waited to take us to the hardstands. Before hopping aboard, I strapped on the chute and slipped my head through the Mae West.

Arriving at my assigned aircraft, *Cactus Kid*, I jumped off the truck and exchanged greetings with a couple of sergeants and the ground crew, who were making their last minute checks. But there was no chitchat. Ducking under the nosewheel door, I climbed the metal steps leading to the cockpit. Instead of settling into the copilot seat, I stowed the flak vest and helmet behind the seat and worked my way back through the radio operator's section to the bomb bay bulkhead door in the center of the fuselage. I wanted to spend a few minutes alone with the aircraft.

Opening the door leading to the bomb bay, I saw in the gloom four 1,000-pound bombs suspended in their shackles—olive drab monsters that sent a ripple of fear through my gut. Instantly, I felt the danger of my situation. Why was I deliberately placing myself in harm's way? I didn't have to be here.

Col. Wilson R. Wood, commander of the 323rd Bombardment Group from November 1943 to February 1945. On July 16, 1943, as squadron commander of the 454th, he flew the first mission of the group and is credited with 29 group and box leads (courtesy Ross E. Harlan).

The fear of combat passed as quickly as it came, never to be repeated. It had to be that way. I turned around, closed the doors and headed forward to the cockpit.

Lt. Oscar Boothe was just settling into the left seat. "Welcome, Captain Rehr," he said. After his cockpit checks, we chatted briefly about the weather. With a high overcast at Earls Colne, we should have no problem joining the formations once we reached altitude. But ground level clouds at the target meant we'd probably have to turn back. Disappointed, I slipped the flak vest over my upper body and settled into the right seat.

Suddenly the quiet English morning erupted into bursts of irregular growls, bangs and whines until all 72 engines roared in a magnificent harmony. As we sat idling waiting for the operations officer to send up a flare signaling "go," I asked Lt. Boothe if he'd flown the D-Day missions.

"No, but this is my 77th mission," he said.

A flare signaled the start of the operation. A lead bomber rolled into position on the centerline of the 6,000-foot runway. Holding the brakes, the pilot smoothly increased the power then gave his aircraft its head. Every 20 seconds, another pilot repeated that performance. We taxied around the perimeter of the runway and waited our turn.

Once in the air, we climbed and then began wide circles until all 18 aircraft of our box were in position. Three groups of six planes made up a box. Six planes led the box. Behind, six more planes flew high and to the right. On the lower left, the last six planes followed. The Marauder in which I rode was not a lead aircraft. Our only job was to follow the pilot who led our group of six. He in turn followed the box leader, who with his bombardier set up the bomb drop. Everybody flew a tight formation, particularly near the target, which kept the bombing accurate and con-centrated the defensive firepower of the .50-caliber guns. I watched Boothe's tech-nique for holding position. Move in close to the lead ship, but leave room for error. No overlapping of wings. We'd taught the same technique back at Del Rio and Dodge City.

After skirting London, we headed for the coast, where hundreds of boats rested at their ports. Joining us over the channel were fighter escorts—the P-38s, P-47s and the British Hawker Typhoons, which swept the skies overhead looking for enemy aircraft. Although I was busy scanning the scene in the air, I did look below. A long convoy of Landing Ship Tanks, or LST's, escorted by destroyers motored toward the French coast. These naval ships carried a seemingly endless supply of troops, vehicles and materiel in support of the ground war in France. Navy minesweepers crisscrossed the choppy channel searching for explosives.

Nearing the coast of France, we flew at 6,000 feet above broken clouds. Mov-ing inland, they thickened. Nearing the target, we could see nothing below. We must have been close to the railroad junction because everybody tightened up the for-mations. I expected enemy fire, but there was none. Then the group began a wide left turn. Apparently the box leader decided to make another pass over the target hoping he might find a break in the overcast. Turning 18 planes around took time. Hanging around the target just gave the gunners on the ground time to take aim at us.

In the end, both box leaders gave up the effort. Nobody wanted to risk drop-ping the bombs on the wrong target. Thirty-six aircraft, still loaded with bombs, headed back to Earls Colne. Decent weather made the landings routine. So this was my first mission. No excitement. No stories to tell Jake and Searle. They knew I was disappointed when we grabbed bikes and headed for a pub.

The following day, I rode with another pilot, Lt. Theodore Witt in *Hell's Belle*. Our mission was to the same target, only this day the skies had cleared. Shortly after takeoff, I asked Witt if I could view the action from the waist gunner's position just beyond the bomb bays. He didn't need me up front, and I wouldn't have many oppor-tunities to be an observer again. I left the bulky flak vest behind because there wasn't much room to maneuver back there. As I made my way along a catwalk between the bomb racks, I noticed that this time we were carrying the 250-pound frag-mentation bombs that propel lethal shards of hot metal in all directions. They had only one purpose: kill anyone in range.

Ducking under the turret gun, I joined the gunner who was kneeling in the waist position between openings on both sides. I waved my recognition to avoid shouting over the engine noise. It was tight back there as we both kneeled to look out the open rectangular windows. His job was to man the two .50-caliber waist guns, one on each side of the aircraft, in case enemy fighters attacked. In the rear of the Marauder, I could see the tail gunner who handled twin .50-caliber machine guns. Overhead were two more guns mounted in the turret. These six rear guns defended the Marauder against attacking fighters. For offensive maneuvers like strafing, there were four, fixed belly guns and a single nose gun, all fired from the pilot's compartment. There was also a flexible nose gun for use by the bombardier. A tightly flown Marauder formation carried a lot of firepower, a fact that didn't escape German fighter pilots.

What a view from back there! The channel was still busy with ship traffic moving in both directions. Just offshore from Omaha Beach, you couldn't miss the breakwater we'd created by deliberately sinking hundreds of boats and barges. Ships passing through this "mulberry" or "gooseberry," as the artificial reef was called, entered calmer waters, making it easier to unload and load men and materiel. Within a few days, an extraordinarily fierce storm destroyed this artificial harbor and 800 ships loaded with tons of essential supplies. The business of war practically came to a standstill until men and materiel flowed again.

But today, the weather gods favored our mission. On a bluff overlooking Omaha Beach was a makeshift landing strip surrounded by small tents and plenty of red crosses so the enemy would recognize this as a place where medical personnel evacuated the wounded.

To the west behind Utah Beach lay thousands of acres of land the Germans had flooded. I'd heard that on D-Day, hundreds of different colored parachutes were visible in the watery landscape. Men must have drowned there. That's what the Germans intended. But from where I knelt, I felt detached from the scene. My thoughts were on the target and our own safety.

This railroad junction was supposed to be a heavily defended target. After yesterday's failed attempt, everybody figured the Germans were ready for us. At 6,000 feet, we were too low for the 88mm antiaircraft cannons to be effective against us. But the Germans must have been firing something, most likely the 40mm guns, because we seemed to be taking evasive action every 20 seconds or so. However, I didn't see the green and yellow tracer shells that should have been arcing skyward.

Suddenly the bomb bay doors unfolded with a roar, and the aircraft slowed. We were on a 45-second bomb run flying straight and level now. Then relieved of its burden at last, the plane rose smoothly upward, and I watched as dozens of torpedo shaped objects picked up speed as they plummeted toward earth. On contact with the target, they burst, sending streaks of red in all directions. Mission accomplished, we pulled a sharp left and reversed course.

As we headed toward the channel, a bizarre scene below shocked me. Broken gliders littered the landscape. Some were imbedded in hedgerows and trees. Others had obviously ground looped and broken apart. I knew they carried heavy equipment and men behind enemy lines. But how the hell did those guys survive? Only a few looked like they'd landed successfully in those very small fields. Later I learned that the Germans had filled some of those fields with sharp poles, called "Rommel's asparagus" after German Field Marshal Erwin Rommel, who masterminded the enemy's defensive strategies at Normandy. The Germans strung these poles with wire connected to landmines, making them particularly deadly to the paratroopers.

This photograph taken immediately after the D-Day invasion shows gliders scattered around a large field (*center*). Others ended up in smaller fields surrounded by hedgerows. The pilots of the first wave of gliders, which carried full loads of men and equipment, were forced to release in the darkness over Normandy, resulting in crash landings and high casualties (courtesy Ross E. Harlan).

As we left the coast of France behind, I happened to glance at the right wing. What I saw chilled me. A flower of aluminum protruded from the top where flak had penetrated from below. Immediately, adrenaline kicked my survival instincts into high gear. I looked for fire or maybe leaking fuel. With red hot metal penetrating the skin, that fuel tank could have exploded, and here I was sightseeing. Everybody knew you couldn't escape a flamer. Maybe from back here.

The problem was figuring out what was going on inside the wing. There was no way of telling how much internal damage there was to the fuel line, or how long the ship would keep flying. Immediately I made my way forward to tell Lt. Witt.

"We took a hit in the right wing," I said.

"The radio operator just told me," he said. "We're breaking formation to land at an emergency field." Landing at the nearest safe field was prudent, so ground crews could have a good look at that wing. On the other side of the channel, near the coast were special airfields designed for emergency landings. Their runways were longer and wider than most, and they were equipped with FIDO or Fog Intensive Dispersal Operation. If pilots had to descend through fog, ground crews lit gasoline-filled pipes that lay in ditches bordering the runways to burn off the fog. We touched down at one of these airfields without incident.

A Brit flying a C-47 gave us a ride back to Earls Colne. Before we boarded, he handed me a .50-caliber shell as a souvenir of this mission. "Take it for good luck," he joked. After dodging barrage balloons, we were home within an hour. I put the shell in my trunk intending to keep it.

Back at Earls Colne, Maj. Alfred Blomberg, the operations officer for the 456th squadron, debriefed Lt. Witt and me. When I returned to the hut, Searle and Jake were sitting outside looking at a magazine. "You're back," said Jake without looking up. "Thought we'd gotten rid of you."

"You guys clean out my footlocker already?" I asked. The personal items of men who didn't come back had their belongings searched to remove anything that might be embarrassing to the families.

"If we looked, there wouldn't be anything interesting in there anyway," said Searle.

On June 13, Gen. Hap Arnold visited Earls Colne and promised all the high mission men that he would recommend their speedy return to the states. The good news cheered our tentmates and took the chill off our relationship. Sometimes when veterans decided to welcome newcomers, they recalled the horror stories of their toughest missions. Why not? They'd earned the bragging rights. But these guys didn't try any of that with me, perhaps because as a captain, I outranked them.

One of them, however, didn't do much of anything but lie on his cot in a dark corner of the tent. Before we'd arrived, he'd been an entrepreneur. He and his sister, who lived in Oklahoma, sold "bombs"—meaning that for a price, the folks back home could receive a photograph of a 1,000 pound bomb with their name on it. This guy wrote the name in bold letters on the side of the bomb and photographed it before it was loaded in the bomb bay. Apparently they weren't hurting for business. The other men resented him because the enterprise had a ghoulish slant. Shortly after we arrived, he disappeared.

The afternoon of June 15, I flew my first mission from the left seat. The target

The Normandy coast, photographed during the 323rd's June 15, 1944, mission to Valognes, France, in support of the ground forces fighting to take the port of Cherbourg (courtesy Ross E. Harlan).

was a fuel supply depot at Valognes, France, just south of the city of Cherbourg, a vital port the Germans still held. Before the briefing, some guy who was headed home to Minnesota asked if he could ride along. It was a beautiful late spring day, and he wanted to have one more flight. He didn't need it, and he wasn't volunteering for any responsibilities. I guess he just wanted to observe the action over Cherbourg. He didn't seem to care that the group had to penetrate heavy enemy defenses to get to Valognes. I had no problem with his request. Nor did Searle, who gave up the right seat—even though this was his first mission—and sat in the radio compartment behind the cockpit.

Jake and I were excited about flying our first mission together, even though our jobs were to follow the leaders. I had to fly a tight formation. Jake had to drop our bomb load in unison with the lead plane. After taking off then joining the group overhead, we climbed to 12,000 feet, the usual altitude for a medium bomber. As we crossed the channel and headed inland at Cherbourg, I wondered what my passenger found so fascinating down there. But I had no time for sightseeing.

Preceding us to the target were Marauders called "window" aircraft. Their job was to drop thin metallic strips similar to aluminum foil that created chaos on the

White Tailed Marauders from the 323rd score a direct hit on an enemy fuel or ammunition depot. Billowing smoke nearly reaches the bombing altitude, 10,000–12,000 feet.

enemy radar screens and confused the antiaircraft gunners. It must have worked because those of us in the first box came home with almost no damage to our aircraft. By the time the second box arrived on the scene, the gunners were organized enough to damage 12 of the 18 aircraft. But in the end, photos showed heavy fire and smoke boiling up from the fuel depot. The bombing was accurate.

After landing, my passenger thanked me, and I never saw him again. It would take a lot more experience as a combat pilot for me to understand why he wanted to stick his neck out for one more mission. Eventually, I realized that some men felt married to this business of war. Heading home meant separating from a unique wartime family held together by esprit de corps. Ending a tour of duty brought conflicting emotions—relief and guilt; joy and sadness; confidence and dread. A returning soldier faced the added stress of trying to please well-meaning family and friends, who just want him to be the same person he was before heading off to war.

Around midnight of June 15, the blast of an air raid siren roused everybody out of bed. Headed toward the base were V-1 buzz bombs that the Germans had just begun launching against random sites in London. These 19 foot bombs had wings, a little engine, and a programmable guidance system, which couldn't have been working too well if they ended up in the Earls Colne area. There may have been bomb shelters near our hut, but I don't remember seeking shelter. Several of us stood outside and watched.

As they whump whumped at 2,000 feet overhead, their pulsing, red-hot tail and flame lit up the darkness. Then came a few seconds of silence after the engine quit, and finally the explosion. Frankly, it was exciting seeing them pass overhead, because they fell well beyond the perimeters of the base. The following night, warning sirens roused us out of our beds four times.

A couple of days later, I headed north on my bike to watch a demolition team work on an unexploded German bomb that lay in its crater. Along the way, I watched one of these V-1s pass overhead. The throbbing continued for another minute or so before the menace ran out of fuel and nose-dived to earth. Out in the English countryside, it was easy to ignore the threat of these "doodle bugs" because chances were they'd land in a pasture or grove of trees and do little harm. It wasn't until a visit to London that I realized how deadly and terrifying these bombs could be as the Germans kept up the assault on that city day and night.

To stop the incoming bombs, the British set up antiaircraft guns along the Dover coast. During the day, they also used the Spitfires flying at 400 mph alongside these missiles to disorient the gyroscopes, which caused them to plummet to earth prematurely, hopefully over water or farmland. Our Marauder group responded by continuing raids on their launch sites in Holland and France, which the group had been doing since the beginning of the year.

After only a couple of weeks, Jake and I were growing impatient with dropping bombs on the lead of others. Jake even approached the squadron's operations officer, Maj. Blomberg, to let him know that he and I had enough expertise to be a lead aircraft. Then on June 22, I flew in the right slot directly behind Blomberg. He was leading the first box of 18 aircraft to a significant target, the railroad marshalling yards and fuel dumps at Armentières, near the border of Belgium.

This was a hastily called mission in the late afternoon that included not only two boxes from our group, but also Marauders from several other groups and some British Havocs. Flak was heavy going in and out of the target area, although we escaped serious damage because we were among the first to reach the area. Those who followed were not so lucky. Flak damage to three of our aircraft forced them to turn back before dropping their bombs. Twenty others made it back to base badly shot up, a few with wounded on board. When we left the target, there was smoke below. But as more planes dropped their bomb loads, the inferno sent flames and smoke as high as bombing altitude, 12,000 feet. More than likely, we'd hit an ammunition train.

Riding with Blomberg was a group photographer, who knelt in the waist gunner's position for an unobstructed view of the action. As we approached the English Channel on the return flight, he pointed his camera at me and with cautious hand signals directed me to move in tighter to Blomberg's right wing. The late afternoon air no longer bubbled with thermals. So I called Blomberg on the radio and told him I was moving in for a photo shoot.

"OK, I'll hold position," he answered without hesitating. If he changed altitude

A formation of Marauders from the 386th Bombardment Group leaves the coast of France behind after a bombing raid in late June 1944 and races home across the English Channel to England. The high bomber is *The Yankee Guerrilla* (National Archives photograph 342-FH-3A1822-51754).

or decreased his power, I could run into him. Gently I increased the power. Slowly, carefully I moved in close enough so that our wings overlapped—the kind of close that could make pilots nervous if they didn't trust each other. There was no way to relax as I concentrated on holding the position. Finally, the photographer waved me off. Slowly, I eased back on the throttles and dropped behind.

Later when Blomberg and I studied the close-up photos of my Marauder, which appeared to dominate the skies as it passed over the French coastline headed for England, he joked that he didn't want anybody flying that close to him again. "On your next mission, you and Jacobs will be flying a lead position," he said. Those were the words Jake and I had been waiting to hear. We'd now be leading flights of six, which gave Jake and me more flexibility in setting up the bomb run.

By the end of June, I had eight combat missions behind me, which must have entitled me to a 48-hour pass to London. Returning, I learned that on June 29, Lt. Oscar J. Boothe had flown his last mission against a gun battery on the Cherbourg Peninsula. It was his 81st. There had been plenty of flak and machine gun fire. His plane, *Klassie Lassie*, was on its 100th mission and took a direct hit. The explosion littered the air with debris that damaged a couple of ships behind. Nobody saw any parachutes. His was the only plane lost. At the end of the day, six men had their names added to the list of MIAs, missing in action.

Word was he was supposed to be heading home in a couple of days, but he volunteered for just one more. Everybody knew volunteering was unlucky. Why Boothe's Marauder was the only one lost that day is another mystery of war.

4

Bridge Busting
and Night Bombing,
Beaulieu, England

July–August 1944

July brought continuous drizzle and ground hugging clouds, the worst weather that England and the Continent had experienced in 50 years. Except for local training flights, the Marauders at Earls Colne remained grounded for the first 17 days of the month. This was good for the Germans. With impunity they replaced men and equipment in key areas of Normandy, like St. Lô and Caen. Without bomber support to knock out German lifelines, especially bridges, our ground forces could not advance beyond Normandy's hedgerows and pastures.

For bomber crews, briefings and missions were normal. Sitting through briefings day after day only to have them scrubbed—sometimes three or four times a day—was abnormal. To prepare the body and mind for a difficult target only to return to stuffy, tin hut for a poker game or to a mist-shrouded field for another volleyball or baseball game was abnormal. Flying a mission was preferable to standing by, which only prolonged the war.

Waking up every day to a gray world was depressing. Saying good-byes to the departing crews didn't help. Farewells are always easier when you can head off to the daily routine. I hadn't been around long enough to share in the sentiments. But as men tossed their trunks and duffel bags into the back of transports on the first leg of their journey home, the malaise of those left behind only deepened.

In July, the group lost nearly 10 percent of its experienced crews. Most of the replacement pilots were second lieutenants right out of advanced training, where they trained on twin-engine aircraft like the docile AT-17, called the Bamboo Bomber, with its 245 horsepower engines. Like Searle, most had barely 300 hours flight time when they were commissioned, and many had never seen a B-26 before.

After earning their wings, they headed directly to war with no opportunity for transition training at Del Rio or Dodge City. Col. Wood had no choice but to set up a training program and turn these new arrivals into copilots on the Marauder.

I participated in the training program by preparing the current copilots for the left seat. If the ceiling lifted even for a few hours, I enjoyed flying with these men, who like Searle, needed all the advanced training they could get in the Marauder. With barely 2,000 feet, conditions were tight for handling speed and power settings, which gave them excellent practice. After climbing out, they had to power back to limit the speed and maintain visual contact with the airport. Reaching altitude, they slowed down even more to maintain an approach speed, around 160 mph. The big thing was to build their confidence.

After they became proficient with take-offs and landings, we practiced single engine landings. If this war continued much longer, there'd come a day when they'd have to coax a crippled Marauder back to a safe landing. They had to feel secure about their abilities to fly and land on one engine. Searle was advancing quickly, but he needed more combat experience in the right seat before I turned him loose with his own crew.

Around the middle of the month, the whole group, nearly 2,000 men, moved to a base in southern England to be closer to the action in France. This new station, Beaulieu Airdrome, was located just inland from the coast near Southampton and Bournemouth.

One morning, shortly after we arrived in at Beaulieu, word came that Hitler had been assassinated. I happened to be standing near the operations office when someone made the announcement. Walking to the edge of a nearby runway where low clouds and almost no visibility kept things eerily quiet, I tried to imagine a sudden end to this war and couldn't. It took years for Hitler to create his war machine. Killing the mastermind wasn't going to make a difference.

I'd seen firsthand his spellbinding power over the Germans during the summer of 1938. After graduating from Culver Military Academy in Indiana, my roommate, Gardner Johnson, and I boarded a ship for England. Touring Germany was part of our itinerary. We were high-spirited teenagers, newly liberated from the regimens of a military life. For us, Germany's nationalism was just another adventure like biking in Great Britain, hiking in Switzerland and seeking pleasure in a Paris brothel. In retrospect, the signs of impending war were everywhere, even beyond Germany's borders. But few seemed to notice.

Shortly before our arrival in Munich, there had been a large rally for Hitler. In the heart of the city, parade bunting and flags adorned with swastikas still hung from buildings. Apparently he'd emerged from his alpine retreat at Berchtesgaden to get himself adored. Germany was out of the doldrums, and Germans had Hitler to thank for the good life. They had jobs, and their money was worth something again. Munich's famous beer hall, the Hofbrauhaus, exploded with energy. Tables of singing Germans saluted one another with wine, beer, and schnapps. When Gardner and I attempted to speak the language, they invited us to join them. All were welcome.

As we staggered back to the hotel after an evening of carousing in the beer-hall, we passed a troop of marching soldiers in their late teens carrying polished shovels. Strong and healthy looking, they stared straight ahead as drilling soldiers do. But what struck me was the intensity of their commitment. Nothing could have caused them to avert their eyes, not even two foreigners, teenagers like themselves.

While waiting at a Munich rail station for a train to Berlin, we noticed railroad cars that once belonged to Austria. Just three months before our arrival in Europe, Hitler had annexed this neighboring country, which was also his birthplace. In a crude display of power, the Germans had painted "Deutschland" in big white letters on the sides of the cars, barely covering the "Österreich" underneath.

On the train to Berlin, Gardner and I shared a compartment with a high ranking German officer in full dress uniform. He carried an ornate, ceremonial mace, a symbol of his authority. Sitting rigidly near the doors of the compartment, he showed no desire to converse. Gardner had a gift for ingratiating himself with strangers. But this guy wouldn't even look at us. Here was a genuine Nazi stuck in a first class compartment with two American teenagers. Gardner and I drank and laughed, and generally behaved like asses. The German, who sat next to me, stared straight ahead. When the train stopped in Nuremberg, he stood up, turned at the door, and looked directly at us. Raising his mace he said contemptuously, "Heil Hitler." Then he turned and left. Speechless, Gardner and I just stared at each other.

That was the first time I'd ever seen anybody salute Der Fuehrer. However in Berlin, the epicenter of Hitler's power, citizens leaving restaurants saluted the other diners with "Heil Hitlers" and "Seig Heils." In this city, political genuflection must have been essential to survival. But for two military academy graduates like Gardner and me, the sight of civilians saluting one another struck us as amusing, even absurd. We were too young and self-absorbed to recognize the consequences of such fanatical devotion.

In Berlin, Dad, who traveled from London to meet us, suggested we tour the city in the motorized trolley that stopped there. Only a handful of tourists joined us. The driver and guide told us he was a Jew from Brooklyn. Throughout the tour, he repeated several times, "You will not find me here after September. I'm getting out of here." For the first time since entering Germany, I felt uncomfortable. Only later did I realize that his status as an American probably insulated him—at least for the moment—from laws that prohibited German Jews from working. But he must have felt the pressure. The marching soldiers we saw from his trolley carried rifles, not shovels, and stared straight ahead as though mesmerized. I imagined them breaking the steady rhythm of their leather boots on the pavement and surrounding the trolley to arrest our guide. The whole scene was disquieting long after he parked his vehicle in front of the hotel, and we had thanked him for the tour.

With the exception of our guide, Berliners, like the revelers we joined in Munich, seemed oblivious to the darker side of Hitler's politics. The Haus Vaterland, a large hall offering four floors of entertainment, rocked with exuberant oblivion.

Within a few hours of the assassination attempt, Hitler broadcast assurances to his people that he still lived. I wondered how ordinary German citizens felt now about this dark and shrill little man, whose physical appearance mocked his vision of a master race. He was their twentieth century pied piper, whose mesmerizing

I took this photograph of soldiers marching in the streets of Berlin in 1938 while touring the city. My guide was a Jew from Brooklyn, who repeatedly said, "You'll not find me here after September. I'm getting out of here."

rhetoric led them down the path to war. Some in his inner circle wanted him dead, but they had failed. Their botched effort accomplished nothing except to inspire new fanaticism and cruelty in Hitler. His demands for absolute obedience from his troops and citizens only intensified.

By late July, his armies still held key positions in western France, which prevented Allied ground forces from barely moving beyond Normandy's hedgerows. The job of medium bomber groups was to do whatever it took to protect the lives of those men on the ground. Destroy the enemy's supply routes, marshalling yards and ammunition dumps and kill their troops—whatever the risks. A couple of days before the assassination attempt, Marauders from our bomb group, along with nearly 2,000 other Royal Air Force and U.S. heavy, medium and light bombers dropped 12,000 tons of bombs on a defended area east of Caen. The mission was in support of British Gen. Bernard Montgomery's troops, who had not yet claimed the city. When the bombing was over, a mass of smoke and dust obscured the destruction and human misery below. That's the way it had to be.

With so many bombs falling, there was always the possibility of accidentally dropping them on our own troops. It happened on July 25 in a similar massive bombing effort in support of our offensive at St. Lô, called Operation Cobra. The mission

British infantry release smoke screens to mark their positions near the Rhine River as Marauders from the 323rd Bomb Group fly over.

called for nearly 2,000 bombers from the Eighth and Ninth Air Forces including 36 Marauders from our group, to drop tons of bombs along a stretch of highway running between St. Lô and Périers. Our ground forces had orders to wait out the bombing 1,200 yards from the bombing line instead of the 3,000 yards mandated by the Eighth and Ninth Air Forces. Unfortunately, drifting smoke obscured targets, and some of the bombers, including Marauders from our unit's first box, bombed too early. Accidental bombings like this were called "shorts." When this snafu was over, Allied bombers had wounded nearly 500 men and killed over 100 U.S. troops, including Lt. Gen. Lesley J. McNair, who, apparently, ignored repeated warnings from General Eisenhower not to take unnecessary risks.

When the news of the tragedy reached the base at Beaulieu, crews were shocked and grieved. An angry Col. Wood didn't have to remind us that our job was to save the lives of our ground troops, not trap them in a deafening barrage of death. Even though I had not taken part in the St. Lô bombings, I felt the responsibility of the group. In the end, these tragic losses at St. Lô were offset by the extraordinary success of the operation, which sent the Germans into retreat and enabled our ground forces to move rapidly eastward.

Beaulieu, England. My crew and I before boarding our Marauder for a mission. We wear Mae West life jackets. *Standing left to right:* Lt. Victor Jacobs, bombardier; Lt. Joe Searle, copilot; Capt. Lou Rehr, pilot. *Front row left to right:* Sgt. James Knight, engineer/gunner; S/Sgt. James Alexander, radio/gunner; Sgt. Charles Allen, tail gunner.

As a lead bomber crew, Jake and I approached this war with the conviction that our only job was to hit each target dead center then bring our crews home safely. I looked forward to missions because I believed that every sortie we flew was weakening the German position in France and saving American lives. Before boarding the Marauder, I made sure Searle and my three enlisted men understood the importance of each mission.

If we had to abort because of weather or a mechanical problem, I wanted them to be as disappointed as Jake and I were that we could not complete the job.

When the weather improved in late July, Jake and I established our reputations for precision bombing with bridge busting. Bridges—railroad and highway that spanned the Seine, the Loire, and the Orne Rivers—were the lifelines of the Germans. Bridges kept replacements of men and equipment flowing to the enemy. Prior to D-Day, Marauder groups had done a hell of a job knocking out bridges along the Seine, which isolated the Germans who defended Normandy by disrupting their supply routes . But the task was not easy. Destroying one bridge had required an average of 91 sorties. Then under cover of night, the Germans rebuilt many of them.

Hitting a narrow bridge with 4,000 pounds of bombs required precise movements from both the bombardier and pilot, who together often had to make last minute adjustments for wind speed and drift or changes in altitude due to cloud layers. Missing the target by even a few feet might not cause any damage to the structure at all. Bombs that passed through steel girders resulted in only minimal damage. Dropping prematurely or too late could result in civilian casualties. If the Marauder crews didn't get it right the first time, they often flew the same mission the following day, where the German gunners awaited their return.

Jake figured we could do better. One day, as we sat around waiting for clouds and drizzle to go away, he said, "Look, Head." That was his nickname for me. "If we're going to destroy these bridges, we're going to have to do a two-minute bomb run."

I stared at him. The usual Marauder bomb run was around 45 seconds. At that point, the pilot's job was to keep the aircraft as level as a billiard table. No more weaving through the sky to evade the gunners below. Up in the fishbowl nose of the bomber sat the bombardier, his mind focused like a laser on his bombsight. Never mind the black bursts bruising the sky. Or worse, the heart of the flak, the occasional orange ball that appeared right there on the nose—the moment of truth before the burst turned black. For 45 seconds, bomber crews deliberately offered their lives to the moment. And Jake wanted two minutes.

Once pilots began the bomb run, they no longer took evasive action against the flak bursts. For at least 45 seconds, pilots and bombardiers ignored the aerial minefield and focused on precision bombing of targets (National Archives photograph 342-FH-3A-18213-51513).

Marauder pilots and bombardiers were known for their accuracy in destroying a narrow span of railroad bridge.

I knew he was right. Hitting a bridge was not like a raid on a sprawling marshalling yard, where bombs dropped anywhere near the target could do significant damage. I also knew that as leaders we had the freedom to set up a longer bomb run because the strategy for hitting bridges was to approach the target in individual flights of four and six aircraft rather than the traditional box formation. I weighed the risks against our experience and teamwork.

After a few seconds, I said, "OK, we're out here to win this war. If that's what it takes, I'll follow you."

We never discussed our more personal motivations. Like me, I'm sure he wanted his family to be proud of him. My British stepmother, Louisa, took great pride in my role as a bomber pilot. London was burning, and the Germans had to be stopped once again as they had been in World War I. Five years at Culver Military Academy also taught me to respect those who sacrificed for their country. There was honor in hanging our butts out. But I didn't enter this war believing I would die. Dying happened to the "other guy" like Lt. Boothe. Soldiers had to think that way. How else could we do what was expected of us? For me, firing up a ship, taxiing out ahead of a line of powerful bombers and roaring off to a target was a real test of my spirit.

Jake and I did not discuss with others our plans for the extended bomb run against bridges. Those who dropped bombs on our lead had no choice but to follow. On July 24, our first target was the Nay railroad bridge that stretched across a tributary of the Erdre River just north of Nantes. Now that we were flying from southern England, our Marauders could reach targets well south of the Cotentin Peninsula. The mission called for Jake and me to lead the second group of 12 aircraft. We awoke to heavy haze over Beaulieu and had to hang out all day for the briefing at 1545 hours. Takeoff wouldn't come until three hours later.

Between the briefing and take-off, we stuck close to operations in case there were any changes. Maybe the visibility would improve or worsen over the target. Maybe the mission would be scrubbed. Hanging around, men smoked, wrote letters or bullshitted about a movie they'd seen in town on a liberty run. I just wanted to get going.

Then word came to board the aircraft even though haze was still a problem over England and the target. Thirty-seven aircraft from the group lifted off and headed across the channel. As we leveled off at 11,500 feet, Jake crawled in, head first, to the bombardier's compartment. Behind me, the gunners fired their weapons just to make sure they worked, but no one expected German fighters on this mission. After D-Day, they'd made themselves scarce over Normandy. It was the heavies on missions to Germany that got their attention.

As we roared south toward Nantes, visibility improved. Below lay a vast patchwork of farmland. Thousands of rectangles, squares, and irregularly shaped fields and pastures lay between occasional clusters of development. Roads in no particular pattern threaded through the landscape. Ahead lay a broad, gently curving river surrounded by the quilt of farmland.

After nearly an hour and a half of cruising, Jake called the initial point over the intercom. A loud rush of air filled the ship as I opened the bomb bay and brought in more power to stabilize the ship against the drag of those doors. There was no turning back. Nothing mattered but hitting the target. Not the flak bursts, not the sounds of the Marauder's skin deflecting and absorbing the sharp metal.

From then on, I followed Jake's instructions. As he corrected for drift, I centered the needle of a Pilot Direction Indicator (PDI) that was linked to his Norden bombsight. "Right 10 degrees, right, hold steady," he said. " Head, tweak it left." To avoid any unnecessary movements, I deliberately slowed my breathing to hold altitude and heading. The last 30 seconds, I left the corrections to Jake. That's when a pilot can really screw things up. I let him know we were 50 feet too high, and he worked his magic keeping the target in the crosshairs. In an instant, a hot orange ball exploded directly in front of us then disappeared. It's over. Can't worry now. Keep the hands steady. Got to hit the target.

Then came his "bombs away." Four thousand pounds lighter, we shut the doors and reversed course to lead the others home. After climbing back into the cockpit, Jake was sure that we'd hit the target "dead center." The next day, the photos of the bombing proved him right. Billowing smoke caught in various stages of expansion showed how the first and third group of Marauders damaged the tracks on either side of the bridge. But only one set of bombs sent smoke surging upward directly over the span. While Jake and I were elated over our success, we knew the other

White tailed Marauders head east across the English Channel on a mission to France (courtesy Ross E. Harlan).

pilots were complaining about our extended bomb run tactics. If our mission targeted a bridge, we would stick to the plan, and they would have to follow.

A week later, the target was the Le Manoir railroad bridge located southeast of Rouen. This bridge was a major artery spanning the Seine. Attempts to hit it prior to D-Day were only partially successful. What the Marauders destroyed, the Germans quickly rebuilt. This time, however, the Germans were determined to use extraordinary firepower to protect this vital span. During the briefing, we were warned Le Manoir would be a dangerous target with plenty of guns protecting it. Pictures of the bridge showed dozens of bomb craters clustered in the fields surrounding the tracks and a few scattered in fields within a couple of miles. We needed to knock out this bridge completely to force the Germans in the area to retreat. In addition to the 37 aircraft assigned to hit the bridge, three window aircraft led the formations to draw off the guns. Fighters, the P-47s, also accompanied us.

I was leading the last six planes in the first box. Twelve other planes would be dropping ahead of us. We took off in the morning, but had to return to base when fog prevented our fighter escort from joining us. By late afternoon, the weather improved enough to permit bombing from an altitude of 11,000 to 12,000 feet. Close to the city of Rouen, the Seine River wound like a snake through the rich farmland.

A direct hit on the Le Manoir bridge shows the accuracy of Capt. Victor Jacobs, my bombardier, who preferred two minute bomb runs for hitting bridges spanning rivers in France (courtesy Ross E. Harlan).

Once again Jake called out an early IP. Nothing changed in our strategy. Up ahead the flak began, first low. Then as we held steady, angry black plumes climbed higher and higher into our path, taunting us. There was power in ignoring their threats and the clattering metal hitting the fuselage and wings. Finally, bombs away! Once again Jake was sure we hit the target dead center. He was right. The photos showed Jake's bombs dropping directly on the bridge. Clouds of smoke dispersed over the fields surrounding the bridge where the bombers ahead of us had dropped. The smaller puffs concentrated right over the span came from the later bombs dropped by Jake and the bombardiers who followed his lead.

Although we returned to base with just a few holes, others were not so lucky. Nine of the group's attacking aircraft returned to Beaulieu with significant damage. Three airmen were wounded.

The following day, accompanied by P-51 Mustangs and led by window aircraft, we destroyed the Chartres railroad bridge. Just on the other side of the bridge stood the spires of its famous cathedral. More than likely, the buildings near the bridge were nothing but rubble, but with such a large population center, we had even more reason for bombing accuracy. There was very little resistance from the Germans here, and once more, Jake and I led a direct hit on the bridge. Knocking out three bridges in one week made us feel like we were making a difference in this war. And despite the riskier strategy, our bombing accuracy brought admiration from the entire squadron, including the ground crews.

Part of our success as leaders came because I made certain that those who followed kept the formation tight, especially when we were close to the target. The Marauders carried a lot of firepower in those twelve .50-caliber guns, and German fighter pilots were reluctant to take on a tight formation. If I noticed a pilot dropping back or sliding out, I called him on the radio and told him to bring it in. I didn't like sloppy flying, because I had to know where everyone was. Some guys bitched because keeping together was hard work. Once out of harm's way, I let the formation loosen up. During the debriefings with the operation officer, I complimented these pilots, many of whom were still trying to get comfortable with combat flying. "Hey you're doing a great job," I'd say. "I enjoyed flying with you and watching the way you handled yourself." As their skills improved, I let them know I noticed.

In the two months since my crew and I joined the 323rd, I had come to know many of the men in the squadron. From early on, I made friends with the ground crews out on the line, the guys who patched up holes and inspected all the parts. I followed them around as they explained their fixes and repairs. That way, too, I learned the idiosyncrasies of each plane. I wanted them know we were a team. We depended on each other.

One day in early August, operations announced that the group had been assigned to fly night missions. Since our entry into the war, the RAF had pressured the U.S. to share in the night bombing. Finally, some desk-sitting general back at the Pentagon yielded, believing it would be a good idea for the U.S. to compete with the RAF's night bombing Mosquitos. Marauders from the 322nd and the 323rd pulled the hazardous duty—despite the strong objections of the highest U.S. Army Air Force commanders overseas.

Men on the front line don't know anything about the politics behind these decisions. When morale is high and the spirits strong, they don't question the purpose of missions. They follow orders because there is a war to be won. But the directive to bomb at night gave the Marauder men pause to think.

The Marauder was never intended for night missions. Bombing had to be done by individual aircraft heading toward the target in "streams" rather than formations. This meant that each crew was on its own when it came to navigating and releasing bombs. Pinpointing the exact location of the target required Pathfinder aircraft that flew ahead of the incoming bombers. These were specially equipped Marauders that navigated using a series of ground stations that broadcast radio beams. When the beams from two separate stations intersected, the plane was directly over the bomb release point. For night missions, these Pathfinders were supposed to locate the target and then illuminate the bombing area with flares. This, of course, gave the German gunners plenty of opportunity to take aim and call in night fighters. Even with the target lit up like Christmas, pinpoint accuracy on the bomb run was not possible without daylight.

Darkness handicapped the crews in other ways. To reduce the red glow from the exhausts, the mechanics installed flame suppressors, which reduced engine power. The gunners who rode in the tail, turret and waist had no way of seeing approaching German night fighters, much less distinguishing friend from foe. And if searchlights surrounded the target, pilots who didn't keep their eyes on the instruments inside the cockpit became blinded, then disoriented.

As an instructor, I'd done a lot of night flying before heading overseas. Flying in AT-6s and BC-1s back at Kelly Field, we trained our men for the eventuality of night bombing. Each cadet received 13 hours of night formation flying that often lasted until 0300 hours making this dangerous, tiring work. Landing at night was also challenging. The runways in Texas were marked with low powered "blitz" lights that were hooded and could only be seen on the final glide slope. We adopted these from the Brits, who used them to protect their airfields from nighttime raids. Sometimes in Texas the only light was a large bonfire in the middle of the airfield, and cadets had to figure out how to land. Inevitably several advanced students flying alone were killed on night cross-country flights. Midair collisions, botched landings, and fog developing over the Bandera Hills northwest of Kelly Field were a constant threat to the inexperienced. I also gave Marauder trainees at Del Rio and Dodge City plenty of night cross-country instruction to destinations all over the country, especially if a trainee wanted to fly back to his hometown. But no amount of training could prepare men for the hazards over Europe.

Our bomb group began practicing for these night missions in June back at Earls Colne. But as far as I was concerned, these exercises were more dangerous than flying over enemy territory. We'd take off sometime around midnight, climb up to 4,000 feet, fly around for a couple of hours then land. Two planes flying in formation covered a sector. Sometimes we'd make several landings in these practices. You couldn't see anything, and there did not seem to be any coordination with other aircraft, British or American. Several times, my Marauder rolled violently from side to side because we blundered into the wake of some unseen aircraft. I don't know what the point was really, except to see if we could go out and come back without getting lost.

Early in July, the ill-fated 322nd Bombardment Group flew one of their night missions to the Château de Ribeaucourt in northern France, where, according to the French underground, V-1 technicians and engineers lived. Despite the miserable weather during the day, that night sky was clear and moonlit. Some of the group flew shiny natural metal aircraft with no olive drab paint for camouflage. Shortly after crossing the French coast, searchlights filled the skies. They were sitting ducks not only to the gunners on the ground, but to a group of 40–50 German night fighters that had been waiting to ambush some RAF bombers that were late in arriving. The Germans shot down nine aircraft. Two crash-landed. One aircraft with over 1,000 holes in it limped back to England but never flew again. When it was all over, 78 men were missing in action. Tragically, the bombs only straddled the chateau, leaving in doubt the fate of its occupants.

When it was our turn to bomb at night, that mission of the 322nd weighed heavily on many of men of the 323rd. But not Jake, who was eager to take on any challenge. He thought we should volunteer. We'd done a lot of night bombing exercises together at Barksdale, which for some reason, he really enjoyed. What appealed to me was the idea of flying a mission without the restraints of keeping a formation together. But I was more cautious. "We don't know the details," I said. "These missions could turn into a turkey shoot." I was in no hurry to volunteer for a suicide mission.

Over the next few days, there was a lot of discussion among the pilots about night bombings. There was concern over midair collisions and accuracy. Wouldn't daytime bombing be more effective for spotting the target and any attacking fighters? Orders were to bomb on either side of 12,500 feet. But the way we figured it, we'd be better off down low, not only for better visibility of the target but to provide safety from the 88mm guns. One of the veteran pilots, Col. Robert Kelly, approached Col. Wood for a change of orders permitting bombing altitudes from 2,500 feet up to 13,000. The possibility of attack by German night fighters was always there. But a lot had happened since the 322nd's disaster at the chateau, including the German retreats at St. Lô and Caen. I was willing to bet enemy fighters would not be a factor, especially if the targets were in the Normandy area. The first mission fell on August 6-7, and Jake and I asked to be scheduled.

The target was an island, the Île de Cezembere, near St. Malo, south of Cherbourg. Defense batteries located here along with gunboats in the St. Malo Harbor kept American troops in the area pinned down. The 323rd was sending out 36 Marauders to destroy five boats anchored in the harbor. We took off sometime around 2300 hours at 20-second intervals and leveled off at assigned altitudes between 2,000 and 3,500 feet. Despite our eagerness to participate, my crew and I could not relax for a second. This was a clear moonlit night, which spooked my rational mind. What if there *were* German night fighters prowling the skies above us?

Over the intercom, I called to my tail gunner, "OK, Allen, keep your eyes open. I am counting on you." Sgt. Charles Allen was a free spirited, wiry built California boy, who barely reached my shoulder—perfect for squeezing into the tight quarters of the tail. If we came under attack, engineer Bailey, who kept an eye on the B-26's instruments, and radioman Alexander, who monitored the radio transmissions, would leave their posts to operate the top turret gun and waist guns.

Sitting in the compartment behind the cockpit was a navigator whose name is lost in memory. He'd transferred from another squadron and needed only 15 more missions. Volunteering to navigate for night bombing gave him more points, which would get him home sooner. He had a good record, and I was lucky to have him on board. After I leveled off at 2,500 feet, he guided us over the moonlit waters of the channel steering clear of the Cherbourg Peninsula and the Isles of Guernsey and Jersey, from where the Germans could fire at us with their antiaircraft guns. He and I breathed oxygen to improve vision, but there was no way to relax knowing there were other Marauders near us. Everyone was supposed to maintain a different fixed altitude, which kept us separated. But the crew and I continually scanned the night sky looking for any threatening shapes.

For at least half an hour, the dark contours of the Cherbourg Peninsula slid past our left side. Here the navigation was tricky as we maintained a position between the French coast and the Channel Islands.

Finally, up ahead, brilliant white lights lit up a square of dark water like some gaudy carnival. The Pathfinders had marked the target. I opened the doors, and we raced toward the lights. Only then did I see another Marauder off my left side. I do not recall any flak or explosions. Jake dropped the bomb load as we passed over that little piece of rock, but in the darkness, there was no way of telling what they hit.

Reversing course over the channel, I climbed up to 4,000 feet. Once we cleared the Cherbourg Peninsula, it was easier to relax. Sgt. James Alexander, my radioman, entertained us with harmonica playing. Alexander was a jazz pianist, a fact I discovered months later when Searle and I walked into a Paris bar and realized that he was the musician entertaining the crowd. Hearing soulful tunes like "I'll Be Seeing You" and "Sentimental Journey" piped over the intercom was bizarre, but so was the whole mission. When he finished playing, he said, "You guys are nuts."

Perhaps Jake and I were nuts. We volunteered for the remaining four night missions, scheduled for around midnight on August 9, 12, 13 and 14. We may have been the only crew to fly all five night missions. These were scattered targets, mostly ammunition and fuel dumps located well inland from the French coast. Bombing altitudes continued to be between 2,000 and 3,500 feet. Fortunately there was little enemy resistance, only some light flak in the target areas. Still I took no chances after the bomb drops. To avoid any German night fighters and ground defenses, I dropped down even lower as we raced across the Normandy countryside back to safer skies over the channel. I took the props out of sync, creating an uneven pulsating effect meant to confuse anybody on the ground. I'd learned that trick from instructing students who had trouble synchronizing the engines. Anyone standing on the ground would have difficulty pinpointing the source. Once over the channel, I brought the engines back into harmony, the signal to the crew that we were now safely over water and returning to our assigned cruising altitude.

The most memorable of these night missions occurred on August 13 against German positions in the Argentan-Falaise Gap. In this area south of Caen, the allies were closing in on the enemy, trapping them in round-the-clock barrages of artillery and bombs. That night, we targeted enemy troops and a fuel dump at Flers. Gen. Eisenhower knew he had the Germans on the run and instructed "every airman to make it his direct responsibility that the enemy is blasted unceasingly by day and by night, and is denied safety either in fight or in flight."

Much has been written about the horror and chaos in the Falaise from eyewitnesses on the ground. Gen. Eisenhower, who visited the site after the German defeat there, called this "one of the greatest killing grounds of any of the war areas." Approaching the targets from the sky, we Marauder pilots were lucky to be above the unimaginable suffering to which we were contributing. Below tons of our bombs left the enemy dead, crazed, buried alive, or wounded. Some of the lucky Germans who managed to escape ended up stunned prisoners of war.

I didn't feel remorse. And in light of what we know now about the atrocities of the Germans under Hitler's rule, I still have no regrets. Our duty was to stop the enemy, throw their battle plans into disarray, demoralize them and force them into surrender.

The night was clear. As we headed across the channel toward the target, everything ahead of us looked like it was on fire. I turned to the navigator and joked, "I hope we're winning." Nearing the battle, I was in awe of this ground war that did not stop. In the darkness, the conflict resembled an enormous world of horizon-to-horizon fireworks—antiaircraft gun muzzle flashes, exploding shells, tracers, search lights, flares, flashes of exploding bombs, incendiaries and fires everywhere. There was no rest for the ground troops, who unlike us, could not escape to the safety of England, although we certainly worried about our own skins too.

Finally these night missions ended. No crews or ships from the 323rd were lost in the effort. However on the night of the 13th, at least one crew strayed off course on the return flight and ended up too close to the Isle of Guernsey. According to Lt. Ted Harwood, who was flying his first mission as copilot for the 456th, the Germans sent up an aerial flare that illuminated the entire sky and nearly blinded the crew. "Almost simultaneously, the German artillery opened fire on our position, he said. "The sky was still lit up, so we could not see the flash of the immense cannons below until the flare faded. Eventually, the artillery fell away behind our aircraft." They landed safely without injuries or battle damage.

The previous month, the 322nd Bomb Group was in the wrong place at the wrong time. Airmen in battle expect these tragic losses. In August, when it came time for the 323rd to take its turn at night bombing, the Germans were on the run. Their night fighters were nowhere to be seen, and the light flak was no threat. The Marauders may not have been the best aircraft for night bombings. But if nothing else, the men who flew these missions deprived the Germans of their sleep and their hopes of defeating the allies—at least for the moment. Flying these night bombing missions, the Marauder men played a role in driving the Germans eastward back to their border. By August 25, the allies had liberated Paris.

The following day, August 26, we moved to Lessay, France, on the Normandy coast. We were cut down to one barracks bag and told to ship our footlockers home with the excess. The living conditions were about to change. We'd be setting up a village of tents on a makeshift airbase with no pub in sight. Still with the retreat of the Germans, everybody figured this war would soon be over.

5

On Leave in London

Summer 1944

Before the group moved to France, I enjoyed a couple of 48-hour leaves to London. I felt at home in this city, where my British stepmother Louisa still had close ties. I first traveled here with my family during the summer of 1936. We made that crossing on a large ship from the North German Lloyd fleet. At that time, no one saw the Germans as a serious threat. In fact, they were known for the best service on the North Atlantic. However, one strange thing occurred during the crossing. I carried with me a small short-wave radio, which I listened to at night, then tucked under my pillow during the day. Shortly after we sailed, the radio disappeared. I thought it was stolen, but my father suggested that I let the incident go. I have often wondered if the German crewmembers, worried that someone might monitor their transmissions, confiscated it.

During that summer, we lived in an apartment on Kennsington Road near Hyde Park. But Louisa made sure that my sister Judy and I visited the East End of London, the "bow bells" section, where she grew up. Anyone raised within the sound of the bells from the medieval church, St. Mary Le Bow, was a true cockney, and she was proud of her heritage. She also showed us rebuilt sections around St. Paul's Cathedral and the Liverpool Street railroad station where German zeppelins had dropped their bombs during the First World War.

Louisa's insights and perceptions were well ahead of her time. In the late 1930s, she recognized that once again England would be forced to go to war against Germany. In 1938, when Dad, Gardner and I returned to London after our stay in Berlin, we told her about a German who shared the train compartment with us. He was a good looking man in his late 20s with a receding hairline and penetrating hazel eyes that he fixed on us when he spoke. His English was nearly perfect, and he called himself by the phony name "Mr. England." I'd seen him earlier standing on the platform saying good-by to a beautiful blond. He was pleasant enough, but there was an air of intrigue about him. Dad noted that he carried a considerable amount of

Prewar London 1938.

British currency, which was illegal under Hitler's rule. He remained with us even after boarding the ferry to England. In the evening, he joined me on the deck and pointed to the clear sky. "Our futures lie in the stars," he said repeating a common belief among Hitler's followers.

"He's a fifth column," Louisa said referring to the name given to enemy supporters or infiltrators who commit acts of espionage, even sabotage. "London will burn again, and this time it's going to be worse."

Two years later on September 7, the Germans began the blitz of London—eight months of terrible bombings intended to demoralize its citizens. Nearly every night, Londoners sought shelter from heavy bombs or raced into the streets to fight huge fires as a cacophony of bombers, bomb blasts, guns, sirens, and screams filled the air. Now, Londoners faced a new menace—these V-1 bombs that fell day and night around the city.

On the first leave, Searle accompanied me. We boarded a train at Colchester for London. Nearing the city, we passed through entire neighborhoods where nothing remained but stone skeletons. After arriving in London, we checked into the Cumberland Hotel, on Oxford Street near Marble Arch. Nearby was a Red Cross club called the Mostyn, which kept 3,000 modest but clean rooms for servicemen on leave. But this trip, we opted for the more luxurious accommodations of the Cumberland. Across the street stretched the broad lawns of Hyde Park, where once I enjoyed picnics with my family. Now antiaircraft guns squatted on the grass ready to thwart attacks by the V-1s and German night bombers.

The first thing I did was hail a cab. I'd promised Louisa that I would visit her childhood friend Kate Dewdney, who was a schoolteacher. My mission was to bring her children a gift from Louisa: packs of Juicy Fruit gum I'd carried with me since leaving south Florida. British children craved the sweet taste of chewing gum and often begged American soldiers for it with the phrase, "Gum, chum?"

Unfortunately, her school was located in one of the most bombed out sections of London, the East End near the docks. There were supposed to be armament factories in the neighborhood, which made the area a frequent target of German bombs. Hitting the warehouses and docks also disrupted the flow of war materials to the front lines.

The cabby, a man in his 50s, seemed eager for the fare. American sol-

Gardner Johnson (*right*) and I in London following our graduation from Culver Military Academy in 1938. During the war, Johnson served with the 93rd Bombardment Group.

diers on leave often held out a few bills—either because the currency confused them or they just didn't care—and let the cabbies help themselves. I settled into his seat and gave him the address. He balked. No bloody way would he take me there. Too dangerous. Robot bombs came right up the Thames over there. Sorry. Only after I offered to pay him a hefty fare did he reluctantly agree.

I couldn't blame him. It was only the end of June, and Londoners were just getting used to this new threat they called "buzz bombs," "robot bombs," or "doodle bugs." Riding in a cab or bus, you couldn't hear their menacing whump, whump. But you saw people on the street look upward, then duck into a building or lie flat on the pavement. In between these deadly and unpredictable attacks, office workers, housewives and deliverymen continued the business of living.

As my driver negotiated the streets, frequent air raid sirens and explosions rang out. Every neighborhood we passed through had burned out, shrapnel-scared, windowless, and roofless buildings. This guy was so nervous, he hunched down over the steering wheel ready to duck in case the glass windows of the cab shattered. If there were such a thing as a civilian with combat fatigue, he was among the casualties. I told him I was visiting some school kids, but he only shook his head. He finally pulled over at the entrance at what was once a former winery.

"I'd like you to wait for me," I said.

"Can't do that, Cap'n," he said.

"I won't be long, and I'll pay you for your time." What the hell. If little kids could make it through the streets everyday to get to this underground classroom, he could risk hanging out a little longer. I convinced him that he was better off standing in the street than riding in the cab. At least he'd be able to seek shelter if he heard the last cough of that rasping motor.

Kate's well-lit classroom lay deep underground protected by thick stone walls. If children had to go to school in a dangerous city, this was a very secure place. Many people in London lived below street level, especially in the subways, where families huddled together on bedding pushed up against the walls. There were so many lined up, it was easy to step on people as you walked along the platforms. Others spent the night in basements beneath their apartment buildings or in hallways outside their apartments where they were protected from flying glass.

Kate greeted me with an enthusiastic hug. Her distinctive looks hadn't changed much since the last time I saw her four years ago. She still twisted her thick, black hair into a bun, and wore those tiny horn-rimmed glasses. She and her mother lived somewhere in London in one of those typical row houses with narrow stairways and a tiny garden in the back.

Inside her classroom, 10 children sat quietly at their miniature desks.

"Children, this is Captain Louie," she said, introducing me with my childhood name.

"Hello, Captain Louie," they responded in unison. The kids were only six or seven years old. The boys sported suits and ties, and all the girls tied their hair back with large bows. I don't recall whether or not they knew I was coming and dressed for the occasion. But they sure looked cute. One by one, they stood and introduced themselves.

"Captain Louie, tell the children what you are doing here in England," Kate prompted me. As I studied those eager faces, I hesitated for a moment before answering. "I'm a bomber pilot sent here to help England win the war against the Germans," I said.

No need to gloss over anything. These children knew better than I what this war was all about. They, not I, had spent the last four years living in fear of these deadly bombings. If their fathers, uncles and brothers were still alive, they were away fighting this war. How many nights had terrified mothers and grandparents awakened these kids and shepherded them down stairways leading to dark and crowded basements? Maybe home was a cot shoved up against a wall in the underground. Now this new threat, these buzz bombs that landed randomly throughout the city, violated their childhood.

When I was their age growing up in Cleveland Heights, Ohio, my friends and I played sidewalk marble games and built go-carts. When somebody shouted "Airplane! Airplane!" all eyes lifted skyward to watch a mail-carrying Curtis Jenny descend into Cleveland Airport.

Here in London, kids playing in the streets probably took little notice of the roar of hundreds of aircraft passing overhead. But if the engine of a deadly V-1 suddenly gasped then quit, children had only 15 seconds to find shelter or end up dead. It would take a few more weeks before the government could organize mass evacuations of London's children to communities with less risk. In the meantime, with Kate's help, they bravely carried on with their schooling.

When one child finally asked me what I had in the bag, I realized the real purpose of this mission: to give them a taste of what it is really like to be a kid. To have a surrogate "uncle" surprise them with a treat—to bring a fleeting moment of kidhood to this wine cellar shelter turned classroom. As Kate and I passed out the gum, the kids let loose with squeals of delight. They folded the sugary sticks into their mouths, filling the air with the unmistakable fruity smell of the gum. Before I left, each child lined up to say farewell with a sticky kiss and a hug.

As I was leaving, Kate said she'd be writing Louisa immediately to let her know I'd delivered the care package. "Take care of yourself, Lou," she said as she gave me her own farewell hug. As I stepped out into the street, the cabby was still there, urging me to get in the cab fast so we could get back to the Cumberland. Maybe he thought all those guns in Hyde Park made the neighborhood safer.

I caught up with Searle and suggested we visit some of the places I'd known before the war. We walked over to Piccadilly Circus, but not for the women. Every GI looking for a good time knew the Piccadilly "commandos" worked round the clock waiting to snare an American with a pocket full of money. The war had mothballed Piccadilly Circus' most famous landmark—the statue of Eros, the cupid figure who is poised to shoot his arrow of lust. Only after the war would he be returned to his pedestal above the bustling intersection. Even in his absence, his spirit lived on.

Searle and I detached ourselves from the scene and headed for Scots Top of Haymarket, a restaurant just around the corner from all the action. My family and I used to eat here, and I had fond memories of being with them. Like the time I ordered "white fish." When the waiter brought the plate, my stomach went into spasms. Piled there were dozens of little fish that still had their heads, eyes and tails. I could not, would not, eat them, which sent my family into peals of laughter. After that, I stuck to beef. Six years later, the place still had the look of a Scottish club with tartan lounge chairs and thick oak tables. There was, however, no seating near the windows in case of an attack.

We also took in one of the London shows, although many of the theaters had closed. Since the start of the V-1s, few people ventured out to the theaters and cinemas. But one theater remained open throughout the war—the popular Windmill that entertained audiences with scantily clad girls and smutty jokes. I don't recall viewing this burlesque show, but maybe we did. I do remember the nightclubs, most of which existed underground. Inside, we were kept informed of the dangers in the streets above by a sign hung near the entrance or on the bandstand. One side said "Air Raid" and the other "All Clear." In the theatre district, a doorman stood next to a discreet sign at the entrance of one of these clubs. Apparently his role was to screen out any undesirables. Our dress uniforms and officer status apparently met with his approval. We descended two levels before entering a posh underground bar. There, strikingly beautiful women smoked and conversed with young men who were obviously free of military service. Maybe they were out-of-work show people. We sat at a little table watching the scene, but frankly, I resented these healthy Englishmen, who were not obligated to fight in the war.

Before hitting the sack, we heard from some other officers in the lobby that the roof was an ideal place to watch the inbound V-1s over the Thames. Half a dozen of us climbed several flights of stairs before reaching the flat top of the building. The scene was awesome. Below, only the muted lights of an occasional taxi illuminated the blackened streets. But to the east, we could see the red glow of the V-1s as they raced up the Thames at 400 mph. Then the flames died, and within seconds, a neighborhood exploded creating an instant fire that illuminated a mass of rising dust and smoke. That night, no bombs dropped on our sector. But those of us who watched the show from the roof never strayed too far from the stairwell leading to safety below.

Returning to Earls Colne, Searle and I had to switch trains at Kings Cross, a large central station through which many trains passed. There, we came across bomb dispersal units examining what was left of a German bomber shot down by British guns. The wreckage, which looked like the aircraft had exploded on impact, lay in a huge crater. The dispersal units were looking for any unexploded bombs, but passersby didn't pay much attention. Some tracks were destroyed, but not all, and the trains still ran. We just had to walk a little distance to board one headed for Colchester.

While stationed at Beaulieu, south of London, I had another three-day pass to London. This time, I visited the city alone. Searle preferred spending leave time in a quaint coastal village with narrow, cobblestoned streets called Lymington, just south of Beaulieu. He'd befriended a bicycle shop owner and his wife, who offered him a room and treated him like family. Many British families welcomed Americans military into their homes, sharing what little rationed food they had. Their hospitality took the edge off the homesickness many men—especially those who were married—felt while stationed in England.

From southern England, the train ride was crowded with military and British families. For nearly two hours, I stood as the train lurched and rocked along. Once we arrived in the city, I hopped off at Kings Cross and hailed a cab for the Mostyn Club that was just down the street from the Cumberland.

Early evening, I boarded a crowded double decker bus for Piccadilly. As soon as I jumped off the rear platform, a neatly dressed women slipped her arm into mine. Like so many of the women milling in the crowds, she must have been spotting prospects getting off the busses. I was in my dress uniform, obviously an officer. From her point of view, I was probably respectable and carried money. My instant date was an attractive redhead in her early twenties with a strong Russian accent.

I didn't object when she hailed a cab and directed the driver to take us to her apartment.

Why not? I didn't have any ties with women back home. Not any more anyway. Some of the guys who had married before heading overseas made pacts with other married men to remain faithful. These were the airmen who spent a lot of time writing letters home, watching movies and hanging out in the officers' club bar. Then there were the unmarried men who became attached to British women they met at the dances held off base around Earls Colne and Beaulieu. This was not my scene, but many guys married these women and eventually brought them home as brides. I wasn't looking for a permanent attachment.

Just before heading overseas, I had broken off a five-year relationship with a striking brunette named Gwen. She was a student at Stevens College in St. Louis, Missouri, and I'd met her several years before at a riding stable near her family's summer home on Lake Erie. With her hazel eyes and wide smile, she was the only distraction in my life outside of airplanes.

Without her help, I might not have become an Army Air Corps pilot. When the recruiters came to Washington and Lee, I met all the qualifications—a single white male with two years of college; 20/20 vision and height of at least 5'4"; acceptable performance on stress and balance tests and during an interview with the visiting military staff. But I needed to gain five pounds to meet the 155 pound standard for my 6'1" height. As luck would have it, Gwen landed a job in the War Department in Washington. Through her efforts with a Pentagon official, I was allowed to take a second physical. For six weeks, I consumed lots of bananas and milk to gain the weight.

She made frequent visits to Fort Worth, San Angelo, and San Antonio, Texas, during my eight months of cadet training. She was with me when word came of the bombing of Pearl Harbor, December 7, 1941. That was during my last week of basic training at Goodfellow Field in San Angelo. We'd driven out in my Mercury convertible to the cattle ranch of Louis Farr, a good friend and excellent horseman from Culver. I just wanted to say good-by before heading on to Kelly Field, 200 miles to the south. Returning to the base that December evening in a heavy rain that muddied the dirt roads leading away from the ranch, Gwen and I heard the news over the car radio. The Japanese had bombed Pearl Harbor. My immediate reaction was, "Where the hell is Pearl Harbor?"

When I earned my silver wings at Kelly in February 1942, I had a jeweler engrave "To Gwen, Love Lou" on the back. Louisa was not happy that I had given them away.

"You've earned those wings," she said. "You should wear them with pride on that uniform."

In retrospect, she was right. I also think she understood something about Gwen that I would not admit. This wasn't going to be a permanent relationship. I could see it in the way she flirted with my friends. She even joked about her liaisons with other men. However, just before I shipped out from Dodge City to begin transition training, she visited me one last time. In her view, now was the time to get married. Fortunately, common sense ruled. I couldn't do it. For lots of reasons, I wanted complete freedom. Still haunting me was something in Dabney's last letter.

> But how's about Gwen, he wrote. Are you married or are you going to or what
> the hell! My advice from a seasoned old married man of two months before it was
> cut short is to take that step. Nothing like it. Lou, I would trade anything for the
> short while we were together…

I made the right choice. Frankly, neither of us was mature enough. There were no tears, no passionate good-byes. She just accepted my answer, then told me she had to catch a train. As a footnote, when I returned from the war, I called her parents' home trying to get her number. I really just wanted to let her know I had made it through. I placed the call with an operator who asked Gwen's father for her phone number. I heard his chilly reply, "If she wants to talk to him, she'll get in touch." She never did. Who knows? Maybe her father never told her I'd called.

The cab dropped the Russian and me off at an apartment building in London's West End nearly two miles from Hyde Park. We climbed a set of stairs to a second floor flat. It had two bedrooms, a living room, a kitchen and an upstairs room for a maid. It reminded me of the apartment my parents rented before the war. The Russian shared this place with another woman who was playing cards with a British officer when we arrived. We joined them, and the four of us had a great time drinking scotch and playing poker in the smoke-filled living room. On the fireplace mantle, I noticed a picture of a Russian infantryman, who my partner explained was her husband. I did not ask for details. Everybody knew why we were here. Distant sirens warned of incoming bombs, but there was nothing close enough to interrupt our party and drive us into a shelter. Finally, the women decided it was time to get down to business, and we exchanged money and disappeared into the bedrooms. Ours was a spacious room with a fireplace, sitting area and brass bed. Black out curtains covered the windows facing the street.

The Russian was fast. Before I'd even untied my shoes, her clothes were on the floor. Quickly, she helped me undress, and then pulled me to the bed. Eros' arrow had hit its mark, and this woman's zeal for lovemaking kept my whole body joyously alert. She had my full attention.

Suddenly, we were surrounded by the deafening booms of the antiaircraft cannons coming from Hyde Park, which sounded like the end of the world. The V-1s must have been right over head. From the sounds of the barrage, there were probably bombers up there too. A narrow band of red and white flashes penetrated the darkness at the back of the bedroom. A window, hardly big enough for a cat to crawl through, faced a side street or alley, and no one had bothered to blacken it. I was ready to drop to the floor and roll under the bed. But the noise and danger only aroused the Russian's passion. I followed her lead. This was a holiday and nothing was going to bother me—including the shaking building.

The next morning, there was a tentative knock at the door. A brunette in a skimpy outfit brought us breakfast of toast and scrambled eggs. She kept her eyes on the woman—I guess so she didn't embarrass me. After breakfast in bed, the Russian began dressing in a Red Cross emergency rescue uniform. She offered me the opportunity to remain in bed while she went to work—which I assumed was an invitation to enjoy the brunette. Enough was enough. I dressed and accompanied her out to the street, where we walked to Hyde Park and then separated.

I headed for the Mostyn Club to get some rest. Some guy on the elevator was telling his buddy about the woman he'd picked up the night before. Apparently, the barrage of bombs and artillery had terrified her, so he ended up with her in a cramped bomb shelter in the basement of her apartment building.

After a shower, I crashed onto the bed. As soon as I dozed off, a V-1 cruised right down our street no higher than 2,000 feet. I wasn't taking any chances this time, so I rolled onto the floor and under my bed to avoid being cut by shattering glass. These attacks continued throughout the day. The hotel wasn't damaged. But frankly, I looked forward to returning to my steel cot in Beaulieu with its thin mattress and coarse sheets and blanket. At least there, it was possible to get some decent sleep until they woke you for a mission.

Part II

FRANCE

Denain-Prouvy
February–May 1945

Lessay
August–September 1944

Paris

Laon-Athies
October 1944–February 1945

Chartres
September–October 1944

The 323rd Bombardment Group's bases in France, August 1944–May 1945.

6

The Germans Retreat and Regroup: Flying Missions from Lessay and Chartres, France

August–September 1944

Below on the sunlit waters of the English Channel, military ships flowed in both directions—between the port of Southhampton and the port of Cherbourg. Troops, vehicles, armament, supplies streamed eastward to conduct the business of war. Ships headed west carried the vanquished: thousands of German prisoners headed for POW camps in the United States. For them the business of war had ended.

On this day, August 26, 1944, I could relax at the controls of the Marauder and study the scene below. For the first time, I was flying to France with no bombs on board—just my crew and the few personal belongings we carried to Lessay, our new base south of Cherbourg. Twenty-four hours before, our troops had marched into Paris. The Germans were on the run. And the 323rd Bombardment Group was about to make history. We were the first Allied bombers to launch from France since 1940.

Within an hour of lifting off from Beaulieu, I spotted the newly created runway just inland from the French coast. Five thousand feet of pierced steel planking lay stretched across what had once been a grass runway used to launch German fighters. Arriving over the field, I circled to size up the scene. A few tents dotted the cleared fields surrounding the runway. But the remaining shelters, hundreds upon hundreds of olive green mounds, lay waiting for 2,000 airmen to set up a tent city. The town of Lessay, a couple of miles northwest of the field still had a few stone walls standing, but most of it lay in ruins.

I'd never landed on pierced steel runway before. So I concentrated on making a smooth touchdown. Humming along the nubby surface, the wheels slowed so quickly, I didn't have to use any brakes. I loved it. Unfortunately, that same surface

Weary Willie Jr. and my crew on the pierced steel runway which the U.S. Army engineers laid down at a former German airbase at Lessay, France. *Standing left to right:* Capt. Victor Jacobs, bombardier; unknown, navigator; Capt. Lou Rehr, pilot; Lt. Joe Searle, copilot. *Front row left to right:* Sgt. Charles Allen, tail gunner; S/Sgt. James Alexander, radio/gunner; Sgt. James Knight, engineer/gunner.

drag worked against us on the take-off. With a full bomb load, the Marauder used nearly the whole 5,000 feet before lifting off. Any moisture, even morning dew, made the surface so slick that one pilot was actually killed when his plane skidded into another. Adding to our difficulties were the large power-reducing dust filters installed on the Marauder's carburetor intakes. But we managed.

As I taxied to a parking spot, we passed what remained of a large maintenance hangar—two white walls. Printed in bold letters on the inside of one of the walls was the warning "Rauchen verboten," no smoking. Just behind, rows and rows of jerry cans covered an area half the size of a football field. Gasoline was a precious commodity. The Germans must have cleared out of this place in a hurry.

Assigned a spot near the end of the runway, my crew and I hauled planks for a floor before staking the tent and setting up our cots. Some guys actually preferred living in tents rather than in an enclosed Quonset or Nissen hut. Of course, it was still summer. And we knew this station was temporary. Like summer camp.

Some distance behind the tent, we dug a trench for a latrine and covered it with a canvas hut for privacy. Several other tents used the facility, one man at a time. As airmen, we were accustomed to amenities such as running water and electricity, but nobody complained much about the crude bathroom facilities, including having to shave and bathe out of helmets. Near our tent, Searle and I dug a five-foot deep, S shaped foxhole we could dive into in case of an enemy attack. We didn't really believe

Aerial view of Lessay, France, which suffered significant damage during and after the invasion (courtesy Ross E. Harlan).

the Germans would stage a comeback at Lessay, but we had to be prepared for surprises. When guys from other tents became restless or bored, they took a shovel and dug the trench deeper. Anybody stumbling around at night had to be careful not to fall into what had become a serious foxhole.

At mealtimes, we waited in long lines, mess kits in hand. Afterwards, we headed to large garbage cans of boiling water heated by coals, where we stood in another line to clean the aluminum plate, cup and utensils. The worst part of living in field conditions was dodging the aggressive yellow bees that swarmed relentlessly around our food and drink. They seemed especially fond of whiskey. The only way to escape them was to fly a mission. At night, we lit our tents with fuel from those jerry cans. By pouring gasoline into a bucket filled with sand and lighting it, we were able to play cards, write letters home and shoot the bull.

I didn't do much letter writing after I arrived in England. An occasional note to my parents or sister was about all I felt like scribbling. It wasn't that way during the two years I was instructing. I wrote and received letters all the time. There were the guys at Washington and Lee, the good friends I left behind when I joined the Army Air Corps at the end of my junior year. They were the Class of '42, and they were going to graduate without me. A couple of guys wrote me a letter dated April 29, 1942.

For the 323rd B.G., living in field conditions at Lessay meant waiting in long lines for food and cleaning the mess kits in large garbage cans heated by coals.

They still lived in a place we called the "Castle." For them, life went on as if there were no war. There was lots of drinking every night because it was their last semester—or because their futures were both certain and uncertain. There was lots of bravado about the "sinking the social sirloin at a great rate." Somebody even managed to set the Upper Castle on fire, but everybody got drunk afterwards including the volunteer firemen. And, of course, they wished I could be there partying right along with them. I must have sent them a picture of me sitting in the AT-6 because one guy said I looked like the mouse in the movie *Dumbo* sitting on top of that "big damn airplane."

The day they wrote that letter, April 29, 1942, was also the dateline on the article somebody sent me about 2nd Lt. Robert Boyce's midair over the Florida orange groves. He was the first Washington and Lee graduate, Class of '41, to be killed in the war, but I can't be sure the Castle boys heard the news.

I also corresponded with some of the cadets who completed their advanced training with me and headed off to the Pacific or Europe. There was the second lieutenant, who became a B-17 or B-24 pilot. He wrote me from Honolulu in September 1942 on his way to Australia. His V Mail ended with "wish you were here to help do a good job." A year later, when I was a Marauder instructor at Dodge City, word came he was killed in a fierce battle for some island in the Pacific.

Then there was his classmate Jack Zawada, the best damn pilot of them all. When he and I rat raced around the Texas skies, I just could not shake the kid. His dream was to fly a fighter, especially the P-38. But he ended up flying the C-47 transport in North Africa. He had no college credits, just a high school diploma. No matter how well he flew, they couldn't make him a second lieutenant at graduation. Instead, men like him were called sergeant pilots with no authority over officers, who often shunned them.

Zawada wrote long, chatty letters. One dated June 12, 1943, was upbeat. He was real excited to hear I was instructing in the Marauder, and said he'd love to fly one. "They pass us up in flight as if we were anchored up there," he wrote. Then he told me that I'd really like it over there in North Africa and sent me a list of what to bring when I was shipped overseas: "First a good folding cot with a pneumatic mattress, and good pillow and several pillow cases and if possible a GI type sleeping bag with a couple of sheets. Bring plenty of socks, under clothes and khakis. And don't forget a good, light, folding chair, lawn type. The rest leave home."

Nearly three months later I received another letter dated August 29, 1943. There was some good news. He was promoted to second lieutenant. "It sure makes me feel good because as staff sergeant pilots and flight officers, we were treated as second raters and always played second fiddle."

But mainly, the tone was sober. He'd been flying combat missions for nine months, which he said felt more like two years. He wondered why we weren't sending replacement pilots. Then he wrote, "On our last mission, we lost our squadron commander, who was a major, and our operations officer, a captain. We sure took a beating. My DC-3 had 463 holes, no hydraulic, no brakes, no flaps and both ailerons' wires cut by ack-ack, a big two-foot hole in the rudder. How we got home only God knows. I only hope we don't have to go through that again."

That was the last letter I received from him. I don't know if he survived.

Bikes were essential transportation for getting around the bases. Jacobs, with bike, checks out my skills with a washboard.

While I was at Waco giving twin-engine training, a former cadet wrote me from the Hotel Tampa Terrace on December 17, 1942. The following day, he had to show up at MacDill Field, the B-26 Marauder training site that acquired the reputation of "one a day in Tampa Bay." This was a guy who was scared of flying, even though he had completed pilot training. At Waco, I tried to build his confidence by giving him extra instruction in the AT-9. We'd do loops, stalls, steep turns and single engine landings. But he never became friends with the aircraft.

In his letter, he thanked me for helping him out. But he added, "I lacked the most essential requirement for flying, and that is confidence.... Just sitting here in this room thinking about it gives me a scare. I wish you were here to straighten me out." I never heard from him again either.

Funny how they all wished I was there. And while I was stuck in San Antonio, Waco, Del Rio and Dodge City, I wanted to be there too, sharing in the spirit of flying missions in combat aircraft. But now that I was overseas and in the thick of the conflict, I didn't write anybody and say "wish you were here." The friends I'd made in the squadron and the group, and especially my crew—they were enough to worry about. Besides, this was the summer of 1944, and even the Castle boys had to be on duty somewhere.

Shortly after our arrival at Lessay, we briefed for missions against the port city of Brest, which lay just to our south on the Brittany coast. Three divisions of Gen. George S. Patton's Third Army surrounded the city. But Brest remained in German hands because Hitler was determined never to surrender this port that harbored his U-boats. He even ordered his SS to execute any German soldiers who showed signs of fatigue or despair.

Gen. Dwight D. Eisenhower had his own ideas about Brest. He needed this port to keep up the flow of men and supplies to the front lines. His other problem lay 400 miles to the east at Metz, near the German border. Here Gen. Patton's troops had stalled out in an attempt to seize an ancient and fiercely defended fortress. Gen. Patton needed his three divisions there.

Air power was essential to end the stalemate at Brest. But clouds and rain during the first few days in September scrubbed several planned attacks. With so many U.S. troops on the ground, the bombing had to be accurate. Finally on September 5, hundreds of medium, heavy and light bombers briefed for Brest strong points. Three boxes from our group would be the first to arrive on the scene, followed by the others throughout the day. We launched despite cloud cover. Bombing altitude would have to be below 5,000 feet.

That day, I led a flight of six to Brest. Taking off to the west, we passed over the Channel Islands of Guernsey and Jersey. While at Lessay, rumors circulated that German holdouts on these islands fired on our aircraft. But I never knew of anyone who experienced this hostile fire.

Heading south just inland from the coast, we had quite a view of Mont St. Michel, the ancient French monastery. The formidable fortress, caught between powerful tides from Normandy and Brittany, towered above a huge expanse of sand flats. A single road ended at the base of a massive pile of turrets, walls, abbeys and impossibly steep streets leading to the towering spires of the cathedral. A lot of guys from our group hitched rides here to climb to the top.

"Searle, next time you and I have a training flight, remind me to bring a camera," I said. A few days later when the weather was decent, Searle piloted a Marauder south along the coast and circled the monastery below 500 feet. Sitting in the right seat, I captured an historic photo of Mont St. Michel. The only vehicles parked near the base of the massive granite structure and traversing the causeway were military jeeps and trucks carrying sightseeing warriors eager to explore this fortification. The photo captures the remoteness of the old cathedral and presents a stark contrast to the acres and acres of parked cars and tour buses that characterize the entrance today.

We dropped our bombs on Brest with surprisingly little resistance from the Germans. Maybe even the SS figured it would have been suicide to mount a last ditch defense against a massive Allied air attack. The following day, September 6, the skies opened up enough to permit another low level run on Brest. This time, our group's bombers took off in the late afternoon. Flying on my right wing was 1st Lt. John

When airmen from the 323rd weren't flying missions, they made liberty runs to sites like Mont St. Michel located just south of Lessay. I took this photograph from a Marauder.

Guldemond. He had been overseas since May 1943 and flew as a copilot on D-Day. Even though we were in the same squadron, I didn't get to know him until we moved to Lessay, where he lived in an adjacent tent. He often joined Jake, Searle and me outside of our tent to share the generous monthly whiskey ration—gin, scotch, bourbon, cognac and champagne. Guldemond was an easy going guy with a ready laugh, and I liked having him around.

On this second mission to Brest, Guldemond carried a group photographer, Wilson A. Reidy, who rode in the waist gunner's position. Apparently, Reidy had boarded Guldemond's plane at the last minute, so there was no time to brief him on the mission.

Once again, the proximity of our ground troops to the targets required accurate bombing. The briefed altitude was still below 5,000 feet. But by the time I arrived at the target area, smoke and fire from all the bombing of the past two days kept Jake from seeing anything on the ground. Passing over the target, we encountered only feeble antiaircraft fire.

"Jake, let's make another pass at 2,000 feet." I said over the intercom.

"Do it, Head," Jake said. "Otherwise we bring the bombs back."

Then I radioed the pilots who followed. "We're going around and dropping to 2,000 feet," I said. "There's a bottle of cognac waiting for anybody who follows."

"You mean we have a choice?" somebody called over the radio.

Once a month, the men received a whiskey ration. *Left to right:* Rehr, pilot John Guldemond, Jacobs and Searle set up the bar at Lessay. In the background is the latrine.

"Yes. Anybody who doesn't want to follow can go home," I said and meant it.

All five planes followed as we circled and descended for another pass over the target area. "As soon as the bombs drop, dive then scatter" I said. "Form up again at 5,000 feet for the trip home."

I figured right. Other than the concussions from our own bombs, this was a milk run. However, as Guldemond dove his plane through the acrid smoke and intense heat, photographer Riedy didn't know what was happening. He was sure they'd been hit and were going to crash. When Guldemond called over the inter-com, "Are the bombs out?" Riedy thought he said, "Bail out." So he jumped and landed just inside of our lines, where the Army picked him up. The next day, he showed up back at Lessay. Guldemond recalls how he "caught hell from the old man," meaning Col. Wood, for that mix-up. But Searle—who was Guldemond's copilot that day—remembers Col. Wood smiling through the reprimand.

It would take another few days for the Third Army to mop up the area so they could join Gen. Patton at Metz, where German resistance was much stiffer. Ironi-cally in the all out effort to wrestle Brest from the enemy, our bombs had rendered the port useless. More importantly, after the breakout at St. Lô back in July, the Allied armies had advanced eastward toward the German border so quickly, that Brest was too far away to serve as a vital port.

The rain and thick clouds of summer continued into September, frustrating our attempts at bombing and giving the Germans a chance to regroup. With lots of free time, men visited bombing sites that from England were only points on mis-sion maps. Towns where there had been heavy fighting, like Cherbourg, Avranches and Granville, also drew the curious.

Normandy in the aftermath of the invasion lay wasted. Not far from the base, pieces of M-1 rifles, empty shells and grenades, remains of plastic explosives, and the personal equipment of the casualties littered the fields and hedgerows. Our base at Lessay was so large that I never smelled the death until I explored the area on foot. Carcasses of dairy cattle and horses lay bloated in the fields where they once grazed—victims of the hedgerow fighting and land mines. There, too, in cordoned off areas lay the swollen bodies of dead Germans. The Graves Registration teams had their work cut out for them as they reclaimed bodies, both American and German. Cleaning up the area was going to take a long time.

One day I was with a dozen or so of men from my squadron walking the fields and narrow lanes where hedgerow growth filtered the daylight. We entered the shaded roadways without fear of attack. But just a few weeks before, when the area was hot with Germans, a man would have to be scared shitless moving along these narrow lanes with no way of knowing if snipers lay hidden in the thick tangle of growth on either side. I'd rather take my chances with the flak gunners. At least we knew where to expect them.

Separating from the group, Searle and I crossed an open field. Beyond, in a small woods, he spotted what looked like an overturned jeep. We had to be careful. Already a couple of guys, tempted by abandoned jeeps, inadvertently found themselves approaching the vehicles through minefields. Demolition teams were doing their best to identify and destroy the land mines that still lay hidden throughout the area. But even well traveled roads swept by mine detectors still concealed explosives that resulted in deaths and severe injuries of civilians, livestock, pets and our own men. One airman lost his leg when his jeep hit a mine. One day, a Frenchman who was walking across a road near the base stepped on a mine that lay hidden in the center of the road. Men who heard the "thump" of the explosion ran to the site to help. But all that remained was a mangled body.

Searle and I scanned the ground for potential problems. Near the jeep, pieces of bent and torn metal lay scattered. There was nothing left here to salvage. As I studied the ground, something caught my eye in an area of thick undergrowth. A piece of a uniform perhaps. Drawing closer I could see through the tangle of bushes and vines the decaying bodies of two American soldiers.

"Searle look," I said.

He moved closer and touched one of the bodies with his boot. "Jesus, they've been there a long time," he said. "There isn't much human left here." I had no desire to study the corpses.

"I'll get the Graves Registration people," I said. "You stay here."

Earlier, we'd passed them and their truck in a cordoned off area digging up shallow graves. Approaching through the field, I watched a couple of these guys grab the boots and shoulders of a dead German and fling the body into a pile where some other German uniforms lay.

Returning with the graves men, I hung around just long enough for them to read the dogs tags of the two dead Americans. Both men were from West Virginia. They were probably just kids who signed up together and vowed to protect each other. Maybe a sniper caught them off guard or a German patrol ambushed the jeep.

It didn't matter now. They were two young guys who should have been back working on the farm, camping in the mountains, or taking their girl friends dancing.

"Be careful how you handle them," I said. I had a feeling that to do that job day after day, these guys had to overlook the humanity of these corpses.

The whole scene saddened and angered me. Dead bodies aren't part of an airman's daily routine. If a returning bomber lands with dead on board or crash lands, emergency crews stand by to assist. When a plane spirals down in flames or blows up, nothing remains but a few personal effects next to cots. When it comes to seeing death up close, pilots fight a cleaner war. After that day, I didn't go out of my way to explore a battlefield that hadn't been cleaned up.

There were still a few French living around Lessay, and they were grateful to have us as neighbors. Some of the women offered to do our laundry in exchange for cigarettes and chocolate. Others sold us bottles of their potent apple brandy, Calvados. We'd try anything, but some of that stuff could make a grown man cry. One day, a couple of locals approached my tent and indicated they wanted to buy one of the bikes we'd carried over from England. It didn't take me long to realize I didn't have much use for it here in France. There was no place within peddling distance to get a good meal or a beer. Like Lessay, most of the surrounding towns were in ruins, caught in the crossfire of the invasion. Airman who wanted to leave the base for places like Cherbourg and Omaha Beach hitched rides. Among the military, there was an unwritten rule that if you stood with your thumb out, you'd get picked up either by American or British soldiers—preferably American, because British transports often ended up broken down on the sides of the roads. Apparently a large number of their newly manufactured three-ton trucks developed cracked pistons almost immediately. Many of the trucks we hitched rides on were part of the Red Ball Express that carried men and supplies from the port of Cherbourg and the beaches to the front lines. These Frenchmen had more use for the bike than I did. After entertaining them with a demonstration of peddling backwards to show how well the bike worked, I accepted their offer of a few francs.

One day, Jake, Searle and I struck out to visit Cherbourg, the vital port town that our bombs helped liberate back in late June. We were looking for K and C rations arriving at the piers. The best C rations had boneless chicken preserved in some kind of liquid. And K rations, which the troops carried with them, had cheese and biscuits and some sweet things in them along with cigarettes and toilet paper. Our mess cooks tried their best with dehydrated eggs and vegetables, mystery meat, and marmalade sandwiches. But the rations just tasted better. There was another problem with the food and probably the water. An epidemic of gastritis laid guys up for at least a couple of days with chills and diarrhea, leaving them weak as kittens. Rations were probably safer than field food. I would have given a month's pay for the care package of Spam my sister Judy sent me while we were still in England. She didn't know, but we had plenty of that canned pressed pork. I ended up giving most of it away. Here in France, Spam would have tasted like prime ribs.

For the trip to town, the three of us dressed in clean pants, puttees, shirt and ties, and leather jackets. We figured that looking our best would give us easier access to the supplies.

Left to right: Searle, Rehr and Jacobs dress up to hitch a ride to Cherbourg in search of K and C rations to fill their bags.

We hitched a ride on a weapons carrier to the center of town, which was about an hour away. Along the way, we passed through villages where families actually lived in bombed out shells of buildings surrounded by piles of timber and stone. Lying on beds or hanging up laundry, they had no privacy.

Cherbourg was a city of contrasts. Some parts teemed with vitality like the cobble-stoned square where we jumped off the truck. This area was crowded with French citizens, some on foot and bicycles, others in horse-drawn farm vehicles. Business was brisk at the Crédit Lyonnais bank, which appeared to have escaped damage. Although street level shops were closed, people occupied many of the apartments over them. But we didn't have to walk far to see where the shellings and street to street fighting had taken their toll. The only thing standing in one intersection was a bronze statue of a horseman waving a flag. Everything else, including a small church, melted into the piles of stone and plaster.

The busiest part of town was the harbor, where offshore, U.S. cargo ships floated. Just two months earlier, German mines made access from the channel impossible. Clearing the mines and restoring the port of Cherbourg had been a model of wartime efficiency. Military police didn't allow people any closer to the docks than a quarter of a mile. But somehow the three of us found a way to get closer. Inside the secure area, we had a good view of the amphibian landing craft that ferried men and supplies to a convoy of Red Ball Express trucks waiting on shore. From the docks, these trucks, driven mainly by Black soldiers, fanned out across the French countryside in an effort to catch up with our rapidly moving troops. Food, gasoline, ammunition, blankets, boots, bombs —whatever it took to run a war passed through this port and a few Normandy beaches like Omaha. The drivers stopped only for

Top: An ancient French warrior stands triumphant amid the ruins of a street in Cherbourg, France. The city was liberated by Gen. Omar Bradley's troops on June 26, 1944. *Bottom:* Cherbourg was a vital port for maintaining the flow of war materials to the front lines. This African American soldier was a driver for the Red Ball Express, which delivered supplies hundreds of miles to our rapidly advancing troops on the front lines.

fuel, repairs and unloading. But that was where wartime efficiency ended. What Jake, Searle and I could not know as we watched the scene at Cherbourg was that poor roads, distances as far as 300–400 miles, and protracted autumn rains would delay the deliveries and ultimately the end of the war. As hard as the men and equipment worked, the system provided only a fraction of what was needed to defeat the Germans. By the end of September, our ground troops wouldn't even have enough gasoline or ammunition to keep up the advance. Our bombs, too, would be in short supply.

Before the military police ordered us out of the loading area, we managed to fill our sacks from a large pile of unlabeled canned food, much of which was dented. The contents turned out to be Vienna sausage, those tiny hot dogs, which like Spam are still around today.

We ended up standing alongside a road that still offered a distant view of the harbor activity. "Holy shit, look at this," said somebody standing nearby. Approaching from the south were thousands of marching soldiers. At least six rows stretched as far as the eye could see. The closer they came, the more remarkable the scene appeared. At the front was an American enlisted man dressed in khakis flanked by six high ranking German officers These wore great coats and full uniforms, despite the mid September warmth, and they marched together in perfect step. Suddenly, the American stretched out his arms and commanded in German, "Halt!" The order rippled through the lines. The vanguard stood within 20 feet of us. The faces of the German commanders showed no emotion. Behind them, their soldiers appeared exhausted. Dark circles outlined their eyes, which stared straight ahead. They could have been survivors of St. Lô and the Falaise Gap.

When the American enlisted man received a signal from the docks to move forward, he commanded, "Marsch!" In perfect step, the troops followed their commanders. Their final destination would be prisoner of war camps in the U.S. But it would take most of a day to load them on to the ships waiting offshore.

"Looks like this war could end soon," said Jake.

With thousands of captured Germans ready to step off the continent, it was easy to believe the war wouldn't last. But I was more cautious. "Maybe," I said. "But there are plenty more where they came from." Here were soldiers stripped of their weapons and forced to march to the commands of an American enlisted man. Yet, they remained united in their resolve and arrogance, and I was reminded of the marching soldiers I'd seen in Berlin and Munich in 1938. As I watched these prisoners march stoically forward, I felt certain that any hopes of a swift end to this war were an illusion.

"Those guys are gonna be eating steak and eggs while we're out here screwing around," said Searle. He had a point. We had to scrounge for standard military rations, and these POWs were headed for three squares a day somewhere in Alabama or Oklahoma.

"Yeah, but these can't hurt us anymore, said Jake.

Shortly after we observed this scene at Cherbourg, stories circulated around the camp of a massacre carried out by German soldiers in a town called Oradour-sur-Glane south of us near Limoges. All we really knew was that shortly after D-Day, the SS gathered up a whole village and killed everyone in it. Details unfolded very slowly, fragments only. Nobody wanted to repeat them. Nobody wanted to believe. According to a handful of eyewitnesses who escaped, the Germans rounded up the men and machine-gunned them. Then they crowded the women and children into a church, suffocated them with smoke, and set fire to the structure.

Five years as a cadet at Culver and three years in the Army Air Corps had not prepared me for that kind of soldier. I could understand how prisoners of war clung to their dignity. But how could soldiers carry out orders to massacre unarmed civilians? Where was their honor? Who could order such acts? By all accounts these victims were not the French Resistance. If the events at Oradour-sur-Glane were true, I felt certain that captured airmen would never see the inside of a prison camp. Afterward, I made sure my crew and I wore our pistols, standard issue Colt .45s, on every mission in case we were shot down.

By the middle of September, we awoke to frost on the tents. Hundreds of miles to the east, Gen. Patton's troops endured cold rains, mud and the flooding Moselle River as they tried to figure out how to storm Fort Driant, a mass of concrete and guns near Metz that sheltered 2,000 German defenders. Five times, our bombers attempted missions to the Metz area. Twice we launched, but because cloud cover extended right down to the ground, we returned to base with fully loaded bombers. These were long missions lasting nearly four hours. It was obvious that we were going to have to move closer to our targets.

One morning, I returned to my tent after operations briefed then scrubbed a mission to Metz. Thick clouds over the target, which was just north of Nancy, were not going away. Waiting at my tent was Capt. Chester "Spike" Gist, my good friend from Dodge City. After his arrival at Earls Colne, he was assigned to another squadron, the 453rd. I ran into him occasionally, but squadrons develop their own sense of identity and camaraderie—sweating out missions, enjoying time off, and enduring losses together. But Gist and I had shared so many good times back at Dodge City and Shreveport, I was always happy to see him. He was a skilled Marauder pilot, and we shared an eagerness to make a difference in this war. Like me, he looked forward to a promotion to major and a position leading box and group formations.

Gist looked serious. "Lou, Browning was shot down over Italy," he said. "A flamer. He took a direct hit to the fuel tank."

I was stunned. "Son of bitch, no." Bob Browning was another Marauder instructor who shared our barracks back at Dodge City. He headed off to transitional training at Barksdale the same time Gist and I did. The last time we'd seen him was at Borinquén Field in Puerto Rico. Over rum and cokes in the officers club, we discussed our final destinations. He was headed to North Africa, not England.

For as long as I had known him, Browning's passion was to spend the rest of his life on a farm in Virginia. I'd promised to visit him there after the war. Hearing the news of his death, I cursed the war, the Germans, the loss of a good man and a hell of a good pilot. Shit. A flamer. The fuel tank explodes, and there is no escape. The Marauder rolls on its back and spirals to earth. The G-forces keep everybody pinned down. I liked to imagine how a pilot could open the hatch over the cockpit

A direct hit to the left engine engulfs this White Tailed Marauder in flames. The bomber begins to roll, which will lead to a spiral earthward. The forces of gravity make it nearly impossible to escape. This February 5, 1944, mission was to a V-1 launch site in France.

and use every bit of his life force to escape out the top. But this "never do" procedure wouldn't have worked. I knew that, and so did Browning in those last seconds of his life.

I wiped my eyes and let go the anger.

I preferred to remember his style. Like the suspenders he always wore when we gathered around the barracks bar. Then there was the time he lost an engine on take-off and landed gear up in a cornfield. Everybody walked away. "Remember his bent propeller we hung up behind the bar?"

"Yeah, we couldn't have anything ordinary hanging there," said Gist.

Then there was the train ride to Savannah. After Shreveport, we boarded a troop train bound for Savannah, Georgia, where we were scheduled to pick up a Marauder for ferrying overseas. Jake and I filled our barracks bags with ice, 150 proof rum and some coke. We settled into the caboose with Gist, Browning and several other guys for one last party. Every time the train stopped, we jumped onto the tracks and took a few pictures with our arms around each other or in reckless poses hanging off of the caboose. Then, sometime in the night, the train came to a screeching halt. We were in Macon, Georgia, where military police boarded and ordered every last man out of the train. They lined us up along the tracks and lectured us about our behavior. That was all. Even the MPs understood, we were men heading to war, letting go of a little tension.

Browning was a modest and considerate guy, who made an impression on my stepmother Louisa. Before we shipped out from south Florida, my folks, who had a winter home in Delray, took a group of us out to dinner. When I wrote Louisa about his death, she dedicated a water fountain at the local library in his name. I always appreciated the gesture, but visiting the place after the war didn't bring much satisfaction. The sense of loss never goes away.

On September 18, I had orders to lead an advance echelon of six aircraft to what would be our new base at Chartres. But low clouds and drizzle hung over a wide area of the continent. There was no way I could launch in the morning. So I sat around waiting for some improvement. Chartres was about an hour flight from Lessay, but with marginal conditions, I needed a navigator. Operations assigned 1st Lt. Frank Burgmeier to ride in the right seat. He was the squadron's lead navigator, one of the best in the group. Since flying his first mission on December 22, 1943, he'd been through a lot of action, including D-Day. Because he flew only in lead aircraft, finishing his tour of duty, 65 missions, wasn't going to happen in the usual six to eight months. We'd seen each other at briefings, but I really didn't know him. I was happy to have a navigator like him ride along to scout out this next base.

When he joined me on the flight line, he had just won $2.25 in a game of gin rummy. He was one of those guys who kept the tedium at bay by playing billiards, card games, or ping pong and taking in a movie now and then.

"I've heard a lot about you and Jacobs," he said. I appreciated the recognition, especially from one of the seasoned veterans of the group.

Burgmeier couldn't have been more than 21 years old, but he looked and acted much older. A thin, dark mustache arching over his lip added to the image.

"I've been flying pretty regularly with John Sterling," he said, "but he'll be heading home next week. They treat us navigators like wild cards. I never know who I'll be flying lead with until I see the loading list."

"I hope we'll be doing a lot more flying together," I said.

"More than likely. I've still got nine more missions before I hit 65," he said. "Then I can go home to my wife."

Burgmeier was married in July 1943 at the base chapel at Avon Park, Florida. "I borrowed $50 and went AWOL for a honeymoon to West Palm," he said. "The unit was on alert to ship out, so we only spent a couple of nights together."

It was obvious he really missed her. Burgmeier's story made me think of Bill Dabney. "Nothing like marriage," he wrote one month before he was killed. "Lou, I would trade anything for the short while Kitty and I were together." I didn't envy married men like Dabney, Searle and Burgmeier. Guldemond, too, had married just before shipping overseas in May 1943. A couple of days of passion followed by an emotional farewell, worry over letters that did or didn't arrive, and resisting the temptation of other women would have sapped my emotional energy and compromised my focus. All I needed was a little fun once in a while with a girl in London or maybe Paris. Say "good by" and never look back. I had to be free to get the job done.

Burgmeier was different. As the man responsible for leading an entire formation to the target, he had to be giving 100 percent to every mission. He had the discipline to separate devotion to duty from devotion to his wife. Tedi, who was 18, supported him with daily letters and frequent packages, so when he returned from a mission, he had something to look forward to—making him the envy of his tentmates.

But today's flight was no mission. The ceiling finally lifted to around 2,000 feet. Burgmeier and I decided to give it a try. Halfway there, weather forced us to turn back.

With clear skies the following day, September 19, the group spent the day moving to a former German fighter base on the outskirts of Chartres. I was happy to be living closer to the action, where maybe, just maybe, we could do more to bring an end to what was looking like a stalemate. I made a couple trips that day to transport supplies. With only Searle flying with me as copilot, I lifted off from Lessay for the last time. There was plenty of activity on the ground as the men packed up, so I decided to give them a little diversion. Loaded with equipment, I climbed out, turned around, dropped the nose and dove to pick up speed. At 250 mph, I roared over the field. Too low, I remember thinking at the time as I skimmed over a pile of lumber at the end of the runway. I was below 200 feet, which was my imaginary line separating show-offs from jerks.

With good visibility, the base at Chartres was easy to find. It lay just outside of the city where the twin spires of the ancient cathedral could be seen for miles towering over the flat landscape. The runway needed some repair, but it was usable. The rest of the airfield was a disaster. Crippled German fighters—ME-109s and FW-190s—littered the area as did shallow pits piled high with live ammunition for loading onto the fighters.

Nearby, a camp with 25,000 German prisoners of war provided plenty of labor. We'd bring in truckloads of them to dig latrines, clean up land mines, and repair the runway and buildings. Except for an occasional German officer who demanded better treatment, most prisoners cooperated cheerfully. Hell, this duty was better than serving on Hitler's front lines, and they knew it.

Day and night the Red Ball Express rumbled along the roads surrounding the base. They called these main roads "Red Ball Highways." At night their continuous beams of light cut the darkness. But still the shortages continued. We needed everything, including rations, blankets, boots, warm clothes, aircraft and vehicle parts, even bombs. Some of our men flew back to England to bring back supplies. Others got lucky and raided some former German warehouses loaded with goods. One of the biggest caches was a stash of champagne and cognac, which mixed together became a potent drink known as a French 75 or a German 88. When the Germans swept through France in the spring of 1940, one of their objectives was to control the great wine producers in regions like Champagne, Burgundy, and Bordeaux. They even appointed "weinfuehrers" to make sure the French were not hiding their best wines or committing acts of subterfuge like shipping inferior vintages stamped with the labels of extraordinary harvests. Many vineyards managed to get away with both acts of rebellion. Nevertheless, the Germans either looted or paid low prices for millions of bottles of wine, much of which was still stored in warehouses throughout France.

Landmines continued to be a problem, and the demolition teams cordoned off large areas of the countryside. Still Searle, Jacobs and I managed to visit Chartres and its 12th century gothic cathedral. From a distance this massive structure with its towering spires appeared to be the only building left unscathed in a city of rubble. But up close, sections of this city were open for business. Our men frequented the shops including a butcher, where they bought steak and hamburger to cook back

The spires of the Chartres Cathedral tower majestically over a landscape of rubble.

Top: The airfield at Chartres was littered with hundreds of wrecked German aircraft. Here Joe Searle sits atop a German fighter, the FW-190. *Bottom:* At Chartres, I look inside a German fighter, the Me-109, surrounded by what remains of a hangar.

Capt. Arthur Noble (454th B.S.) sits atop a German bomb, part of the wreckage at Chartres. Noble and I graduated together from Kelly Field (42B). He joined the 323rd at Beaulieu after instructing in the Marauder at Del Rio, Texas. An experienced Marauder pilot, he is credited with 17 box and group formation leads.

at the base. Searle figured it was really horsemeat. We could also get a decent meal with wine at some of the cafes.

The three of us drove a jeep to the railroad bridge that we'd bombed back in July. Our engineers had restored the bridge, which passed over a stream now choked with dead trees and debris. As we stood at the site, a train carrying supplies chugged across the makeshift span. Surrounding the bridge was a cluster of bombed out stone buildings, including an old mill. As Searle stood in front of tons of stone, dirt and lumber, I snapped a photo so we could kid the other pilots about how inaccurate *their* bombs had been on that mission.

Our stay at Chartres lasted a little more than three weeks, but I'll never forget a couple of missions flown from there. On September 29, three boxes took off to bomb the Julich warehouse, 50 miles inside Germany. This was our longest penetration into Germany yet, and the mission would take nearly four hours.

I was leading a flight of six in the first box led by Maj. Roscoe Haller, squadron commander for the 456th. Long before the bomb run, heavy and accurate flak bursts filled the sky. Suddenly an orange explosion burst under Haller's left wing. His Marauder began a rapid descent. Burgmeier was in that bomber. I'd seen him at the 0330 briefing. He told me he wasn't even on the loading list for this mission. Somebody woke him up and asked if he'd take the lead navigator slot. "You know what they say about volunteering for missions, Lou," he joked.

Top: German prisoners of war from a camp near Chartres were trucked in each day to clear the area of landmines, booby traps and piles of ammunition. *Bottom:* The German POW work detail heads back to camp.

Haller was a high mission man with the reputation as "a pilot's pilot." It looked to me like his engine was shot out, but he must have shut it down immediately because there was no fire from the wing. Still, I didn't envy his position. He was dropping so rapidly that his options were limited: bail out over enemy territory or risk surviving a crash landing on German soil. Unless Haller could slow the descent, there was no way the crew could make it back to the safety of our lines.

After returning to base, we waited around for any news of their fate. Finally one of our Marauders arrived back at the field and signaled its approach with orange flares. A bombardier on board was wounded. The plane was loaded with 12 airmen including Haller's entire crew, who were hitching a ride home.

I was relieved to see Burgmeier step out of the plane. He told me that after dropping out of the formation, Haller was able to keep them aloft long enough to milk the aircraft to a newly captured airfield just over our lines. The runway was bomb-pocked, but they didn't have any choice. They prepared for a crash landing, but with the all the skill of a seasoned Marauder pilot, Haller kept the bomber rolling down the runway. What they discovered after stopping were hundreds of cans of gasoline-filled jerry cans lining both sides of the runway. Losing control during the landing rollout would have turned the Marauder into an instant inferno. Following closely behind was Haller's number two wingman, who was preparing to set down on the same runway. But Haller's crew fired flares warning him to remain airborne until they found a suitable landing area on the airfield.

"That was one of my roughest missions, Lou," Burgmeier admitted. "When I thought we were going to have to bail out or crash land, I said to myself, 'I'd give anything to make our mess tonight.'"

The story didn't end there. The following day, the crew chief of the rescue plane showed Burgmeier a shattered magneto from one of the engines. Each engine had its own magneto system that supplied electrical current to the plugs. When the crew chief inspected the right engine and removed the magneto, it fell apart in his hand. The only thing holding this vital part together was a single wire wrapped around the outside. If that magneto had shattered during the take-off roll or immediately after lifting off, the result would have been an engine failure on that side. With an increased load, even the most experienced pilots would have their hands full. The odds of 12 men surviving a dangerous swerve into the dead engine while still on the runway or a crash landing after lift-off were slim. This wasn't the first time Burgmeier had been a tough spot. Back in June his lead crew almost bailed out over the English Channel when the turret gunner's guns ran away and shot up the Marauder's tail. Fortunately, the Marauder held together as his pilot nursed it back to Earls Colne.

With real hazards facing aircrews every day, we couldn't waste mental energy on the what-ifs. Afterwards, if we survived, there would be plenty of time to ponder the whims of fate.

October 8, just before we moved to another base further east and closer to the action, I had the worst mission of my life. The target was a railroad bridge at Euskirchen, southwest of Bonn, Germany. We'd bombed a supply depot there the day before, but German resistance was fierce and the gunners damaged 19 of our aircraft. This was going to be another long mission, nearly four hours. I was leading a flight of six, but my take-off was delayed because of some equipment problem. Shortly after takeoff, I ran into low-level clouds. For a while I could still see my wing-men. But then they disappeared as the clouds closed around me. We often flew in and out of cloud layers. But this was solid—a bad situation. I was in a box with 18 aircraft, all heading in the same direction, and nobody could see anything. I announced to the box leader and the pilots who followed me that I was going to keep climbing to get on top of the clouds. I figured it was the safest route to avoid a midair collision. I assumed my formation would follow. Finally, at 14,000 feet, I broke out. I flew in circles briefly, but nobody joined me above the clouds.

"What do we do now, Head?" Jake called on the intercom.

"Let's stay on this heading to the target and see if we can find a hole," I said, motivated by an eagerness for dropping bombs on the target no matter what.

For over an hour, we headed east—alone. We might have been close to the target, but there was no way of knowing where we were. Nothing but solid gray clouds passed beneath us.

Suddenly a huge back explosion appeared to our right. I took evasive action to the left where another flak burst exploded directly in front of us. I evaded, but another ragged burst blocked our path. Shrapnel pinged all over the plane. "Somebody's got

German flak gunners have this 323rd Marauder in their sights.

This aerial photograph of German 88mm flak positions shows the deadly potential of such concentrated antiaircraft firepower. Craters from bombing efforts dot the surrounding fields.

a fix on us," I said. "Let's get the hell out of here." I dove, then steeply banked the plane until we came around on a westerly heading.

"Lou, I think we overshot. That's probably Bonn down there," said Jake.

Around major industrial areas, the Germans had radar systems that directed the flak. Even after we got turned around, they kept following us. Taking evasive action was futile.

"Jake, drop the bombs," I said after opening the bombays. Cold air rushed through the Marauder. "Bombs away," he called. We had no idea what lay below. It could have been an industrial complex or a residential neighborhood. It didn't matter. Somebody down there was trying to blow us out of the sky. The taunting lasted another five minutes as we raced west. All we needed now were a couple of FW-190s on our tail. I called the gunners. "Keep your eyes open. We're over some rough territory." They probably had a few choice words about the mess I put us in.

Finally back over the safety of France, I had time to think. What a lousy, fucked-up mission because I tried to outguess the weather. I wondered if anybody made it to the target. I had only myself to blame. After landing, I marched over to operations to find Maj. Lawrence McNally, our operations officer.

"Sorry, Larry. I got carried away," I said. I wasn't going to cover up anything. "I headed out alone, got too high and ran into trouble with the big boys up there in Bonn. I'm embarrassed and pissed off. I can't tell you what happened to the guys following me."

Under these circumstances, coming clean with my mistakes was the only way to maintain and build trust.

He just laughed. "Everybody had trouble out there today," he said. "A couple of your guys came home after they couldn't find you. Nine planes never formed up, but we still had enough to hit the target." He also told me the group ran into some heavy flak over Germany, which damaged 16 of our planes.

"By the way," he said, "Haller has approved you for permanent flight commander."

After our dance with the flak gunners that day, I should have been less eager to lead formations over increasingly hostile territory. But right up front ahead of a box of 18 planes or leading the entire group was just where Jake and I believed we could do the most good.

When I got back to the tent, Jake and Searle had already downed a couple of French 75s. They poured some cognac and champagne in a tin cup and handed it to me.

"That was quite a ride," said Jake. "Where'd we go?"

"This stuff tastes pretty good," I said enjoying the extra kick in the bubbly. "By the way Jake, after today, you and I are going to be leading boxes."

"You mean, you screw up and we get promoted," he said with obvious pride at hearing the news.

Then I turned to Searle. "Joe, it's time you had your own crew," I said. He flew the Marauder well, and I knew he could handle tough situations with a cool head.

"I just hope you learned something out there today," I said.

7

The German Offensive: Flying Missions from Laon-Athies Airdrome, France

October 1944–January 1, 1945

October 13, 1944, Searle, seated in the left seat of the Marauder, circled the spires of the Chartres Cathedral in a final farewell before piloting the Marauder to our next base. Laon-Athies was another abandoned airfield where the Germans once launched their night fighters. It lay northwest of Reims and close to the German and Belgium borders. For a change, the October skies were clear enough that Searle was able to level off at 6,000 feet. From the right seat, I studied the lighter shades of green and brown defining the trenches of World War I that stretched north and south as far as the eye could see. Twenty-six years later, and the scars remained—faint outlines where the flesh and bone of millions fused with mud and rusting metal to mark the legacy of the "war to end all wars."

I was born four months after the signing of the Armistice that brought an official end to the fighting in those trenches. But powerful images of those war years remained to shape my youth, my values. For as long as I can remember, factory whistles all over Cleveland blasted their tribute to the Armistice at the eleventh hour of the eleventh day of the eleventh month. Our German housekeeper, Miss Martha Eichler, who had immigrated to the states before that war, often spent evenings conversing with another German woman. Their talk inevitably led to how terrible the war years had been for them here in the states. As German immigrants, they were always under suspicion as spies or traitors.

During the 1920s, the popular culture loved World War I. When I was eight, my father took me to see my first movie, *Wings*, a World War I aviation story about two hometown buddies who fall in love with the same girl then join the Army Air Corps. The film was silent, but our local theater in downtown Cleveland created live sound effects behind the screen. The rapid machine gun fire followed by screaming planes diving toward earth terrified me. Trapped in the darkened theater, I squeezed my eyes shut and covered my ears.

Nevertheless, the danger of aviation warfare and the daring of those pilots gripped my imagination. At the local dime stores, I discovered pulp fiction with titles such as *Aces* and *War Birds*. These books even taught the rudiments of flying with lines such as "He pulled back on the stick to evade the Hun." One of my favorite books was a collection of World War I oil paintings by the French artist and bombardier Henry Farré, an eyewitness to many of the scenes depicted in his impressionistic paintings. The Caudrons, Spads, and Nieuports in battle over the French landscape fascinated me—in particular one print that depicted two German aviators dropping to earth from their burning plane. Those pilots wore no parachutes.

At Culver, I lived with the trappings and traditions of World War I. Cadets wore a variety of uniforms, coats and hats, all modeled after the World War I styles. Those of us in the Field Artillery mastered handling the horse drawn caissons and firing the French 75 cannon. Barracks with names like Argonne and Château-Thierry were reminders of the World War I battlefields we now flew over. Culver even named a sidewalk after Gen. John J. Pershing, Commander of the American Expeditionary Forces.

Loyalty to country, dedication to duty, and respect for those who served and died in the military were values Culver instilled it its cadets. Outside of the library imbedded in the pavement was a bronze star dedicated to the 85 Culver graduates who had died in World War I. Before entering the building, we stopped in front of the star and saluted. No one dared step on this symbol, not even in jest. Occasionally, I'd study the portraits of these men hanging in a gallery on the second floor of the library. Their youthful features belied the reality of their deaths. While I honored their service and sacrifice, I saw no relevance to my life. This Culver experience was one of the ways young men prepared for promising futures.

If somebody had asked me the perennial high school yearbook question, "Where do you see yourself five or ten years from now?" my answer would have been "Flying airplanes." But flying bombers over these same killing fields where my predecessors died never entered my imagination. Like the outlines of those trenches stretching endlessly in both directions, World War I never really ended. The old hostilities remained, camouflaged by new rhetoric from new leaders. There had been some advances in the hardware—planes, guns, vehicles, bombs—but no progress in what really mattered, avoiding wars. Men still fell from the sky and died in the trenches and suffered prejudice. When it was over, there would be more bronze stars dedicated to those who had sacrificed their lives, more hero-generals to welcome home, more memorials to honor the sacrifices at places named Pearl Harbor, Omaha Beach, Bastogne and Dachau.

Living and flying missions from Laon-Athies tested the spirit of every man in the 323rd. As we settled into tents and makeshift shelters amid a sea of mud, no one believed the situation could get much worse. But it did. The wettest summer and fall in 50 years turned into the coldest winter in 100. Yet, adversity brought the men of each squadron closer as we shared talents and resources to cope with the living

Top: I spent five years as a cadet in the mounted Field Artillery at Indiana's Culver Military Academy. The unit demonstrates their skill with the horse drawn caissons (courtesy of the Culver archives). *Bottom:* I load an artillery shell into the French 75 cannon during exercises at Fort Knox, Kentucky, summer 1937.

Aerial reconnaissance photograph of Laon-Athies airbase shows the extensive bomb damage before the 323rd occupied the site. Engineers did not have time to repair it before the group moved in. The 456th Bomb Group set up their tent city in the large forest on the right (courtesy Ross E. Harlan).

Top: Following the ground troops, the 323rd Bomb Group moved five different times after D-Day. The Rehr crew, *left to right*, Jacobs, Allen, Alexander and Knight, take a break from unloading equpment after arriving in Laon-Athies in early October 1944. *Bottom:* My crew waits for orders before heading off to the woods to find a tent site.

Jacobs introduces these two puppies, which he found abandoned near Chartres, to their new home at Laon-Athies. Flak Bait on the right shared the tent with the Rehr crew. Another tent adopted the white one. Many men kept dogs, which traveled from base to base with their masters.

and flying conditions at Laon. The move also brought us closer to our targets, which gave us confidence that we could end this war sooner, not later. But nobody believed the Germans would give up easily.

What helped when we weren't flying was a seemingly endless supply of champagne and cognac. This was the champagne region, and our airmen must have liberated a huge cache destined for the Third Reich. The German appetite for the bubbly was insatiable, and during the occupation, French wine growers were forced to ship as many as one million bottles of champagne a month to Germany.

Searle touched down smoothly on the only usable runway left after our B-17s got through pounding this place. Literally thousands of bomb craters dotted the surrounding farmland. As Jake headed off into the woods to find a spot to pitch our tent, I helped unload the plane, which included two puppies Jake found abandoned somewhere near the base at Chartres. Somebody could write a book about the dogs the group kept as pets, everything from mutts to Great Danes. Even the war correspondent Ernie Pyle, who visited the group back in April, commented on their numbers. Nurtured by our men, these loyal creatures provided a link with a normal home life.

The 456th settled into a wooded area, which the French called the Forêt de Samoussy. When the Germans occupied here, they hid planes and munitions throughout these woods. Beneath some undergrowth, Jake discovered a concrete foundation raised well off the wet ground. By some miracle, nobody else had claimed it. There were even steps leading to what became the entrance to the tent. After clearing the area and staking the tent, we used flooring from an abandoned hospital to make a door. Raiding the countryside for building materials was essential, because other than a few skeletons of buildings, there was nothing left standing here. A few lucky airmen found a former German equipment depot that had some pre-fabricated shelters. But most of us had to settle for ripping out flooring from abandoned

October 1944, the 456th B.S. set up a tent city in the muddy woods at Laon-Athies. Tents offered the only shelter during Europe's coldest winter in 100 years. Airmen built wooden walkways to reach the mess and latrines, but heavy fall rains often left these floating in the mud.

buildings, cutting down telephone poles, and dragging home sides of wrecked trains. Then using all of our creative energies, we fashioned makeshift shanties. To negotiate the boot-sucking mud paths leading to the mess and latrines, somebody laid down planks for walkways. Sometimes the rain was so heavy, these literally floated.

Outside every tent was a woodpile for a little stove inside. Chopping wood from the surrounding forests was a daily chore—even though the French farmers complained bitterly to our commanders over the loss of their trees. One of the men in our squadron was a forester, an expert in felling. He and I pulled a double handled saw through the trunks, which very often rang out with "chink, chink" from all the shrapnel imbedded in the trees. Afterwards, Jake axed the logs into small pieces. Despite all our efforts, there was always a shortage of wood, so we only fired up the stove in the morning and evening.

Everything we needed to keep warm was in short supply, especially blankets. Once, weather forced several hundred B-17 crewmembers returning to England to divert to our base. That night, our men shared their tents and cots with these Eighth Air Force men. The following day, when these crews returned to England, they carried extra cargo—our blankets. Col. Wood demanded their prompt return, and their commanders obliged. But our Marauder men lost respect for those B-17 men who left them shivering on the front lines, while they returned to warm huts and then headed off to the nearest pub.

At Laon-Athies, chopping wood each day was essential for keeping the small stoves running inside each tent. Jacobs swings an axe in front of the tent, which was erected on an old foundation. Flooring from an abondoned hospital served as a door.

Sharing the tent with Jake, Searle and me was 2nd Lt. Reddis N. Morris, a replacement copilot who was now part of Searle's crew, and Flak Bait, one of the two puppies. He usually curled up with Jake. Awakening in the black cold, I listened to the weather outside. Fog surrounded us with silence. Rain and sleet tapped the canvas. Wet snow, which sagged the tent's roof, dripped from the trees. We took turns starting the fire in the stove, but Jake liked to awaken early, so he often took over. As the smell of smoke filled the room, I lay in the warmth of my sleeping bag, which I supplemented with long underwear, flight suit, and a knit hat. If I had a mission, I looked forward to getting up. But after we established the base at Laon-Athies, adverse weather grounded our bombers for all missions except two in late October. These targets were a couple of railroad bridges on the other side of the Rhine.

Before heading out to the latrines, I dressed in my sheepskin lined bomber jacket and asked the fire starter. "You gonna warm up the latrines too?" These were nothing more than a long slab of wood with holes in it laid over a deep trench. Usually, a layer of frost coated the only seats in the house. If the food didn't leave men constipated, it gave them diarrhea. There was no such thing as privacy, and more often than not, the toilet paper was an old copy of the *Stars and Stripes* newspaper.

Despite the weather, we still had a war to win. The weathermen did their best, but we often launched into the unknown. Quickly developing low clouds or layers of clouds with haze in between complicated our missions. Frequently the bombers couldn't even form up after launching. Or if they made it to the target area, they

At Laon-Athies, a Marauder crashes and burns on landing. Formerly a base for German night fighters, Laon-Athies was heavily bombed by our B-17s before the 323rd moved in. Bomb craters surround this runway, which was only used for taxiing.

often faced a towering wall of clouds. Returning to the base with full bomb loads became routine.

Out on the flight line, there was always tension and excitement after missions, especially because Laon-Athies was so close to all the action. Officers and enlisted men gathered at the hardstands and along the edge of the runway hoping for the safe return of friends and a successful raid. Who didn't make it back? How badly damaged were our Marauders? It was not unusual for a bomber with a damaged landing gear to slide, scream and spark as it ground its metal belly into the runway. There was even more tension when a Marauder signaled wounded on board.

Even strangers arriving at the field created excitement and sometimes tragedy. There was a P-47 fighter base about four miles away. Once, one of their pilots nursed a really shot up fighter toward an emergency landing at our field. Just shy of the runway, he lowered the flaps. But only one extended, and the plane rolled on its back and smashed into the ground. He died instantly. In one terrible "Oh shit" second, that guy had to know that surviving the dogfight and using all his skills to coax his crippled fighter home didn't count. This mission had his number on it.

Because medium bomber pilots flew *in* the weather, not above it, recognizing shifting weather patterns and clouds was an essential skill for all our pilots. But making decisions based on those readings was primarily the responsibility of the flight leaders. When I brought the planes back from a bomb run, I preferred to begin our descent several miles out from the field. This made the approach and landing easier and safer for those who followed, especially pilots with engines shot out, damaged landing gears or wounded on board. Letting down early also saved fuel.

Returning from a mission one day in November, I saw a wall of clouds up ahead. At 11,000 feet, the temperature inside the unheated cockpit was minus 4 degrees. Rather than climb higher, I decided to drop beneath and lead the formation of 18 planes back at low level. But rising terrain and increasingly poor visibility forced me to reverse course, climb above 11,000 feet and regroup above the overcast. Repositioning took a lot of time and energy and was a bad mark for my efforts as a leader.

To make matters worse, I'd drunk too much coffee that morning. We'd been up since 0400 hours for the 0750 takeoff. We ate our meals in an open-air mess, half of a former maintenance shop built by the Germans. Before we moved in, Allied bombers had destroyed the other half of what had once been a large building. Those of us scheduled for missions ate first. We sat across from each other at long tables set up under what little roof remained as we downed a breakfast of oatmeal, bread and coffee. It was chilly, and drinking an extra hot coffee just felt good. If I hadn't tried to outguess the weather, we'd have been on the ground by this time. With a full bladder demanding my attention, I had difficulty concentrating on anything else.

Somewhere near my seat was the relief tube, but I could only grope blindly for it. My copilot was 2nd Lt. Jim Siegling. He was one of the newly commissioned replacements with only 260 hours of flight time when he was shipped overseas and assigned to the 323rd. He had trained in a twin-engine UC-78 or Bamboo Bomber, but he never saw a B-26 until he showed up at Beaulieu back in July. For the next few minutes, however, he was going to be in charge of the formation.

"Keep this thing right side up," I said. "I've got a problem."

Then I fumbled frantically to get all the gear off me—seatbelt, parachute, flak jacket. Pissing on the floor was looking like my only option. I'd never live that down. Finally, at the last second of painful endurance, I found the tube stuck behind the bulkhead. They don't call that thing a relief tube for nothing. The transition from pain to pleasure was instantaneous.

Finally settling back into the left seat, I led the group home where we circled and descended through cloud layers in carefully timed intervals for the landing—never an easy process after a mission. Breaking out beneath the clouds, we had to stay clear of the clusters of bombers circling left waiting for others ahead of them to land. After that experience, the first promise I made to myself was never, never drink coffee before a mission. The second was to learn how to read the weather around Laon.

The town of Laon, which rose nearly 1,000 feet above the surrounding farmland, lay several miles to the west of our base. I quickly learned to trust the reliability of the cloud formations that developed in the morning over the gothic towers of the Cathedral of Notre Dame, which stretched skyward at the top of the plateau. If the clouds rested high above the cathedral, chances were they'd still be there when we returned from the mission. Then I could begin the formation's descent early. But skuddy patches of clouds wrapping around those towers meant that within a couple of hours after taking off, low clouds would settle over the area, and we'd have to arrive over the field and circle down.

The damp, raw weather brought another dilemma that I had little control over: a sinus infection that plugged the cavities in the left side of my face. In the dry winter air of Texas, I rarely had to endure the pain brought on by changes in altitude and pressure. But here in the raw, damp air, a descent from an altitude above 5,000 feet caused excruciating pain. Tears streamed from my left eye, but I still had the use of the right. Once I landed, it took hours for my head to open up. The squadron doctor tried to fix it up with some medicine, but nothing really worked. I'm sure lots of airmen suffered from the problem.

Sunday November 19, I awoke at 0500 hours with the usual stuffy head. I was leading one of three boxes that day. Briefing was at 0550 hours, so Jake and I dressed quickly and downed some breakfast. Entering the briefing tent, I shielded my eyes from the glare of the high powered lamps used to illuminate the maps suspended from panels in the front. I settled into a seat up front alongside the other box leaders.

Suddenly, everyone stood as Col. Wood entered the tent.

"At ease, men," he commanded. Then he took a seat up front. He never said anything, just listened to the briefing like the rest of us.

The target was choice: a command center located in Merzig, Germany, a heavily defended town lying on the east banks of the Saar River. From there, the Germans controlled all activity in that sector, which included Metz, where Gen. Patton's Third Army was still bogged down. Apparently Gen. Patton was fed up. In his inimitable way, he had passed an angry message through Air Corps commanders that he wanted a "revenge bombardment from the air to teach those sons-of-bitches that they cannot fool with Americans." Fifty-six Marauders from the 323rd—three boxes of 18 bombers and two window aircraft—along with medium bombers from other groups, were ordered to destroy that command center at Merzig.

Bombing altitude for this mission was 12,700 feet. Surprisingly, the briefing officer gave no minimum altitude for the bombing. This omission gave flight leaders much more flexibility on the bomb run. I don't know if somebody just forgot to mention it, or they were giving us a silent carte blanche to do what we wanted. An overcast sky at the target area did not favor the mission. Flying time to the target was approximately one hour and 15 minutes. There would be no fighter escort to accompany us. I would be leading the second box.

Arriving at my bomber, I greeted the crew chief and asked, "Is she all ready to go?"

"Affirmative, Captain." And that was all I had to hear. How these enlisted men endured working outside in subzero temperatures and freezing rain changing spark plugs and patching up damaged aircraft with their bare hands was a tribute to their dedication. And I trusted them completely. In the same spirit, the armament people worked through the night with minimum lighting to load the bombs on 56 aircraft. Occasionally the entire mission changed, and they had to switch bomb loads, say from the four 1,000 pound bombs to eight 250-pound fragmentation bombs. Today we carried the four big ones.

Burgmeier climbed into the right seat. He'd been flying steadily with me since

My crew poses with *Hell's Belle*, during the fall of 1944. *Left to right:* Jacobs, me, navigator Lt. Frank Burgmeier, who joined Jacobs and me to assist in box and group leads, and copilot Lt. Jim Siegling.

I began leading boxes back in late October. This was his 62nd mission. He needed only three more before his tour was finished, and he could head home. But once in the cockpit, nobody spoke of such things in the face of a difficult mission. The focus now was on performing our jobs with skill and accuracy. Copilot Siegling was also on board, probably as an observer.

The weather at Laon was good enough to get to altitude in a hurry. But as we neared the German border, the landscape disappeared, shrouded by thickening clouds. Pinpointing that building in the heart of the town wasn't going to happen. "You're within 10 miles of the target," Burgmeier announced over the intercom.

"Tighten up your formations," I called to my pilots. We'd been flying in close formation for over an hour, and it was easy to get sloppy.

We had to be approaching the Saar River. The first box was at least a mile ahead of me. Suddenly flak bursts surrounded those Marauders. From photos in the briefing, I knew just where the guns were positioned—on a hillside just east of the command center.

The first formation took no evasive action. Nor did the aircraft open the bomb bays. Metal clattered against our fuselage as we took our turn through the aerial minefield. There was nothing but solid cloud beneath us. Not a break anywhere. I followed the group leader's box with a slow left turn away from the target area. The ack-ack followed, and then gave up the chase. As he headed west, I figured he was going to set up for another pass. But he held altitude and continued on the westerly course.

"He's headed back to the base," I said to myself. Then I looked below and saw what appeared to be layers of clouds, not solid overcast.

Aborting the mission was his decision, and I respected it. But as the second box leader, I was determined to lead my group down through those layers. "We can do this," I announced to my pilots. "I can see openings. We're circling down for another pass at the target."

With 17 planes following in close formation, things didn't happen quickly. To keep everyone in position, I set up a wide sweeping turn, well west of the target area and wove my way downward through the broken layers in and out of clouds. Quickly Burgmeier shed his seatbelts, stood up and removed his flak jacket. Then he knelt directly behind Jake's position in the nose. He knew the landmarks. If he could find them quickly, Jake could set up the bomb run.

Although Burgmeier remembers heavy flak as we circled downward, only the pain under my left eye distracted me. As we descended from 12,700 feet, I braced myself. It didn't start out as much, just a twinge. Then pricks developed into throbbing stabs. The tear ducts in my left eye burst as we dropped through 7,000 feet. "I can still see. This isn't going to last," I told myself.

I focused on weaving through the layers and looking for the bottom with my good eye. More and more of the terrain came into view.

"I know that intersection," Bergmeier said. "Lou move left, just a little." As I maneuvered, I leaned right to look over Burgmeier's shoulder and get a glimpse at what he and Jake saw through the nose. We didn't have far to go to break out.

"OK," Burgmeier called, "that road will take you to the IP. Lou, move left. Line up with it. See it there? Yes, there!" Just as we broke through 6,000 feet, the entire landscape opened up. Ahead the muddy Saar spilled over its banks. There wasn't much time to set up the run. The target was just on the other side. I leveled off at 5,700 feet and took my lead from Jake.

"I got it," said Jake. "Open the doors, Head." The rushing sound filled the aircraft. "Tighten up back there," I called to the pilots. "This is it." How many pilots still followed, I did not know. Roaring across the river, we rode out the tracers that arced and crisscrossed in our path. They didn't matter. The target, a large building standing several stories high right in the middle of the town, lay in Jake's crosshairs.

Then bombs away! I led the group in another sweeping turn to the left and headed for home. Burgmeier settled quietly into his seat. Jake crawled out and calmly announced we'd "hit the fucker dead center."

When we returned to base, Col. Wood, with a Texas sized grin, met us on the ramp. Apparently an observer from Gen. Patton's troops had watched the bombing from the other side of the river and called the base to let Col. Wood know. He was ecstatic. Our bombs flattened the target.

"You guys are going to get the DFC for this one," he said.

An aerial view of what General George Patton called "the splendid bombing of Merzig" on November 19, 1944. Bombardier Jacobs, navigator Burgmeier and I each received a Distinguished Flying Cross (DFC) for this mission.

The Distinguished Flying Cross! How he knew within two hours of our bombing that the three of us would be recognized, I don't know. But official word came three days later.

What helped was a letter from Gen. Patton himself to Maj. General Samuel E. Anderson, commander of the Ninth Bombardment Division. Copies quickly made their way downward through the ranks and ended up in my paperwork.

> The splendid bombing on the German town of Merzig on the morning 19 November by over 160 medium bombers of your command is producing excellent results. This bombing, coupled with your afternoon effort on the ordnance Depot at Pirmasens, I am certain will materially assist this Army in cracking the Siegfried Line and defeating the German nation.
>
> The willingness of your airmen to go in against heavily defended targets is an inspiration to this Army.
>
> For all the officers and men of the third United States Army, I wish to express to you our appreciation for your cooperation and our admiration for your magnificent efforts.
>
> G.S. Patton, Jr.
> Lt. General, US Army, Commanding

The Distinguished Flying Cross has been around since 1927 when President Calvin Coolidge presented the first one to then Capt. Charles Lindbergh for his historic flight across the Atlantic. By a special act of Congress two civilians, Wilbur and Orville Wright, received the DFC in 1928 for their 1903 flight at Kitty Hawk. From 1941 to 1943, a lot of guys picked up DFC's for racking up missions against the enemy. Gen. Hap Arnold wasn't happy, and after a visit to Europe to assess the situation, the Army Air Corp established new criteria for the award. As of August 1943, men earning the DFC had to distinguish themselves by heroism or outstanding achievement while participating in aerial flight. Recipients were supposed to do something that clearly set them apart from others in the same circumstances.

I did not know all that history at that time. I was just happy to get some recognition for the three of us who hung our asses

I receive my first Distinguished Flying Cross, for the November 19, 1944, mission to Merzig, Germany.

out there. The "outstanding achievement" was the result of the combined talents and dedication of three experienced airmen. Cheers from our commander and recognition from a small group of friends was enough. This was war, and we got a medal. That was nice. But the war was not over. Besides they never even pinned the bronze cross, engraved with a four-bladed propeller, on our dress uniforms until March 1945, four months later. Burgmeier had gone home. It wasn't unusual for some guys to receive theirs posthumously.

Thursday November 23, the group celebrated Thanksgiving. If the weather hadn't been so miserable, we'd have been flying. But we hadn't had a mission in two days. The mess cooks tried to make it seem like home with turkey, mashed potatoes, string beans, dressing, fresh French bread, cake, apple and raisin pie and coffee. As we sat in the open air mess, some men chatted about their own family traditions—the early morning trek into the woods to bag a deer or a pheasant, the foods like Aunt Margaret's sweet potato pie or Mom's giblet gravy.

My own memories of Thanksgiving were from the years at Culver. Christmas was the only holiday we spent away from school and with family. Tradition for me meant a Culver football game and the Thanksgiving Formal, one of the few times we invited girls to the campus. As I recall, they came from some private girls' schools in the area—virgins in white gowns gracing the arms of cadets in full dress uniforms.

I don't remember any fooling around. Their visits were just too well organized. I was sure Culver carried on these traditions even during the war, but I did not speak of them here at Laon-Athies.

That holiday dinner made a lot of guys sick. Some of the turkeys shipped from the states had spoiled. How the cooks missed the smell of rotten turkeys, I don't know. But this outbreak was severe.

I escaped that problem only to awaken on November 29 to a double dose of illness, the flu and some intestinal problem. I was scheduled to lead a box that day, but I was too sick. I made my way to Gist's tent to ask if he'd take my lead. Gist was such a friend, he didn't even hesitate. I never had to make a request like that before, and the strain and anxiety of sweating out Gist was far worse than if I were leading a mission myself. The target was a German barracks area. He returned safely and came to my tent to let me know the mission was "routine." Just some minor flak damage to the plane. "Lou I have some other news," he said, and I knew something bad was coming. He maintained a pipeline of information with the other Marauder groups, and he knew a lot.

"Bob Farrell was shot down over the Rhine," he said.

"Christ, who's next," I said, almost too sick to feel sorry about anybody but myself. Farrell was the fourth Dodge City instructor who traded boredom and restlessness for war.

He didn't share the barracks with Browning, Gist and me, but he always showed up when the drinking light was on. He was a fun-loving guy, and I always enjoyed having him around.

"Wasn't he the one who set our barracks on fire?" Gist asked.

"Yeah, he shoved too much paper or wood in that pot bellied stove," I said. It overheated, and the barracks wall burst into flame. Between our efforts and the base firemen, there wasn't much damage. But after that, the brass viewed us as troublemakers, which was part of the reason they shipped us out.

Gist and I were the remaining survivors—so far. How many more friends was this war going to claim? Inexperience killed Dabney and Boyce. But Browning and Farrell were seasoned pilots like Gist and me. Experience did not count for shit when the ack-ack had your number on it.

As I lay there feeling sorry for myself, something struck me. I no longer wanted the responsibility for the lives of the men in my plane or for that matter, all the crews that followed my lead. What I really wanted was to fly solo. If I were going to die, I didn't want to take at least five other people with me. When I felt better, I marched over to headquarters and applied for a transfer to a P-47 Thunderbolt group. Occasionally guys transferred from bomber to fighter groups and vice versa. Or if they really liked being where the action was, they'd finish a tour of duty in say a B-17 and request transfer to fighter group rather than head home. The P-47, nicknamed the "jug," appealed to me because like the Marauder, it was rugged and highly maneuverable. It also carried significant firepower with its eight .50-caliber machine guns.

But Col. Wood ignored my request. His aide dismissed me as if he had heard this stuff before. Instead they gave me a new assignment: assistant operations officer with even more responsibility. My new job was to help the operations officer, Maj.

Lawrence McNally, to ensure everything was in place to get the bombs to the targets. We were responsible for organizing crews, making sure the planes were flyable and the bombs properly loaded, and handling any emergencies that could delay a launch like a collapsed gear or crash on take-off. They also promoted me to major.

In retrospect, they were right. Just thinking about the steep dives and climbs required of fighter jocks made my sinuses cry for Mother.

December turned the raw rains of the last two months into snow, sleet and freezing rain. Ice coated the trees and bushes encasing them in brittle glass. December 2, I led a box to Saarlautern, just east of the Saar River, to knock out trenches, pillboxes, and dug-in tanks and armor. We were supposed to drop on Pathfinder lead, those Marauders equipped with special instruments for locating targets when weather prevented visual bombing. But their equipment failed, and we brought the bombs home. Weather thwarted the few missions we attempted. Either half the formations were unable to find their leader, or severe icing forced aircrews to give up. We tried, but there wasn't much else to do but shovel snow, cut wood and sit around the feeble tent stove drinking cognac and shooting the bull.

One evening in early December, a replacement pilot from another squadron dropped by to show us a German rifle, a Mauser K98k, he'd found the day before. This gun was the primary infantry weapon used by the Germans in World War II. He joined us for a couple of drinks. Feeling good, he showed off by firing the gun through a hole in the top of the tent.

"Hey if you're gonna do that, go outside," I told him.

So he stepped out into the frosty night and fired his rifle several times into the sky. We all thought this was pretty funny until somebody from another squadron got pissed off and sent the Officer of the Day to investigate. These officers, who were armed, were in charge of discipline and could make arrests.

He confronted our visitor, "What's going on here? Looks like you're asking for trouble."

Ignoring him, the visitor turned and entered the tent.

The officer stepped inside and said, "I'm taking you to headquarters."

The quick thinking guy with the rifle asked, "What's the password of the day?" Laon-Athies was close to the front. For security purposes, everybody was supposed to know the password of the day in case the enemy infiltrated the camp. What he should have said was "glassbottom boat."

Unfortunately, he forgot. Or he was just too stunned to respond. Suddenly, he had the Mauser pointed at him. "You don't know the password," said the visitor. "I'm taking you to headquarters."

We all drew our guns and marched him over there. At the time, it seemed like a pretty funny thing to do. We played it straight until some commander settled things amicably.

Within days, failure to recall the password or that the St. Louis Cardinals won the World Series could get a man killed on the spot. On December 16, Hitler surprised everybody, especially Gen. Eisenhower and the generals under his command, by thrusting a quarter of a million men through the rugged hills and forests of the Ardennes in Belgium, northeast of our base. The historic Battle of the Bulge had begun. Suddenly boredom at Laon-Athies changed to a state of high tension. Word of enemy activity in the vicinity of Reims, just a few miles away, and Laon quickly spread. German paratroopers and English speaking Germans posing as American soldiers committed acts of sabotage. At Soissons, just 20 miles southwest of our base, they succeeded in destroying a large ammunition dump. Located nearby were large supplies of food and fuel, which if captured would be vital to the advancing German troops.

We were on a six-hour alert to evacuate to England or another French airbase if word came that the enemy was going to overrun Laon-Athies. Within two days, the Germans had broken through the allied lines along a 60-mile stretch. Men at the base had orders to destroy strategic communications and materiel that we could not fly out. But the weather had us socked in, and we were unable to take off or launch any missions. There was even some talk of retreating to Paris by foot. Nobody seemed to have a real handle on exactly what was happening. For protection from an attack, I carried my pistol and wore a helmet. Some men even carried gas masks.

Every morning an icy fog shrouded the base and remained until dark. At night, the skies cleared. Night missions were not possible because we were not equipped with blitz lights, those hooded lamps needed to set up the proper glide slope for landing. The Germans, however, had no difficulty launching at night. They'd send out their JU-88s, twin engine bombers, to cruise around looking for our bases. We maintained a complete blackout. But we'd hear the drone of their engines, sometimes as close as half a mile away, and sometimes right overhead. They were low, certainly no higher than 2,500 feet. When they approached, we rolled out of our cots and into the frozen foxhole. Sometimes there was only one aircraft cruising around up there, and he acquired the nickname, "Bedcheck Charlie." But strangely, I don't think any of those pilots knew exactly where they were. They passed overhead several times, and then left. I would have given anything to take off in a Marauder and fly around up there waiting to shoot one of these guys down. But there would be no way to land.

Beginning on December 18, we briefed for missions, hoping that something would happen to change the weather pattern. Because our medium bombers were superior bridge busters, eight Marauder groups based in eastern France were briefed to sever four key bridges that carried supplies to the German troops. The Euskirchen, Ahrweiler, Mayen and Eller bridges lay along an arc running north to south some 50 miles behind German lines. Previously our Marauders had inflicted severe damage to these structures. But they were so essential to this offensive, the Germans rebuilt them practically overnight. Everybody heard the same message. Hit these targets at all cost, at any altitude, even as low as 1000 feet. Some of our pilots even offered to fly single ship, low level attacks. Ground crews rose before dawn to de-ice the Marauders' wings and warm their engines. But every day, an icy fog cloaked the region, enabling the Germans to advance westward.

All the briefings and scrubbings were getting to Burgmeier. He had one more mission to fly with me, and he just wanted it over. We were going to be the lead ship for two boxes from our group. I could see his frustration as day after day, he made out the navigation flight plans only to scrap them.

"You know, Lou," he said after one of these briefings, "they told me they'd make me a captain if I'd fly five more missions as squadron navigator for the 454th. No way! I just want to go home. Tedi thinks I'm headed there already."

After five days of briefings, I began to believe that retreating was a real possibility. We had a grim joke. If the Germans let us keep New York, they could have Paris. Our only hope lay in those ground troops stopping the Germans. What we did not know until later was that German forces routed untold numbers of our infantry into what witnesses have described as a "chaotic retreat" westward. Many of these ground forces were untested recruits, kids right out of high school, who were rushed into battle without adequate training.

During these tense days after the attack began, we had visitors stay at the base. They were seasoned troops, Rangers, on their way to Bastogne, Belgium. They stopped at Laon-Athies to await orders before continuing on to the front. These were hellfire type guys, who specialized in storming difficult German strongholds like the cliffs at Pointe du Hoc on D-Day—with no small loss to their numbers. These guys arrived on trucks mounted with .50-caliber and 20mm antiaircraft guns with all the swagger of men who had survived months of killing. The first night, they headed into Laon looking for booze and the local brothel. One woman turned them down, then locked them out of her basement apartment. Her rejection prompted one of these crazy guys to throw a grenade down her steps. Fortunately nobody was injured. They played by different rules. I was glad to see them leave for Bastogne, where their brand of fighting would do some good.

Six days after the battle began, the weather looked like it might break. Gen. Eisenhower raised our level of expectation by issuing a rare Order of the Day.

> By rushing out from his fixed defenses the enemy may give us the chance to turn this great gamble into his worst defeat. So I call upon every man of the Allies to rise now to new heights of courage, of resolution and of effort. Let everyone hold before him a single thought—to destroy the enemy on the ground, in the air, everywhere—destroy him! United in this determination and with unshakable faith in the cause for which we fight, we will, with God's help, move forward to our greatest victory.

If the weather cooperated, December 23 was going to be a rough day. Turning Hitler's "great gamble into his worst defeat" meant a lot of men were going to die tomorrow. At the moment, Hitler was winning. Emboldened German gunners weren't going to shirk from their responsibility. If we could launch our bombers, the Germans could send up their fighters. "Tomorrow's going to be interesting," I said to anyone in the tent who was still awake before I rolled over to sleep.

The briefing was at 0600 hours. Stepping outside, I felt a cold, dry breeze blowing from the east. Tense with anticipation, our crews settled onto the benches set up in a large tent. Today, Gist and I were leading two boxes to the Eller Railroad Bridge that crossed the Moselle River. I'd led a mission to this vital supply route back in late October, but the Germans quickly repaired the damage. Our bombs were to hit the entrance of a nearby tunnel, blocking it with the debris.

Preceding us to the target were two other boxes from the 397th Bomb Group

Marauders at Laon-Athies line up behind group mission leader Rehr in the silver Marauder, upper left corner. Despite blizzards, freezing rain and bitter cold, tents provided the main shelter. Ground crews worked outside loading bombs and repairing damaged aircraft.

based at Péronne, France, northwest of Laon-Athies. That was the strategy for each of the four bridges—two boxes from two different bomb groups targeted a single bridge, 72 planes per bridge, if they all made it. Sending the 397th ahead of us was only going to stir up the hornet's nest of antiaircraft gunners. Near the target, we'd be following Pathfinder aircraft. Their special radar was essential for pinpoint bombing because, at the moment, clouds and haze still obscured the Eller. We were told to expect heavy and accurate antiaircraft fire shortly after take-off and especially at the Eller, which was protected by an experienced Panzer division. Enemy fighters could appear at anytime, so rendezvous with P-47 escort would occur shortly after take-off.

The skies were lightening as we headed out to the aircraft. A light haze hovered near the ground, but overhead the skies promised some decent visibility. A thin layer of snow covered the fields surrounding the wet taxiways and runway.

Burgmeier settled into the right seat of the Marauder after slipping on his flak jacket. While I ran through my checklist, he organized his charts and equipment. Nothing appeared to distract him from focusing on his responsibilities as lead navigator. The job today was too important. Three hours from now, after he guided us back to the base, he could think about what lay ahead—his journey home and the reunion with his bride. But for now, the only thing that mattered on that morning of December 23, 1944, was doing our jobs with precision and courage.

Take off was 0900 hours. We were so close to the front lines that it was safer to take off on a westerly heading to form up and gain altitude. While I was organizing my box, Gist's take-off was

As lead navigator responsible for guiding a formation to a target, Lt. Frank Burgmeier rode in the right seat of the Marauder. Approaching skies full of flak, he and I donned protective helmets.

delayed for a few minutes when a pilot lost control of his Marauder during lift off. He veered right and smashed into a Cletrac, a vehicle used for moving materials around the field. Fortunately, there were no explosions, only a crushed ground vehicle and a Marauder that was so badly damaged that it never flew again. While ground crews cleared the wreck, I circled with my box waiting for Gist to launch.

As we headed east, I saw bursts of flak off to my right. These were smaller and lighter in color than what the Germans sent up, and they weren't fired *at* us. I figured these were our troops letting us know their positions—probably inexperienced infantry who were afraid we were going to drop on them.

En route, several P-47s joined us. We were the lucky ones. Apparently some fighter commanders didn't believe the weather predictions. Only belatedly did they scramble the escorts. At the end of this day, this lapse in communication combined with haze, which made finding the units difficult, led to extraordinarily high losses for several of the Marauder groups. Some boxes came under attack by estimates of 50 to 75 ME-109s and FW-190s.

Our escorts were busy. This was this first time I'd encountered so many daring and aggressive ME-109 pilots. They came at us from all directions. One would appear, send a shock of recognition through the cockpit, and in the same instant disappear. I relied on my gunners and the P-47s to do their work. Dogfights were all over the sky. But my focus had to be on taking evasive action—gentle moves, no more than 15 degrees one way or the other to keep the formations together. For at least 40 minutes we flew in and out of flak. With decent visibility, their gunners had no problem tracking us with their 88s. As we neared the target, the ragged, black death filled our airspace with impunity.

Over Wittlich, Germany, about ten miles from the Eller, I called over the radio,

Marauders tightened the formation when approaching a target to concentrate the firepower. Each Marauder carried twelve .50-caliber guns for protection against enemy fighters.

"Tighten up. We're near the IP." Suddenly, an excited voice called over the radio, "We're losing a ship. Bostick bail out!" A direct hit blew the left engine off of 1st Lt. Joseph C. Bostick's Marauder named *Circle Jerk*. Instantly flames engulfed the wing, then tail. The plane rolled on its back and fell out of sight behind the formation.

"Stay in formation," I ordered. Ignore the loss of six men and their last seconds. They were gone. History. Hold steady. Get the job done.

No more evasive action. We were on the bomb run. Drop when the Pathfinder drops.

Then bombs away! With a sweeping left turn, I led the formation away from the target and back through the relentless flak barrage. The sheet metal guys who patched the holes and torn skin on these Marauders had their work cut out for them.

We had it easy compared to the other groups. As it turned out, our late arrival at the Eller saved a lot of lives from our group. The two boxes from the 397th that preceded us to the Eller lost 10 aircraft very close to the target. Intense flak knocked out three Marauders in the first box. Just as their second box was turning away from the target, it came under attack by a wave of Me-109s. Only after seven more planes disappeared in flames did the P-47s show up to challenge the enemy fighters.

It would take days to assess the full extent of the damage to the Ninth Air Force Marauders. When I landed back at the base, I knew nothing of the fate of other groups. As I shut the engines down, my crew chief handed me a cigarette though my window. I passed it to Burgmeier.

"Congratulations, Frank," I said. "You're going home."

"Feels great," he said. "I'm writing Tedi, and then have a little celebration."

He added, "Lou, Jake, thanks."

Twelve months of combat flying and 65 missions later, 1st Lt. Frank Burgmeier was heading home to resume life with the young woman whose letters and packages helped him endure their separation. Before joining the Army Air Corps in 1942, Burgmeier was an apprentice toolmaker in a typewriter factory, a job that paid him 30 cents an hour. His dream was to become a pilot. When the Air Corps dropped the college requirement, he was accepted into the cadet training program. Although he soloed in primary flight school, he ended up hospitalized for nearly a week, and could not catch up with his class. When he washed out, he says he "got lucky" when the Army Air Corps sent him to navigation school at Hondo, Texas. He graduated near the top of his class and proudly accepted his commission as a second lieutenant. On October 9, 1943, he shipped out of New York Harbor on the *Queen Mary* headed for combat. The respect Jake and I had for Burgmeier's expertise and professionalism in guiding formations to the target never waned even though it would be 45 years before we made contact with each other again.

As I climbed out of the plane, my crew chief asked, "How'd it go?" I gave him a thumbs up then followed him around the ship as he assessed the damage. We'd picked up a few holes that day.

Then I grabbed my jeep—a reward for being assistant operations officer—and motored near the edge of the runway to watch our returning Marauders. Overhead, the Pathfinder that I'd followed to the target fired a red flare. The pilot landed with no brakes, overshot the runway and crashed. One man inside was seriously wounded, but alive. The aircraft had over 200 holes in it. Overhead another returning Marauder circled the field, then its pilot called an emergency over the radio. *Lady Luck III* had no hydraulics for operating the landing gear. At 4,000 feet, 1st Lt. William H. Eastwood ordered the entire crew to bail out. We counted them as they dropped through the bomb bay. Six parachutes floated down and landed west of the runway in the farmlands. The Marauder kept motoring away. No one bothered to search for its remains.

Then I heard Gist's voice on the radio. Calmly, he announced that he had an engine shot out. He asked that the area be cleared for his landing. Other pilots left the pattern to await his touchdown. Like the pro he was, Gist landed safely as did 1st Lt. Ellis S. Byers, who also limped back on a single engine. When it was over, there wasn't an aircraft that didn't have battle damage.

When Gist rolled onto his hardstand, I was there to meet him.

"Where'd they get you, Spike?" I asked.

"I was just pulling away from the target," he said. "I shut the engine down right away and told the rest of the box to head home without me."

He was lucky he made it. All that ack-ack and enemy fighters on the prowl for a crippled, lone bomber made him an easy kill. But we did not speak of that.

"Isn't it time for a three day pass to Paris?" I joked.

"It might happen sooner than we think," he said. "Those fuckers are too damned close."

December 23, 1944, has been called a "black day over the bulge" for the Marauder groups that bombed that day. Only two men were known dead. But 227 were declared missing in action and presumed dead. These are the crews who rode their planes down in flames. Thirty more men were wounded. As for aircraft, the eight participating Marauder groups lost a total of 47 bombers. Of these, 39 were missing in action along with their crews. Two were lost when their crews bailed out over friendly territory. Six aircraft were so badly damaged they couldn't be flown again.

How the 397th and the other groups coped with their extraordinarily high crew losses, I can not say. Six men from the 323rd never came back that day. This was not unusual for a rough mission. So there wasn't much talk about our casualties.

Somebody might say, "So and so went down today."

Then a seemingly indifferent response followed. "Yeah, that's a bitch." End of conversation. It didn't do any good to dwell on the unavoidable.

Shortly before I joined the group, Burgmeier's best friend, a bombardier named Dale Rush, was killed on May 20, 1944, during a mission to Dieppe. A flak burst shattered the Plexiglas nose where he sat. Like Burgmeier, Lt. Rush was newly married, and together they made a pact to remain faithful to their wives. The two filled the hours between missions by bicycling around Earls Colne and taking liberty runs to Colchester, where one of the pub owners even adopted them as her "boys." To them she was "mom."

Burgmeier was on leave when Rush was killed. When he returned, no one told him the details. "I guess they were trying to keep me from getting down," he said. "His death affected me for some time, but I didn't talk it over with anyone." Accept the losses and keep going. In war, there is no alternative.

Years later Burgmeier came across a widely published photo of a black burst exploding directly in front a Marauder. Suddenly, he realized that was the terrible instant of his friend's death. That's how it is with war memories. If you live long enough, there is always some serendipitous moment that awakens the pain of loss.

Gist was right about the Germans being "too damned close." Close enough that on Christmas Eve, we saw the artillery light up the eastern sky. Close enough to hear their guns. Close enough to send us diving into our frigid foxholes when the air raid sirens blew. But for the next five days, the weather held. Christmas week, the Ninth Air Force helped turn the tide by disrupting German transportation and supply lines. Gist and I led one more box on the 27th to another German railroad bridge, the Nonnweiler. Then the weather closed in. Without the air offensive, the casualties among the infantry would have been far higher. As it was, there were too many losses. From December 16 to January 2, American infantry casualties numbered 41,315 officers and men—4,138 killed in action, 20,231 wounded in action, and 16,946 reported missing.

For the 323rd's heroic efforts during the week of December 24–27, the group received the Distinguished Unit Citation. This is awarded to a group for displaying "gallantry, determination, and esprit de corps in accomplishing its mission under extremely difficult and hazardous conditions as to set it apart and above other units participating in the same campaign." Because the circumstances are extraordinary, the award designates only a short time period. What is significant about the wording of

During a mission to Dieppe, France, on May 20, 1944, the 323rd formation encountered intense and accurate antiaircraft fire. This flak burst killed the bombardier, Lt. Leo Dale Rush, Jr. (456th B.S.), seated in the nose of *Ole 33 Gal.* He and navigator Burgmeier were both married shortly before they arrived in England and were best friends. Killed also was tail gunner S/Sgt. Johnnie McClelland (National Archives photograph 342-FH-3A-16140-52895).

this award is that it also pays honor to the ground crews, who barely slept during this critical period to keep the Marauders loaded with armament and serviced for combat.

For extraordinary heroism in armed conflict with the enemy. During the period 24–27 December 1944 the 323rd Bombardment Group dispatched a series of highly effective attacks against supply and transportation installations employed by the enemy in reinforcing the counter-offensive in the Ardennes sector. A full-scale attack was staged against a railroad bridge at Trier, Germany on 24 December. Despite fierce opposition from the defending artillery batteries, which damaged 14 of the 44 planes, the gallant pilots maintained formation and released their bombs with devastating effect on the objective. Ground crews labored throughout the night to ready the planes for flight, and on the morning of 25 December, 51 aircraft of the group attacked the key railroad bridge at Nonweiler, Germany with excellent results. At 1400 hours the group again staged a full-scale attack. Despite severe icing conditions and intense opposition from antiaircraft fire, which damaged 16 aircraft, the determined airmen inflicted extensive damage on transportation facilities at St. Vith, Belgium. During the following two days the airmen of this group flew against fierce opposition to bomb three more vital enemy objectives. The inexorable determination and courage and outstanding aerial skill exhibited by the officers and men of the 323rd Bombardment Group in the execution of this brilliant series of attacks reflect a devotion to duty in keeping with the highest traditions of the Army.

By command of Major General Kepner:

Robert M. Lee
Brig. General USA
Adjutant General

As December drew to a close, I tried to write a letter to my sister Judy. But I just didn't have anything to say. There was no way to explain what was going on. New Year's Eve, Burgmeier hitched a ride on a C-47 transport back to England. He ended up at an RAF base and got quite drunk.

The same day that Burgmeier crossed the channel headed west, musician Glenn Miller's aircraft, a Noorduyn Norseman carrying him to Paris, was lost over those dark, chilly waters. It wasn't until the 1980s that someone figured out that probably his pilot lost direction in the bad weather and wandered into an area used to jettison bombs. A bombardier in a British plane saw a small aircraft, a Norseman, hit the water as he dropped his bomb load. The theory is that flying at 1,500 feet and buffeted by concussion waves from the explosions, the pilot lost control of the aircraft.

Shortly after midnight at Laon-Athies, a lone German fighter pilot strafed our field with his guns blazing. He damaged one Marauder before our flak gunners shot him down. He crashed in a frozen field a few miles from the base. Happy New Year.

8

On Leave in Paris

Late Fall 1944

A steady rain tapped the canvas canopy of the transport that carried Jake, Searle and me and three other officers to Paris. In October, shortly after we set up base at Laon-Athies, the brass decided to boost morale by issuing three-day passes to Paris— 18 hours for enlisted men. Scrubbed missions, mud, and the less than adequate living conditions created restlessness, boredom, even complacency. A leave in Paris meant civilization, freedom, fun.

Paris was all these things and more to me. Even as a boy, I knew the monuments, parks, avenues, and the view from the balcony of my great grandparents' apartment adjacent to the Arc de Triomphe. I visited these places through a photo album made by my mother, Margaret Sands. During the spring and summer of 1900, she lived in Paris. She was probably 12 at the time and recorded her experiences through pictures and words. This was the year of the Paris Exposition, a kind of world's fair. Her family business, the Oil Well Supply Company of Pittsburgh, erected a drilling tower among the international pavilions to demonstrate the latest in oil drilling equipment. Somewhere near the Eiffel Tower, they struck water. The story passed down to me was that after the event, the French built a fountain on the spot.

Mother died of leukemia when I was four, but I still have vivid memories of her, particularly when she put me to bed each night. Together we said a little prayer:

> Dear Father in Heaven
> God bless Mommy and Daddy and everybody
> Make Louie a good little boy
> And may he learn to serve Thee.

As her illness progressed, she had to have help in caring for me. Then there was the final car ride from our home in Cleveland to her parents' home in Pittsburgh, where she died. Growing up, I came to know her best through these photos and her

Paris, 1900 (photograph by Margaret Sands, my mother).

hand written captions. Pictures of her reveal a confident and elegantly dressed young woman with a wry smile. Like the Paris women that she photographed as they strolled along the Champs-Élysées or rode in horse drawn carriages on the Avenue de Bois de Boulogne, she wore long dresses with tightly tailored waists and sleeves, topped off with hats piled with ribbons and flowers. She added her own touch, a leather camera case that hung from a strap around her tiny waist. She must have carried that camera with her everywhere. I kept it in its case for many years after her death. Then it disappeared as most objects like that do over time.

Fortunately, her album, this tangible connection with her life, has survived and brought me a lifetime of enjoyment. There are the photos of horned, black goats standing on a street corner, one with her caption, "Goat's milk 3 cents per glass. Produced while you wait." There is a mustached organ grinder with his four children and a donkey carrying a large sign on its back announcing a special concert at the Moulin Rouge. Clear black and white photos of children, puppies, kittens, the baker, the concierge, boats along the Seine, and an occasional dinner on the street show her love for the everyday life of Paris. Long before my first visit there in 1936, I could identify landmarks like Notre Dame, Arc de Triomphe, the Jardin des Tuileries, the Place de la Concorde and, of course, the Eiffel Tower, built for the International Exhibition of Paris in 1889.

I have an intangible connection with her too—something I have never spoken of until now. On missions, when all hell seemed to breaking out around us, I felt

Place de la Concorde, Paris, 1938.

her presence. She was there at the Le Manoir, at Merzig and at that critical Bulge mission on December 23 and others to come. Some essence of her—hard to define but comforting and calming—surrounded me during difficult moments. I sensed that she would be there for me, win or lose.

Even before I shipped overseas, her invisible hands protected me. Several times, I could have become just another killed-while-training-others statistic. Like the time at Kelly when I was teaching V formation take-offs, and I did not realize that my left flap had a jammed linkage and was stuck in the fully extended position. If a wingman had not alerted me with frantic pointing, my aircraft would have rolled on its back after lifting off. The resulting crash would have killed both me and my right wingman, who flew too close to avoid a collision.

The scariest situation occurred at the base at Dodge City. We had a few short-winged Marauders that had been in Alaska. I enjoyed flying the "shorts" because with a top speed of 300 mph, they really moved. One afternoon, somebody from headquarters asked me to test fly one that had an engine changed. The hanger where the mechanics worked was too small to fit the whole aircraft, so the empennage or tail section, which was fabric, remained exposed to the elements. Engineering said the plane was ready to fly. I respected their work, so I didn't bother to check it over. I invited another instructor to come along for a demonstration of how fast this plane could fly at 5,000 feet.

We launched and climbed out at 170 mph. Suddenly the engineer ran forward to the cockpit. "The right engine's pouring oil," he yelled. Immediately, I turned onto the downwind leg, landed and rolled onto the ramp. Getting out of the plane, I saw people standing around the tail. The fabric on the top part of the elevator had torn loose. Weakened by the harsh weather in Alaska and a recent hailstorm, it hung down like toilet paper. With any more airspeed, we would have lost all control and plunged quickly to earth. We wore no parachutes on training flights. Publicly, I always said that broken oil line saved our lives. Privately, I came to believe that in wartime, soldiers need something extra, something beyond the human effort, to keep them from harm's way. How else could some of us have survived?

Wherever my mother's spirit lives, it must have frowned on my less innocent pursuits in this French city. Blame Dad, Paul Rehr, who in 1936 introduced his 17 year old to the tantalizing nightlife of Paris. I suppose the real purpose of our trip was to reconnect me with my mother's past, including a brief visit with an elderly relative. But it was the evening we spent cabaret hopping that I recall so vividly. This was a group tour of several nightspots. We had an English speaking guide and a car to carry us to each place. After we enjoyed the singing and dancing at a couple of small, smoky cabarets, we visited a larger, more elaborate club. We sat at a reserved table right near the stage. There was a lot of excitement and energy in the place.

Dad must have known what was coming, but he didn't warn me. When the lights came up on the stage, there was the most beautiful woman I had ever seen. Blond with short hair, she wore a pair of sequined panties. And that was all. I could not take my eyes off her large and beautifully shaped breasts as she sang and danced. Shocked and embarrassed because my father sat next to me, I also thrilled at her erotic dancing and sexy voice. Adding to my confusion was the black gentleman in the audience who stood and loudly cheered her performance. According to Dad, he was her boyfriend and an American boxer.

Two years later, Gardner Johnson and I were seated on a Paris bound train with some French sailors who had been at sea. They bragged about the sensual delights awaiting us in Paris. So after Gardner and I checked into a hotel, we hailed a cab and asked the driver to take us to a first class brothel.

We got more than we bargained for. The madam escorted into a room with a stage and invited us to sit in some overstuffed chairs. There was nobody else there. When the lights came up, the girls entertained us with an erotic and irreverent skit. The setting was a convent, where a "monk" simulated his secret pleasures with the "nuns," several at once. When the "mother superior" appeared on the scene, she had her own pleasure with the women.

Then as the scantily dressed girls posed on the stage, the madam, with a sweep of her arm, invited us to select the girl of our choice. I just sat there speechless. Recognizing my inexperience, the madam selected for me. This girl was around my age, probably someone the management was breaking in.

We climbed the stairs to a clean, well-decorated room, like someone's spare room in a house. The sex was anticlimactic after the bizarre goings on downstairs. What I remember most about this French girl is something she said while we were dressing. "The Germans are coming to Paris." There was no panic in her voice, just resignation. At first, I wasn't sure what she meant until it dawned on me that high-ranking German officials probably frequented Paris brothels like this one. No doubt they liked to brag about Hitler's plans to take over all of Europe. Trust the Paris prostitutes to have the scoop two years before the diplomats figured out what Hitler was really up to.

From Laon-Athies, Paris was a three-hour ride in the back of a truck. Scanning the landscape, I watched the spires of Laon's cathedral recede as rolling hills of yellowing vineyards, damp forests, and battle-damaged villages filled the space. Perhaps because of the military traffic, we slowed somewhere between the towns of Soisson and Villers. Along the side of the road was a cluster of headstones with their iron crosses marking the graves of German soldiers killed during World War I. Someone was taking care of them by keeping the area clear of weeds and debris. I was struck by the humanity of such an act—the compassion, the honor, and the respect for life and death that transcended these wars.

There was a German cemetery on the east edge of the base at Laon-Athies. I didn't know it was there until one night some other officers mentioned the site and asked if I wanted to see it. The wooden crosses dated 1940 to 1941 meant that the Germans were based there during the Battle of Britain. Somebody had taken care to give these aircrews a proper burial, a tradition among pilots that had its beginnings in World War I. There was even a wooden archway adorned with a swastika and eagle that served as an entrance.

As we stood looking at the scene, one of the men kicked and pushed the wooden structure intending to knock it over. "Stop!" I yelled.

"What do you mean?" he said. "These are fucking Nazis."

"These are fallen airmen." I said. "This is not why we are here."

There was no argument from him or the others.

As our transport neared Paris, the rain stopped, leaving a high overcast. The three of us jumped off in the heart of the city right in front of the luxurious George V Hotel, our living quarters for the next two nights. Even during the war, the place retained its elegance. Beautiful tapestries, inlaid wood furniture, nineteenth-century bronze sculptures and paintings mocked our crude existence at Laon.

After checking in, I enjoyed the luxury of my first hot bath since leaving England. Back in Laon, we had two options: bathe from a helmet or bathe from a bucket placed next to the stove. Now that I had a whole tub, I soaked for at least an hour.

After dressing—we always wore our dress uniforms on leave—I headed for the dining room just in time to see a very drunk Jake surrounded by military police. Apparently, he'd spent the last couple of hours at the bar and ended up in a fight with someone.

"This man is my bombardier," I said approaching the group. "I'll deal with him." I don't know what the MPs would have done with him besides throw him in a brig to cool off, but his arrest could only mean trouble for me, his commanding officer.

After they left, Jake followed me to the lobby. "What the hell's going on here?" I asked. "You can't embarrass Searle and me like this." On the base, we often drank too much in between missions as a way to relieve stress. We'd get loud and do some stupid things. Once I pinned Jake to the tent floor after an argument over a missing bottle of cognac he'd kept under his bed. How I overpowered him I will never know, because he was one of the strongest men I'd ever known. By the next day, it was over. It had to be. Grudges had no place on missions.

But here in Paris, with MPs around every corner, losing it after a few drinks could get complicated. "If you get yourself in a bind like this again, you're on your own," I said. He knew I meant it.

That night, we all drank too much. After dinner in the hotel dining room with its linens, fresh flowers, and chandeliers, Searle and I headed for the bars in Montmartre, which were usually crowded with military. We stepped inside a cubbyhole, where two young women served drinks and played old French songs on a record player. They weren't interested in military types. In our drunken state, who could blame them?

We moved on to another bar. Hanging out there were three English-speaking, middle-aged women. They quizzed us about where we were based, and what we were doing. But Searle and I were too drunk to respond. Then it dawned on me—these women could be Nazi sympathizers looking for information to sell to the Germans. I wanted to tell Searle, but I could not move my mouth. In desperation, I jumped up and shouted, "Let's get out of here!"

The next day, after a long, much needed sleep, I set out alone for the Left Bank to visit some old friends. Monsieur and Madame Flobert owned a small shop of collectibles and antique guns at 3 Boulevard St. Michel. During the summer of 1938, Gardner Johnson and I enjoyed the Bohemian flavor of this quarter with its writers and artists. One day, as we passed the Flobert's shop, I noticed in the window a beautiful set of antique dueling pistols nestled in a small felt box. I had been looking for unusual souvenirs, and these would be easy to carry. We entered their small, neatly kept shop, which smelled of oiled metal. Hunting rifles and shotguns hung on the walls. More pistols lay in the showcases. The Floberts, an English-speaking couple in the early 50s, graciously welcomed us. They were obviously very happy that two American teenagers found their shop so interesting.

After I purchased the pistols, they invited Gardner and me to meet them for dinner in Montmartre. The date was July 13, the eve of Bastille Day, and Parisians were in a festive mood. Music, laughter and dancing surrounded us. During our dinner conversation, Monsieur Flobert told us that because of his expertise in guns, he often testified at murder trials in the Court of the Seine. He was pleased to hear that during one of my years at Culver, I had earned a title of National Rifle Champion.

After dinner, the Floberts pointed toward the famous Moulin de la Galette dancehall that was immortalized in a painting by Toulouse-Lautrec. "You're young. Go dance and have fun," they said. I guess they figured we'd want to find girls. After thanking them for their company and the dinner, we wandered over to the dancehall to watch the partners glide around the floor to love songs and fast stepping tunes. But we were too shy to join the dancing. Somehow the rigid ballroom dancing they taught me at Culver didn't fit in here.

Although our encounter with the Floberts was brief, I never forgot their good will. For a couple of years after my visit, I sent them Christmas cards. I was sure they would remember me. I wanted them to know that six years later, I was part of the Allied effort that liberated Paris.

Holding on to the back of an open bus spewing diesel exhaust, I jumped off at the Louvre and walked along the Seine toward the Pont St. Michel. Surveying the city, I noted how little the war had changed Paris. In sharp contrast to Chartres, no rubble surrounded the majestic structures. There were fewer buses rolling through the streets, but getting around town on them or the underground was no problem. Paris really was a refuge from this war.

Crossing the Seine, I headed for their building located not far from the bridge on the left side of the street. Approaching, I noticed that the shop windows were boarded up. Overhead, shutters concealed the French windows of their apartment. Their place was deserted. I wasn't totally surprised because the war may have forced them to move. Still, I wasn't giving up. I knocked several times on their door before a neighbor finally opened an adjacent entrance. Seeing my uniform, she hesitated to say anything at first. Why should she after years of living in fear under the Nazis?

"Les Floberts?" I said.

She spoke quickly, and I did not understand most of her words. But her anxious look and the word "Gestapo" made it clear the Germans had arrested the Floberts.

I was stunned. I had come to accept the deaths of fellow pilots. They were military men. Flying bombers, we also understood that civilians and even our own infantrymen were sometimes victims of misplaced or stray bombs—like the tragedy at St. Lô back in July. But the arrest of this couple hit me in a different, more personal way. The Floberts were about the same age as my parents, who also enjoyed having young people around them. On that festive summer evening back on July 13, 1938—the eve of France's Independence Day—none of us could have imagined the terrible events that altered our lives forever.

A man who owned firearms shop, and who knew enough about ballistics to testify at murder trials was surely a criminal in the eyes of the Nazis, as was his wife. Under German law, possessing firearms was illegal. Even a forgotten service revolver from World War I that was left rusting in a cellar was reason enough for imprisonment. More than likely, the Germans arrested them soon after they rolled into Paris. I wanted to believe the Floberts worked with the French Resistance. I wanted them to be heroes. But in the end, the only certainty was their fate at the hands of Hitler's henchmen.

Depressed, I retreated to the hotel, unable to enjoy the remainder of my leave. For the moment, Paris offered no refuge, no escape from the realities of this war— a war without end. Amen.

Once again on November 15, my crew and I had an authorized leave to Paris. There seemed to be no plan for issuing these passes because this would be my last break for the next five months. Effective at 1200 hours, we had 48 hours to indulge in whatever Paris had to offer. This time Jake, Searle and I reported to the American Red Cross Club, called the Rainbow Corner, at 8 Boulevard de la Madelaine. After checking in, we were directed to rooms rented out by carefully selected French citizens.

I was housed in a comfortable second floor flat owned by an attractive woman with a very large dog, probably kept for protection. When she opened the door to my room, I looked at the dog and said, "petit cheval," or small horse, which really cracked her up.

On this leave, I was looking for a liaison—for the touch of a woman. The Russian had provided enough excitement to last a while. But this was Paris, and its women had their own style.

As Searle and I headed for Montmartre, I had no desire to seek out kinky entertainment, but if in the course of the evening something happened, I wouldn't resist. He and I ended up at the New Moon, a cabaret crowded with military. After a couple of drinks, I focused my attention on a very attractive singer. A man approached me and offered her for so many francs. I declined, and he moved on to others. I did not like the idea of dealing with a pimp.

Sitting there at the bar, I felt fingers slowly caressing my arm, then sliding toward my hand. Close behind me stood a dark haired woman, maybe in her early 20s. Turning around, I smiled and studied her eyes, which did not move from my face. "Combien?" I asked. We conducted the business part right there in the bar. After I paid her, she led me out of the New Moon and into the damp streets.

We did not have far to go. In the next block, we entered an apartment building. She led me to an ornate second floor flat, like something out of the 1890s. Scrolled wallpaper, heavy drapes and Louis-the-somebody's furniture made me feel like I'd stepped into one of my mother's photographs. French windows opened onto a narrow balcony that overlooked a courtyard. She led me to a bedroom with a canopied bed. I wondered how many Germans had slept here too. Like the Russian in London, she had her clothes off before I could loosen my tie. She lay on the bed and watched me undress.

After that, I don't recall much. I wasn't drunk, just exhausted. Physically and emotionally, I was wrung out. We had sex, then I must have rolled over and fallen asleep. I awoke the next morning alone in this apartment. Immediately, I sat up and focused on the room. My tunic and pants hung neatly on a chair. On a nearby table, lay my watch and wallet. Nothing was missing. I can't say my experience was typical. Maybe I was just lucky.

One month later when the Germans threatened to overrun the Allies at the Battle of the Bulge, I heard these Paris prostitutes got rid of their English phrase books and dusted off their German versions. Adjust to market conditions. That's how the oldest profession in the world survives.

9

Veterans and New Recruits: Flying Missions from Laon-Athies and Denain-Prouvy Airdromes, France

January–February 1945

January brought blizzards, subzero temperatures and new crews. Some of these guys were shocked at the living conditions. They should have counted their blessings. In December, the shortage of infantrymen on the front lines led to the transfer of some of our airmen into infantry units. Tail gunners, radiomen and engineers headed off with field packs and carbines, but with no training. Their casualties were significant. At Laon-Athies, living in a moldy tent and sleeping on straw surrounded by friendly faces was paradise compared to bedding down in a frigid, snowy foxhole that faced an enemy 100 yards away. Having just arrived from the States, these new men had no perspective.

Many of the replacement pilots came to us without crews—other men with whom they had formed a close relationship before entering combat. Some arrived with a balls-of-fire attitude, just daring the Germans to shoot them down. Others lacked the spirit for the greater cause. Perhaps they believed the war couldn't last much longer, that heroic efforts weren't worth the risks. More likely, they were just inexperienced and lonely.

As the newly appointed operations officer for the 456th Bombardment Group, I got to know a lot of these pilots as I motored my jeep around the ramp making sure everything came together for each mission. One day in January, I had all the planes organized for take-off. With relief and pride, I settled into the jeep to watch the coordinated lift off of our Marauders.

Then somebody rolled halfway down the runway and cut the power. What the hell. The pilot taxied back to his hardstand where I was waiting. As he shut down the engines, I realized he was one of the new replacement pilots.

Climbing into the cockpit, I asked, "What happened?"

"The RPM on the left side was a little off," he said. "I didn't think it was safe to take off."

"Get all your people out of here," I said. "You and I are going to flight test this plane."

"With a full load of bombs?" he questioned.

I did not answer him as I settled into the right seat.

The other planes had already left for the mission, so we taxied and lined up for take-off to the east. "Now push those throttle controls all the way," I ordered him. As we slowly picked up power, I could see the left throttle easing back. "Jam it in there and hold it there," I yelled over the roar of the engines.

After we lifted off, he eased back on the throttles for the climb. No problem here as we ascended rapidly to 5,000 feet. For one moment of madness, I thought about catching up with the others. I wanted this guy to complete the mission. But it was against the rules. I hadn't attended the briefing, and we had no crew.

"Let me have this plane," I ordered him.

We had the local skies and runway to ourselves. I put the nose down and swung around, building up the speed as we dove. I lined up with the runway and continued the rapid descent. Our airspeed read 250 mph when we leveled off at 500 feet, and buzzed the field. Not the whole field, but enough of it to satisfy my frustration. Smoothly, I pulled up and leveled off at 3,000 feet before entering the landing pattern.

"There is nothing wrong with this goddamned plane," I said as I shut down the engines. "I'm going to credit this aircraft as acceptable to fly." Without that endorsement, the ground crew would not have received credit for the mission. However, I did direct them to make the minor adjustment to the throttle.

I had never treated an officer or enlisted man like that. The power setting needed adjustment, and he didn't know how to deal with it. Instead of explaining what was wrong and building his confidence, I embarrassed and probably scared him. I should have left that last part to the Germans.

For the first time, I realized this war was getting to me. A year ago, when I was so eager to join the fight, I could not have imagined how living with the dangers of war eroded the spirit. This was one of those times when frustration overcame patience. Intolerance replaced understanding. I thought about my original tent mates at Earls Colne and the indifference they showed my crew and me. No, I wasn't burnt out. I still had plenty of spirit left for the fight, plenty of pride in our Marauders and their crews. I just had to remember that many of these replacement pilots were too inexperienced to be out here.

As it turned out, his aborted mission was a rough one. Of the 35 Marauders that continued on to bomb a German highway bridge, weather prevented all but 11 planes from dropping the bombs. Heavy flak, both inbound and outbound, caused damage to 25 aircraft and wounded two crewmembers. The group lead plane flown by Capt. Robert H. Adams, the newly appointed squadron commander for the 453rd, took a direct hit. His crew bailed out over enemy territory. Six men were declared missing in action. Adams stayed with the ship and was presumed lost until we learned that he'd bailed out safely over Belgium. Another plane took a direct hit from a 88mm shell that passed through the fuselage and damaged the controls. The pilot had to nurse the plane home. Despite the difficulties, the planes that managed to drop their bombs did significant damage to the bridge. So the kid dodged a difficult mission. There would be many more to come.

Apparently, the war was taking its toll on Gen. Eisenhower too. Back in the fall when bad weather and shortages stalled the Allied advance, he became fed up with reports of increased looting, rape, profiteering, and men lying in hospitals with self-inflicted wounds. The number of deserters also increased significantly during the stalemate. In wartime, deserters are court-martialed and sentenced to death. But not since the Civil War had an execution actually been carried out. With so many soldiers retreating in panic during the surprise attack in the Ardennes, Gen. Eisenhower decided to send an unmistakable message to those of us who carried on the fight. He would not rescind the order to execute Pvt. Eddie Slovik, who months before the Bulge disaster ran from his infantry unit twice.

I didn't want to believe the army would actually kill a man for desertion. But they did on January 31, 1945. The story came to us from soldiers who had witnessed the execution not far from us in the Vosges Mountains, southeast of Laon. According to those who were there, Pvt. Slovik stood with his hands tied behind his back and his head covered in a black hood. He was led into a snowy courtyard, tied to a post and shot.

Apparently that same day, two other men stood there awaiting execution for the same crime. But the officers in charge appealed to Gen. Eisenhower to stop the killings. Hours later, he agreed.

I was sickened. The man wasn't selling secrets to the enemy. He wasn't committing acts of sabotage. He was a coward, and soldiers fighting a war despise cowards—those men who haven't found a way to manage the fear, men who'd rather face the scorn of their comrades than serve their country with honor. Throw Pvt. Slovik in jail, disgrace him for life with a tainted military record. But do not stand him in front of a firing squad and execute him. As far as I was concerned, if Gen. Eisenhower wanted to send a warning, his plan backfired. This execution of an American soldier was a crude and barbaric assault on the morale of those of us who were giving everything we could to rid the world of a real enemy.

Ironically, word of the execution didn't spread much beyond the few units based near the execution site in eastern France. This was not the kind of story you'd see printed in *The Stars and Stripes*, the official military newspaper. And even though Europe was crawling with war correspondents, the execution of the first American soldier since the Civil War wasn't the kind of story the censors allowed reporters to pass on to their newspapers and magazines. It wasn't until 1954, when journalist William Bradford Huie published *The Execution of Private Slovik*, that civilians learned the details. Even Slovik's wife didn't know the real story until years later.

During World War II, censors reviewed all radio broadcasts, newsreels, news articles and letters for sensitive information. On the other hand, war correspondents—

if they were courageous or crazy enough—had access to the front lines. Reporters and photographers, both men and women, stayed at the bases, slept in the orchards and foxholes, and observed from bombed out buildings while the ground forces routed snipers. They jumped with the Airborne, flew in bombers, and wrote their stories showing the heroism and sacrifices of our ground troops and airmen. Stories that featured the men on the front lines boosted everybody's morale and fueled enthusiasm for the war effort.

War correspondents periodically joined the 323rd on its missions. Ernie Pyle, the most beloved and arguably the most gifted of all the World War II correspondents, spent a few days with the group in April 1944. With the ease of an old friend, he writes of ordinary men in extraordinary circumstances. "The Flying Wedge," his story of living and flying with our unit, can be found today in collections of his writings.

Others like Ed Goodykoontz, unit correspondent for *The Stars and Stripes*. wrote about the heroism and death during our group's mission in May 1944 to a V-1 installation in France. This was a particularly dangerous mission during which intense flak killed two gunners, wounded 10 airmen and damaged 19 aircraft on the bomb run. Nine Marauders landed back at Earls Colne with an engine shot out. His article, "Beyond the Communique—Plenty," refers to the inadequacies of one line statements such as "Marauders bombed military installations in France," which lose the human drama and tragedy of such difficult missions.

His colleague, staff writer Bud Hutton, frequently flew and wrote about his experiences with our group including his ride on D-Day. William Randolph Hearst, Jr. publisher of the *New York Journal American* showed up at Earls Colne about the same time I did in June 1944, and wrote a series of four articles about his role as "copilot" on one of our Marauders. The men liked having reporters around because they knew if their names appeared in the articles, their friends and family back home would see it.

February 2, I was group lead for a mission to the Ober-Vilkerath Railroad Bridge located several miles east of Cologne. From Laon-Athies, flying time there and back was going to be close to four hours. At the briefing we were told to expect heavy flak. P-47's would be flying cover for us. After the briefing, Col. Wood approached me. With him was a 40ish looking man dressed in a tight fitting flight jacket and military field cap.

"Major Rehr, this is Major Vincent Sheean," he said. "He'll be flying with you today."

Sheean was a famous war correspondent and author of the 1939 book *Not Peace But a Sword,* which predicted World War II. He'd also joined the Army Air Corps and participated in the invasion of Italy. In what capacity, I do not know. But Sheean was no stranger to war. Prior to World War II, he covered the 1927 Chinese Revolution, the 1929 Jerusalem riots, the Italian invasion of Ethiopia, and the Spanish Civil War among others.

One of the most interesting articles he wrote appeared on December 7, 1938, in *The New Republic*. He describes his stay in Rosenheim, Germany as he waits for repairs on his automobile. He recalls some of the same things I saw that same year during my summer tour: the denial of impending war, and the restaurant patrons who blindly demonstrated their loyalty to the Fuehrer with "Heil Hitlers!" and "Seig Heils!" But his focus is on the blatant anti-Semitism he witnesses in Rosenheim. His article reveals chilling examples of the persecution of local Jews.

"Pleasure, sir, to have you along," I said to Sheean as we shook hands. "Be sure to wear the flak jacket." Ordinarily reporters did not ride in lead ships, but Col. Wood must have figured Sheean was seasoned enough to handle the danger. I invited him to sit in the copilot's seat.

What follows is his article that appeared in several stateside newspapers in one form or another. This version comes from the *Charlotte Observer* dated February 4, 1945, and is reprinted with the paper's permission.

Riding Skyways Overseas

Wrecking Bridges is 9th Specialty

NINTH BOMBARDMENT DIVISION HEADQUARTERS, Feb. 3—(by Wireless)—

The Ninth Air Force attacked German bridges east of the Rhine yesterday for the first time in an effort to curtail or interrupt the Nazis' eastward movement of diversion and equipment.

Bridgework is one of the specialties, and they played a great part both in the Normandy campaign and in the battle starting December 16 against Von Rundstedt's counteroffensive. The section of the Air Forces which does this job is the bombardment division under Maj. Gen. Sam Anderson of Greensboro, N.C., who is only 39 and was a colonel a year ago. His force consists of medium and light bombing aircraft with the B-26, otherwise the Marauder as his mainstay. The Ninth bomb division, since the "bulge" battle began, had 25 communications centers and 24 bridges for its targets and has removed these bridges including the big Hermann Goering road bridge, 1500 feet long, at Newied, above Koblenz. Such jobs as this had to be done again every so often because Jerry has shown great perseverance at repairing bridges. At Nonnweiler, for instance, one month after B-26s had destroyed a 200-foot, three span railroad bridge, the Nazis had replaced it with a temporary steel structure. The replacement span was knocked out in January 29 by B-26s only a short time after it had been completed.

To observe one of these bridge operations yesterday, I flew with a group of B-26s to the neighborhood of Engelskirchen, 16 miles east of Cologne. It was a day of bright wintry sunshine and only scattered clouds, which permitted a remarkable view of the entire Rhine Valley, and the flight proved a remarkable demonstration of our astonishing air mastery over it. Between ourselves and our "little friends"— P-47 Thunderbolts—and various other groups coming up, it looks as though this air definitely belongs to us.

Headed for the Rhine

We took off from a bomber base in France at about 9:30 and laid our course to the Rhine, which we crossed not far from Koblenz near a place where the Moselle flows into the Rhine. The beauty of that unique river is visible for a long way in both directions. As we went in, we certainly were visible to German defenses, but they did not speak up. We turned at an initial point east of the Rhine and swept on to Engelskirchen, and without changing formation, which must have sent the inhabitants of entire provinces into shelters.

I was in the lead ship piloted by Maj. Louis S. Rehr of Delray Beach, Fla., a 25-year-old lad with 43 B-26 missions under his belt. Our target was a railroad bridge over which eastward traffic goes out from Cologne and Bonn. After we had dropped our bombs, we went up and around to the southward and got a view of the target, which looked pretty well covered. From this part of the trip we got an excellent view of Cologne, dominated by its towering cathedral as we came near. On our way out, we observed other groups of medium bombers coming in on a similar job. This time the Germans decided to open up, and I have never seen such an even, fixed barrage as was put up over Koblenz. Fortunately, neither we nor any other planes were caught in it, so far as I could see.

Cites Lorelei Rock

As we crossed the Rhine, Major Rehr, who was busy taking some evasive action leaned over and said to me, "I believe that's Lorelei rock down there." It turned out that Rehr had himself made a pleasure trip up the Rhine from Mainz to Cologne with another boy in 1938 when they got out of prep school.

We received a considerable dose of flak from Trier as we passed it to the south. The stuff was breaking above us and on both sides, and we actually acquired two new holes, very small ones, in the ship. There was no serious damage to anybody in our group.

The most striking aspect of the day's doings to me was our absolute, uncontested air mastery. Our formation sailed along in plain view of the entire German countryside and no enemy aircraft poked his nose up. The flak was heavy over some places but by canny plotting of the course, this can usually be substantially avoided.

Looking for Trouble

As soon as we crossed the Rhine our "little friends" abandoned their escort duty and went right down on deck, fishing around looking for something of military value to shoot up. They are so swift and cut so many capers that the Germans normally make no effort to shoot at them, reserving their attentions to bomber formations.

The crew of my ship is typical of the air corps bunch, mostly very young, coming from all parts of the United States. Capt. Victor Jacobs of Anaconda, Mont. was bombardier; First Lieut. John Kuczwara of Chicago, navigator; T/Sgt. James B. Alexander of Middletown, RI, radio gunner; S/Sgt. Charles Allen, Daly City, Calif,. Tail gunner; S/Sgt. James N. Knight, Camas, Utah, engineer gunner; First Lieut. Paul R. Watson, Monmouth, Ill., was extra navigator. I was copilot of a sort.

As soon as we got back into friendly territory, one bar of candy and package of chewing gum were issued to each man aboard. This is the gift of a grateful nation and does not come off the men's normal ration.

For the most part, his account was accurate. The bomb run was smooth, the bombing accurate. On such a clear winter day, the spires of the Cologne cathedral rose majestically above the city's ruins despite intense allied bombings. The heavy flak around Trier, however, scared Sheean. As I took evasive action through the barrage of black bursts and showering metal, he hunched down in the right seat and covered his head with his arms.

"Alexander, give that man a helmet," I called back to my radio gunner. Immediately, he plunked down the protection on Sheean's head. To get him to relax, I pointed out the Lorelei. Why not? If this weren't wartime, we'd be enjoying a spectacular aerial tour of the Rhine River Valley. Then I whipped out a chocolate bar from of my top pocket and handed to him.

He was my guest, and I wanted him to have a memorable ride. He made up that stuff about the entire crew having a ration of candy bars and gum. This might have been done on the heavies on long distance bombing missions. But for us, the only ration we got after missions was whiskey from the flight surgeons. He probably wrote that last paragraph to make the folks back home feel they were doing their part. When we arrived back at the base, Col. Wood was there to escort our guest to lunch.

As it turned out, Col. Wood was only days from heading back home to the states. He had been with the group since the beginning, and not enough can be said about his exceptional leadership as he guided the 323rd through its greatest achievements of the war. As an original member of the group, he had led 29 missions, including the first back in July 1943. This was a guinea pig flight, a last ditch effort to see how Marauders performed on medium level bombing runs rather than at low levels, where the losses were staggering. Many in the Air Corps command were convinced that the Marauder was unfit for combat and should be phased out. Fortunately, that July 16 mission, led by Col. Herbert B. Thatcher, the group's first commander, showed that the Marauder had a place in the war. Had men like Col. Wood, Col. Thatcher and Col. Samuel E. Anderson, the commander of the 3rd Bombardment Wing, not persisted in proving the Marauder's worth, the Allied air effort in Europe would have lost a formidable weapon.

What also made Wood so well respected by his men was that he understood the stresses of dangerous combat missions, the loss of good friends, the inadequate living conditions, and the longing for family and spouses. He allowed his men to relieve the strain of fighting a war with excessive partying, practical jokes, buzz jobs, even fights. He tolerated excesses, but not anarchy. His leadership style set the tone for all his senior officers. I didn't know Col. Wood well, but he recognized Jake's and my commitment to winning this war. As with all his men, he rewarded us for our efforts.

Col. Wood's last official duty was organizing one more move, the fifth since I arrived on the scene. Back in early December, there had been rumors of another move, but now in February it made sense. Targets in the Cologne area and upper Ruhr industrial region around Essen and Dortmond were just too far away from Laon-Athies. By February 9, the group had settled into the Denain-Prouvy Airdrome a couple of miles south of the city of Valenciennes, France. I remember no special farewell for Col. Wood. He was just gone, and by February 14, a new group commander arrived. Around this time, I also, took over as commanding officer for the 456th.

Before the war, Valenciennes was noted for the manufacture of fine lace. When the Germans occupied this coal rich region, they mined the vital resource to manufacture steel and provide power for ships and electricity. Surrounding the perimeter of the base, giant piles of coal stood untouched like the rusting machinery used to dig it from the ground. Some of us settled into wooden barracks that had formerly housed forced laborers that the Germans exploited for their war effort. But compared to the miserable conditions at Laon-Athies, this place was the Ritz. We even had separate cubicles for privacy. Headquarters were in two well-constructed brick buildings. As squadron commander, I even had my own office in a very small building between the barracks and the mess. Other buildings housed showers and a latrine—really just a cement floor with trenches cut through it over which we squatted, taking care not to fall into the pit. Even though the living conditions improved somewhat for some of us, there weren't enough barracks to house all the squadrons. Many men, including Searle, continued living in tents.

Not long after we settled into the barracks at Denain-Prouvy Airdrome, I grabbed a jeep and headed for the nearby village of Herin. Along the road, lay a cluster of modest homes, probably those of the French mine workers. Passing through, I waved to the children standing along the roadside. Suddenly they were pelting my jeep with small rocks. Then I noticed Russian flags hanging from their homes. My guess is that these working families were communists, folks who would have preferred that Russians, not Americans, occupy their neighborhood. Fortunately, this resentment was not typical of the local French people living around Valenciennes.

Defeat of Germany may have been inevitable, but that didn't stop them from shooting down our planes and taking our crews prisoners if downed airmen were lucky enough to survive beatings from German citizens. During the month of February 1945, the 323rd Bombardment Group suffered its greatest monthly losses. Eight planes shot down, 33 men declared missing in action and 11 wounded.

The morning mission on Valentine's Day, February 14, 1945, added significantly to the toll. I led the first of two boxes against heavily defended troop and supply concentrations at Xanten, Germany, north of Essen and just over the border from Holland. We carried the 250-pound fragmentation bombs.

I was loaded with crew this day. There were nine of us on board rather than the usual six or seven. A couple of guys may have been riding along just to get another mission behind them, like the copilot who rode as an observer at the back of the plane. His job was to let me know how well the other Marauders held their positions in the formation. There were two navigators. One sat behind the cockpit with the engineer and operated a sophisticated device called a Gee box. This was a radar navigational aid that within seconds could line up a plane with a runway and was accurate to within 25 feet at sea level. As advanced as his equipment was, the Gee navigator was a backup to the lead navigator who sat in my copilot's seat. I also carried an engineer and two additional gunners.

The target lay at least an hour away. Ahead of the group flew three Marauders called flak suppressors. They were loaded with 100 pound bombs used for driving the flak gunners into their shelters. When the gunners saw the rain of these smaller bombs, they were supposed to run for protection or become so distracted, they couldn't concentrate on us. The technique usually worked. But this time, there were just too many antiaircraft guns protecting the troops and supplies.

Briefing altitude was 12,000 feet through broken clouds. A couple of minutes before the bomb drop, flak bursts surrounded the formation. I evaded with gentle 15-degree turns. I didn't want to lose anybody back there.

Suddenly, the engineer yelled, "Our right engine's hit! We're losing oil!" Immediately, I brought the power back on that engine and cut off its fuel. Simultaneously, I ordered the engineer to close a fuel supply valve leading to the right engine. I turned around to make sure that he didn't get mixed up. Then I increased the power to the left engine to hold altitude and lowered that wing slightly for better control.

"Slow up and stay on the bomb run," I ordered the pilots who followed. With my airspeed below 200 mph, I didn't want them overtaking me.

There was no need to abort the mission. The target was very close. I opened the bomb bay doors, which slowed us even more. Jake made his adjustments. Then we salvoed the bombs. Four thousand pounds lighter, the Marauder was easier to handle.

Very slowly, I began a left turn to get the hell away from the flak gunners. With less power, it would take us longer to reach safety. I lowered the nose and I called the other crews who followed. "You men head home," I said. "I'll see you back at the base."

Once we were free of the antiaircraft fire, I focused on controlling the descent. As we slid down slowly from 11,000 feet, I knew that once we entered the denser air below, I'd be able to hold altitude. This is where experience in the Marauder really paid off. I knew what this plane could do. There was never any doubt in my mind that we would make it home with 3,000 feet to spare.

Shortly after we broke from the formation, Jake crawled out of the nose and into the cockpit. His face and hands were peppered with cuts. The physical wounds were not serious. But he was clearly shaken. "I gotta get out of there," was all he said as he moved back to a seat near the engineer. For the moment, he was OK, and I couldn't worry about him.

Arriving over the base, I could see through the broken clouds that we had plenty of room to make a complete circle for a left-hand pattern. "I'm overhead and descending with one engine," I called to the tower. "You'll see the flares."

"You're number one, clear for landing," someone responded.

Then the engineer released a few orange flares as we descended through the clouds so there was no mistake that this was an emergency.

I broke out on the downwind leg and reduced the power. Even though I knew I was over the field, it was a comfort to spot the familiar landmarks like an abandoned powerplant at the end of the field, which I always used as the turning point onto the final approach. Full flaps down as I turned onto the base leg. We were at 2,000 feet. No problems.

Keep up the airspeed, hold the altitude with full power. As I turned onto the final approach, I extended the gear, which increased our descent rate. I reduced the power, and we dropped even faster. That beautiful 6,000 feet of runway stretched before us. It was all ours.

Suddenly, directly beneath me, I spotted another Marauder. Silver. But definitely not from our group. What the hell is going on? Lost Marauders frequently landed at Valenciennes. But they didn't have the tower frequency, so the old rule "see and be seen" applied. This guy couldn't have seen us because he was determined to land. I had the option of touching down on the grass on one side of the pavement, but I would have damaged our landing gear. People in my plane could be hurt. I had no choice but to go around.

Full power to the good engine. Retract gear and flaps. Keep the nose down to build up energy. At 500 feet, pull up slowly. Climb, climb. We leveled off at 1,500 feet, and I once again turned onto what was now an abbreviated downwind leg. Checking to make sure that stranger had cleared the runway, I lowered the gear and flaps. Somebody in a jeep raced over to him to make sure he rolled clear. Finally, we had the runway to ourselves as I touched down smoothly on the surface.

I'd come this far, I was determined to roll this thing right onto a hardstand located three quarters of the way down the runway and to the right. I had enough energy when I shut the engine down to keep rolling right to the spot. Cheers erupted from the back of the plane. I'd been concentrating so hard on the situation, I missed all the "Oh, shits" and "Christ, what's going on" coming from the crew. Suddenly, I realized how many men were relying on my experience, including the other pilot and his crew. We were lucky. Our damage was minimal, and once we cleared the flak gunners, flying the Marauder was like wearing an old leather shoe. Predictable. Comfortable.

Waiting at the hardstand was my crew chief, who walked over to my open window and handed me a cigarette. When I stepped onto the ramp, he was studying the engine. "Looks like the only thing wrong here is a broken oil line. Thanks, Major." He was right. By afternoon, I was able to test fly the plane and put it back on the line.

I stepped forward to look at the nose. Flak fragments had punctured the Plexiglas in several places leaving ragged holes. "Plexi-flak" is what some guys called the exploding combination of hot metal and glass showering the bombardier's compartment. Jake, who left the plane quickly after landing, had been lucky. Everybody knew the horror stories of bombardiers who'd lost eyes, limbs and their lives. We'd flown nearly 45 missions together, and he never faltered. Even today, he bombed with such precision that I would eventually receive another DFC for this mission. But how long can a bombardier sit in that fishbowl and ignore the kaleidoscopic bursts of flak surrounding him, the dogfights, and the concussions rocking the plane and still concentrate only on centering two cross-hairs on a distant target?

Our situation that Valentine's Day could have been much worse. Perhaps, once more, the invisible hands brought my crew and me home safely. Broken clouds over the target prompted several brave crews to make three and four bomb runs. Of the 39 aircraft launched that morning, at least 12 returned home severely damaged. Two bombers never made it. For those 14 airmen from the 454th and 455th Squadrons, the day ended tragically.

One of their aircraft crash-landed after taking a direct hit, which probably severed flight controls and severely wounded crew members. Those who witnessed the crash saw only one man hit the silks before impact. Landing in the target area could only mean trouble. When the second bomber burst into flame after its right engine caught fire, the enlisted men bailed out at 1,200 feet. The tail gunner was taken prisoner by a German who fired a pistol at him as he fell to earth. The engineer/gunner was badly beaten by townspeople until soldiers intervened. The pilot, copilot and bombardier survived a crash landing. But the pilot had a broken neck and died two days later. The copilot had broken bones. Only the bombardier and radio/gunner were uninjured. These facts came out only after Gen. Patton's army overran their prison camp at Mooseburg, Germany, on April 29, 1945. What we knew immediately was that two aircraft and 14 crewmen were missing in action.

They gave me the DFC for that mission, because despite "withering antiaircraft fire" and the loss of an engine, we "bombed visually and with such precision that a vital enemy supply concentration was greatly damaged." I would not see the paperwork for that award until I returned home in late July. Surprisingly, the citation read that heavy clouds obscured the target, and that I descended to 3,000 feet to drop the bombs. I have to believe that even the guys who kept track of these records were getting tired.

As for the stranger pilot, I never saw him. He returned to his home base, but not before somebody chewed him out, then gave him directions. I was too busy to give the incident any more thought.

There were a lot of changes after February 14. That's when the new group commander, Lt. Col. Rollin M. Winingham, showed up. He had served as the air executive officer of the 397th Bombardment Group, the youngest Marauder group in Europe because it flew its first mission on April 20, 1944. This was also the unit that suffered such devastating losses on December 23. It is never easy for a new leader, an outsider, to break into the inner circle of a closely-knit group. But with fewer combat sorties to his credit than many of our pilots, the high mission men from the 323rd did not consider him their equal.

Admittedly, Col. Wood was a tough act to follow. Like slipping into his cowboy boots every day, Wood fit comfortably into his command, with a relaxed, yet polished style. Lt. Col. Winingham's handsome, angular face conveyed rigidity, which matched his style of leadership. He arrived with his own agenda that included emphasis on conformity and adherence to his rules. He began by imposing what he believed was a more disciplined plan for take-offs and landings, formation flying, cloud penetration and bombing. Despite excellent bombing results from our group during the month of February, he called the planning and the flying "unprofessional" and the bombing "sloppy." He obviously planned on making a career of the military. So he chose a kick butt operating style that include requiring pilots to follow what he called his "proven and improved procedures."

Back at the 397th, he headed up something called the Bombing Analysis Board, with the responsibilities of analyzing the bombing results of lead teams and suggesting ways to improve the techniques. Apparently he often rode along as copilot to see how leaders performed under stress. He never led a mission for our group, but he did ride as an observer with several group and box leaders, including me.

One day in early March, he sat in my copilot's seat. Our target was the Remagen railroad bridge, a huge span crossing the Rhine south of Bonn. Here the Germans moved considerable men and materiel during their retreat eastward. I accepted the fact that Lt. Col. Winingham was new and needed to get to know his senior officers. But as the group lead that day, I flew the way I always did.

Thick clouds hovered over the airfield. After launching, I entered scattered clouds at 1,500 feet and called to the others to spread out before we lost each other in the overcast. We broke out around 4,500 feet, where we regrouped and tightened up. Two Pathfinders joined us as we headed toward the target, over an hour and a half away. During that time, I remember no conversation with the commander. Arriving at the bridge, I could see breaks in the overcast. But we still followed the Pathfinders as they set up the bomb run and drop. Surprisingly there was little resistance from the gunners below. As we discovered four days later, this must have been one hell of a sturdy bridge because on March 7, it was still intact when our infantry stormed across. By that time, it was the Germans who were trying to blow it up to prevent the Allied advance.

When we arrived back at Denain-Prouvy, cloud cover still obscured the area. After the lead navigator announced our position near the field, the formation spread out for the descent. Flying at 200 miles an hour, each group of six descended through the overcast at two-minute intervals. Breaking out underneath, I led the box back to base. Even on the return flight, the new group commander remained silent. As far as I was concerned, everything went smoothly. He must have agreed because after landing, he never called me in to discuss my leadership.

The only conversation that I remember having with him occurred one evening in the officers' club. He approached me to tell me I would be receiving one of four French Croix de Guerres with Silver Star issued to the group from the Ninth Bombardment Division. Officially these came from the French government for outstanding effort in the liberation of France. He told me he wanted to distribute them to the four squadron commanders. I thanked him, agreeing that all of us were deserving of the recognition. He kept his word to me, although I did not receive the medal and ribbon until long after the war had ended, and I had returned home.

10

No Easy Road to Victory, Denain-Prouvy Airdrome, Valenciennes, France

March–April 1945

Nobody asks to be a squadron commander. There is no politicking for the job. You just earn it through skill and dedication. When I joined the group nine months earlier, I just wanted to be a leader, someone people respected. But since my appointment to assistant operations officer for the 456th back in December, followed by the operations officer in January, I'd been on track to take over as squadron commander. On February 16, when my predecessor Lt. Col. Roscoe R. Haller headed home, I stepped into the position.

Back in primary flight school, I had a good friend named Eddie Wagg from Lambertville, New Jersey, who let everybody know his dream was to become a squadron commander. At Washington and Lee, where he was recruited along with me, he excelled at wrestling. But Eddie didn't have a feel for flying. A liaison with a local Fort Worth girl didn't help either at this critical time in his training.

His dream ended one day when there was a posting that announced that he had to fly with a new instructor. If you had to fly with a stranger, there was no way you could pass. You might as well not show up.

"Lou, I've got my final ride out here," he said. "I can't hold my altitude."

"Ok, when you're in level flight," I said trying to help, "use the forward cockpit windscreen to position the horizon."

After his ride, he told me the technique worked. "The guy said I was really good now on holding altitude," he said, "but he still washed me out." Like so many that left flight training early, he was drafted after the war started.

Eddie ended up as crew on a B-17 flying out of England and North Africa with the 301st Bombardment Group. He was never going to be a squadron commander, but he took pride in his wartime role. In December 1942, he wrote me saying that he was "somewhere in North Africa ... showing the world that Boeing makes the greatest plane that ever took off." Then he added, "Lou, I would have made a piss-poor pilot and am one washout who knows it."

Washing out was my biggest fear. And it didn't take much. The first day I drove through the open wooden gates of Hicks Field Army Air Corps Pilot Training Base, an upperclassman scowled at me and said, "Just remember this. Your class will be holding its graduation in a phone booth."

All those years at Culver taught me that the military has its own way of doing things. If I wanted to make it through primary, basic and advanced training, I was better off keeping my mouth shut. In primary, our redneck civilian instructors looked for any excuse to wash us out of training, especially a know-it-all attitude. So I never even mentioned that I had a pilot's license, earned during the summers of 1939 and 1940. And I never told anybody that from my Culver days, I was already a commissioned officer, a second lieutenant in the field artillery. If war broke out, I wanted to be in the air, not on the ground.

Towards the end of this initial training, I came very close to following Wagg out of those wooden gates. We were always running, even to our open cockpit trainers, the PT-19, so it was easy to forget the essentials like fastening the single belt around the waist. In those days, there were no checklists. Flying solo, I decided to practice a spin. As the nose of the aircraft pointed toward the ground, and the fuselage began its rotations, I found myself floating away from the seat. No belt held me in. My left hand grabbed a section of metal tubing on the fuselage. I held a death grip until I slowly eased the nose up. We wore parachutes, but falling or bailing out would have ended my Air Corps career. Fortunately, I was alone and never told anybody about my stupidity.

Having the second lieutenant's commission did pay off when I graduated from advanced flight training at Kelly Field. The War Department in Washington, D.C., notified the base commander that I was already an officer. They issued me a lower serial number with my second lieutenant wings, which meant I had seniority, even over some of our advanced instructors at Kelly.

Now three years later, I was a major, a survivor of nearly 50 missions and one of four squadron commanders for the group—an old man if you measured age by responsibilities, not years. Yet at 26, I *was* older than most of the men in the group, especially the hotshot replacement pilots who tested my patience.

After training exercises, some of these guys buzzed the little wooden building that housed my office. The terrain was flat except for these mountains of coal that rose hundreds of feet into the air. From miles out, they came roaring at 250–300 mph, probably no more than 300 feet off the deck. The funny thing is that I could hear them but not see them until they got close and lifted up over my office. Usually they'd come in pairs, one following the other. Everything in my office shook and slid. I wasn't amused. Sooner or later somebody was going to get hurt. Finally, I met with half a dozen of these characters, all first and second lieutenants.

"You've proven to me that you can buzz faster and lower than I can," I said. "I don't want to see it anymore, or I'll ground you." That stopped the nonsense.

Two months later when I was on duty in Germany, word came that one of these pilots decided to buzz an abandoned coal pile. Starting low and way out, his plan was to zoom up one side, go over the top and nose down on the other side. Only he didn't count on the giant mining rig on the other side. Everybody on board was killed.

We didn't need to lose our crews with that kind of nonsense. The Germans still had a monopoly on killing our men and destroying our aircraft. Crash landings and bailouts were common. Marauders still took direct hits and exploded in flight, adding more names to the missing in action list. Planes still limped back to base with wounded on board. Downed crews who ended up over enemy territory still became POW's—that is if they were fortunate enough to be found by

Cadet Rehr climbs into the cockpit of his primary trainer, the PT-19 at Hicks Field, Fort Worth, Texas, during the summer of 1941.

German soldiers and not German citizens, who sought revenge for the bombings that left their cities in ruins, something they had not experienced in World War I.

During March, the 323rd flew 44 missions, more than any other medium bomber unit in the ETO. Cloud decks, smoke and fire over the target areas frequently required the use of Pathfinders for an accurate bomb drop. These were long missions, four hours or more because our targets stretched into the industrial Ruhr region around Düsseldorf and Essen. The Allies' objective was to cut off supplies and transportation routes leading to the area, therefore isolating the Germans who fiercely defended their turf with accurate and intense ack-ack.

As a squadron commander, my focus continued to be on leading missions, which included eight of the 44 flown in March. Fortunately I had a highly experienced

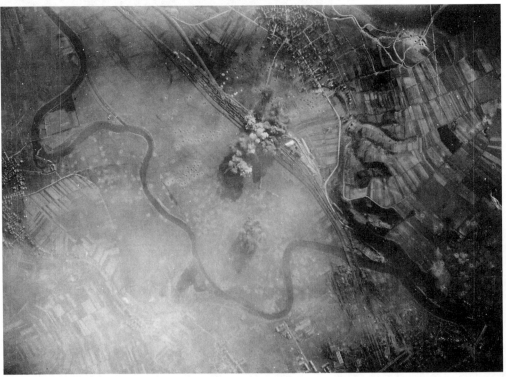

executive officer, Maj. Ross Harlan, and I could not have managed without him. He came from Poteau, Oklahoma, and had joined the Army Air Corp in 1941 after graduating from college. He had been with the 323rd since its inception in September 1942. Before becoming the squadron's executive officer, Harlan had been an intelligence officer and adjutant. He had worked with every commander of the 456th before me, which made

Sitting in my jeep, I discuss a mission with one of my pilots. The jeep was essential equipment for group and squadron leaders before and after missions (courtesy Ted Harwood family).

the transition seamless. Besides managing the housing, feeding and transportation for the men in the squadron, he and his staff took care of my paperwork, which included promotions and demotions and discipline for the enlisted personnel. Our relationship was based on mutual respect and trust, and we consulted often on important matters. His considerable talents relieved me of a lot of responsibility on the ground so I could focus on hitting targets and bringing everyone home safely.

One of the more serious situations he handled was an incident involving profiteering by some of the mess staff. Harlan noticed that the quality of the food was deteriorating—beef stew instead of steak, desserts made without much sugar, weak coffee. Privately, he questioned a corporal who worked occasionally in the mess. "I took him out for a jeep ride," he said. "I knew he would level with me because I got him out of trouble once with the military police."

After assurances from Harlan that he would not be punished, the corporal named the mess sergeant who had a racket going with a Frenchman working in the kitchen. In an effort to pump money into the French economy, the U.S. government urged us to hire locals. The sergeant, who also had convinced a cook to help him, passed along meat, coffee and sugar to his French partner, who fenced the food on the black market. The two then split the profits.

I told Harlan to go ahead and deal with it. He confronted both the sergeant and the cook, busted them down to privates and assigned them to permanent K.P. duty.

"I also told them that if I heard any criticism from other men in the squadron,

Opposite top: Returning from a mission deep into Germany, White Tailed Marauders approach the runway at Denain-Prouvy Airdrome near Valenciennes, France. During March 1945, the 323rd B.G. flew 44 missions, more than any other medium unit in the ETO. *Bottom:* This photograph shows the successful bombing of the Wetzler marshalling yards north of Frankfurt near the Lahn River. I was group lead that day, March 18, 1945.

Maj. Ross Harlan *(center)* had been with the 323rd since 1942, serving as an intelligence officer and adjutant before assuming the duties of executive officer for the 456th B.S. His experience and talents proved invaluable to the commanding officer, me *(left)*. Lt. George Wolfe, photographer for the 456th *(right)*, shot the only known photograph of Maruaders under attack by the Me-262 while riding in my bomber on the April 20, 1945, mission to Memmingen, Germany.

I'd see that the two of them were court-martialed and convicted of grand theft," he said afterwards. The mention of court-martial was a bluff because Gen. Eisenhower had issued an order to defer all trials except in the case of capital offenses until after the war. He just did not have the manpower to handle every case. I had no problem with the way Harlan dealt with the situation. His desire to maintain order, discipline and morale within the squadron drove all his decision making.

With close to 450 men in the squadron, there were always issues that required our attention, especially when it came to relationships with women. Like the drunken corporal who was harassing some French women in a local bar. The French turned him in, and we restricted him to the base for one month.

Once when I returned from a mission, the ground crew was nowhere to be seen. The squadron and I ended up chocking the wheels of the bombers ourselves. When I started asking questions, somebody told me that my men were hanging around a tent that harbored some French girls. Mad as hell, I rounded up the distractions and escorted them off the base.

If men in the squadron wanted to get married, they needed my permission. But these things never worked out. Before long, the stress of the airman living on the base apart from a new wife led to a request for a divorce. That meant a whole other set of problems.

One unique situation involved an enlisted man who wanted to marry a local French woman he'd met back at Laon. Harlan knew that back in the states, this guy had abandoned a wife. Then while based in England, he married an English girl and left her pregnant when we moved to France. Now he was working on the third.

There were also the men who had received "Dear John" letters. Rejections didn't do much for morale, and a few men wanted my permission to go home to patch things up. Permission denied.

Some of these men had been away from home at least a year and a half, and they were lonely. More importantly, they were thinking ahead to life *after* this war. Who could blame them? The German defeat was inevitable. The only problem was that out of fanaticism or fear of Hitler's henchmen, the Germans were not giving up.

In fact, in the aerial war, the Germans now had a far more menacing weapon—the Messerschmitt Me-262, a fighter jet that was capable of speeds over 500 mph. Even parked on the ground, this was a frightening looking aircraft with its shark-like fuselage and two torpedo-shaped engines protruding from the underside of the wings. Mounted in the nose were four 30mm cannons. By April, some of these jets even carried 55mm air-to-air missiles mounted under the wings. Marauders flying in a tight formation with tail, waist and top turret guns blazing were no match for the speed and firepower of what was clearly a technologically advanced war machine.

In early March, a lone maverick Me-262 approached my formation but retreated when our P-51s scared him off. As group leader, I was unaware of its presence until the debriefing. It would not be until April when our targets switched from the Ruhr region to southern Germany that I would witness the deadly capabilities of this new weapon. Marauders from our group and two others would become the special targets of a small group of jet pilots.

During the last two months of the war, stories about death camps and starved and crazed prisoners found in liberated cities like Cologne filtered onto the base. This knowledge strengthened our resolve to bomb anything German. If we could not hit the specific target, every town, city and building became a target of opportunity. I felt no nostalgia for the Germany I'd experienced in 1938. The same Germans who reveled in the beer halls of Munich and Berlin had allowed themselves to become intoxicated with Hitler's venom. While their cowardly leader protected himself in underground bunkers or maybe caverns deep inside the Bavarian Alps, his followers fled cities that now lay in rubble and ash. These could be reclaimed, unlike the humanity that was lost to Hitler's fantastic vision of a universe.

Each mission, I focused on destroying that universe. But I admit it was becoming harder and harder to awaken at 0230 when a corporal on the other side of the door announced, "Sir, time to get up. You have a mission today." I hadn't had a leave since November.

While we were busy flying missions, some headquarters type living the good life in Paris came up with the idea to throw a party for the officers of the 323rd and the 394th, another Marauder group stationed nearby in Cambrai.

I was supposed to drum up enthusiasm among my squadron, but I didn't have a good feeling about this. It wasn't an organized affair like a USO show with professional entertainment. It wasn't going to be anything more than a drinking party for 800 officers in a giant hall in Cambrai. They were even going to invite a few local women. Part of my job was finding some entertainment. My radioman Sgt. Alexander, the jazz pianist, had too much talent to waste on such a large gathering. There was another sergeant who played the fiddle. I recruited him.

The men from our base piled into trucks for the 25-minute ride to Cambrai. Gist took a jeep. I knew what he was up to. He was hoping to meet some woman and head out with her. But he'd started drinking before the big event. He didn't get far from the base when he ran off the road into a ditch and totaled his jeep. Fortunately, he was alone. That put him in the hospital for a few days. I swear that guy had some kind of magic charm that kept him around. I just hoped his luck didn't run out before the end of this war.

It was bizarre standing around a giant hall with a bunch of other men who dressed and acted like us, but whose faces we did not recognize. But with plenty of alcohol, it didn't take long for things to get rolling. Small talk morphed into shouts and raucous laughter until nothing but a continuous roar filled the hall. Over by the entrance, the fiddle player looked like a mime as he earnestly sawed away at his instrument. I felt sorry for him and finally told him to stop and go off in a corner and have a couple of beers.

After that, I joined in the drinking. Frankly things were so out of control, the whole sorry affair was an embarrassment. Not many women showed up. Near my table, a lieutenant ended up on his knees licking the legs of a French woman. She acted amused. But who could tell? Sometime around 2300 hours, somebody signaled the end. It took awhile to round up our men and pile them into the trucks for the trip home.

After Jake's close call with plexi-flak over Xanten back in February, he and I flew only one more mission together. This was in early March, and as he guided me along the bomb run, he lost his patience. "God damn it, Head, I said *five* degrees left." Shortly after that mission, he came to my office to tell me that he preferred flying as an instructor bombardier with other crews.

Maybe after months of defying the odds, he was finally feeling vulnerable. With the war winding down, nobody wanted the distinction of becoming one of the last casualties. I thought the change was a good idea and suggested that he work with crews that I had recommended for lead positions.

On the afternoon of March 26, the group launched 30 bombers led by two Pathfinders to bomb a marshalling yard at Gemünden, Germany, east of Frankfurt and at least two hours' flying time from our base in France. Late afternoon, I motored over to the runway to watch the returning Marauders. Most returned with their bomb loads still in place and barely enough fuel to make it home. Thick clouds with tops reaching 19,000 feet surrounded the target. The box leaders attempted twice to reach the top, then gave up and headed home. Only one flight of six from my squadron reached the top and completed the bomb run, despite the lack of oxygen.

As I stepped out of the jeep, someone ran over to tell me that two squadron planes had not returned to base.

Weary Willie Jr. undergoes repairs to its badly damaged bombardier's compartment and undercarriage. Marauders could take a lot of punishment and still bring their crews home. However, bombardiers were often killed or maimed from the plexi-flak, the exploding combination of hot metal and glass when flak bursts came too close. Denain-Prouvy Airdrome.

"Sir, Captain Flittie's bomber made an emergency landing in Luxembourg City," he said. "Lieutenant Parker was killed."

Capt. Robert Flittie was part of my squadron, and he had recently been assigned a lead position for flights of six. I knew Jake was on board as a bombardier instructor. With two men in the nose, Lt. Donald Parker, Flittie's bombardier, was not able to wear a flak jacket. Later, Tech. Sgt. Richard Tyson, who was part of that crew, told me that a piece of shrapnel no larger than an eraser on a lead pencil pierced Parker's spine, and he died instantly.

Searle, who was following Flittie's lead, was the pilot of the other missing Marauder. No one had heard from him.

When I returned to operations, Jake called me from Luxembourg City. His voice was strained, and he avoided speaking about Parker's death.

"Searle's missing," he said. He was behind us coming home. But he called to say he was running low on fuel. After that, we ran into heavy flak over Koblenz."

"Do you think he was hit?" I asked.

"I can't say. We had our hands full," he said. "I just know we lost all contact with him."

"If Searle ran out of fuel, he can handle himself," I said. "I'm glad you're OK."

"Intelligence really screwed up," Jake said angrily. "We were supposed to have a flak-free corridor around Koblenz."

I waited at operations to see if there was any word about Searle and his crew. Apparently during the flak barrage, Flittie's formation had difficulty following his lead as he attempted to evade. When they joined up again, Searle, who had been following directly behind the left wing, was no longer there.

I returned to my office. I wasn't going to worry about the man from Vera, Oklahoma. This was Searle's 63rd mission. Two more missions, and he was going home to his wife in Savannah, Georgia. Nobody saw his plane explode or drop suddenly from the formation. If bailing out was his only option, he had enough experience to manage the bomber and his crew. Turn off electrical switches and fuel valves, release the bombs unarmed, order the crew to abandon ship with three short rings of the alarm bells two seconds apart, trim the aircraft, and exit through the bomb bay. Maybe he didn't have time to transmit a distress signal. My only concern was the possibility of a bailout over enemy territory.

That evening, he phoned from an Army base in Sedan, France, not more than 50 miles away. Flak blew off the nose of his plane, but he managed to fly the crippled bomber another 100 miles west of Koblenz before exhausting all the fuel in his main and auxiliary tanks. After every one in his crew bailed out safely, they hitched a ride in a jeep to the closest Army unit. I was relieved. But the plane he bailed out of was one of my favorites, *Ole 33 Gal*. She was one of the older, faster models, the ones manufactured before they made changes to the wing to shorten take-off and landing runs. We'd flown a lot of missions together. Jake, Burgmeier, copilot Siegling and I even had a crew picture taken with her. She had endured a lot of punishment long before I arrived. Only recently did I realize that *Ole 33* was the Marauder in which Dale Rush, Burgmeier's bombardier friend, was killed when a burst of black death came too close on a mission to Dieppe. Close scrutiny of the photo shows the tail number, 135033. When Searle and crew bailed out, she became just another casualty of the war, one more missing-in-action aircraft. Well, better to go down as a warrior in battle than to suffer the ignoble fate of being turned into scrap metal after the war.

The next day, we sent a truck to Sedan to pick up Searle and crew. That evening, I visited him and copilot Morris in their tent where they had a new stash of cognac. For some reason during the bailout, Morris shed a pair of fleece-lined boots as he floated to safety. A French farmer ran to pick them up, liked them, and offered to trade some fine cognac for the footwear.

"Lou, I'd like to fly my last two missions as an observer in your plane," said Searle.

"Good," I said. "We'll get you out of here the first week of April."

"Thanks. Vera's got a birthday on the 25th. Maybe I'll make it there for the party," he said.

Since my days as assistant operations officer for the squadron, I'd become good friends with one of the senior officers, Lt. Col. James E. Womeldorff, the group ground executive officer. "Chief," as we fondly called him, turned out to be a trusted friend and mentor. With a receding hairline and rimless glasses, he looked like he was in his late 30's. In civilian life, he had been a successful executive back home in Little Rock, Arkansas, and he applied his considerable talents to whatever tasks ended up on his desk. Col. Wood had appointed him to the toughest job on the base, which was to coordinate all support systems, everything from Band-Aids to bombs. He really knew how to make things happen from setting up and moving bases to acting as a liaison with the local communities and the allied command. He and Harlan were good friends from the time they shared living quarters back at Earls Colne. Before becoming the group's executive officer, he had held that position for my squadron, the 456th, so the two men had worked together a long time.

Like Col. Wood, Womeldorff made a point of coming out of his office to watch the activities on the runway. Back at Laon-Athies, he'd be racing around in his jeep helping the operations officers supervise the clearing of snow and ice or whatever other problems developed. When we returned from missions, he'd be there waiting to see how things went.

Those of us who worked closely with him admired his talents. It wasn't just his organizational skills, but also his ability to resolve conflicts and handle tense situations with intelligence and a sense of humor. When we moved into and out of bases, inspectors showed up to rate the group. At Laon-Athies, he brought order to the muddy chaos, resulting in a "superior" rating from our evaluators.

He and I liked each other immediately, and I spent many evenings in his Butler hut sharing talk and a couple of drinks. Sometimes we speculated about what would happen after the Germans surrendered. Nobody trusted the Russians, and we both wondered if Eisenhower would drive them out of Germany.

One day, Womeldorff stopped by my office to tell me he had submitted the paperwork for my promotion to lieutenant colonel. "You have what it takes, Lou, to be a good leader," he said. "You've earned it." Coming from him, I knew the compliment meant something. For the first time since entering combat, I thought about *my* life after this war. Becoming a lieutenant colonel might be enough of an incentive to stay in the military. Odds were, I'd make it through to the end. Between my five years at Culver and the four years I'd served in the Army Air Corps, I'd spent nearly a third of my life in the military. Why not stay with it? Now, it was up to Lt. Col. Winingham to sign the paperwork.

During the first two missions in April, we lost 13 men when two of our Marauders took direct hits. I was leading one of those missions on April 3 for a bombing run on the Holzmenden Marshalling Yards. Our objective was to disrupt the flow of enemy troops out of Holland and into Germany. This was a day when the changing seasons created an interesting phenomenon in the skies over Europe. When the conditions were right, horizontal rolls of clouds lined up between our base and the targets. We flew perpendicular to these monsters that stretched for miles on either side of us and rose to heights of 18,000 feet above the ground. Without oxygen, we didn't attempt to fly over the top. Flying beneath at 2,000 feet was too low. Instead, I usually stayed around 12,000 feet, and looked for openings large enough to lead the formation through to the other side—two, maybe three miles ahead. When we broke out in clear sky on the other side, it was possible to see the ground for many miles. Sometimes there'd be five or six of these sky ridges along our route to the target. I thought they were beautiful, and I loved the challenge of leading the group through their canyons. Gist, who was as busy as I was leading missions, even coined a phrase: "Follow Rehr to the Ruhr."

On this Holzmenden mission, we expected heavy flak. Ahead of us three window aircraft dropped chaff to confuse the enemy's radar. Despite their efforts, I remember plenty of black bursts filling the sky. But on the bomb run, my focus was on the solid wall of clouds just beyond the target. I'd have to make a sharp left turn immediately after the drop to keep from losing everybody in that soup. Just as I turned, I saw one of the window aircraft disappear into the gray mass.

That Marauder with its crew of seven never returned to base. At the debriefing, we concluded they'd been hit by the ack-ack. But there was no trace of them, no word of a crash landing or of anybody who bailed out and made his way to safety.

Several days later, a well dressed, American civilian appeared in my office. He must have had special credentials to gain entry to the base. He was the father of the pilot of the missing aircraft. He had driven to the base from Paris, where I assumed he had a position.

"Major Rehr, I'm looking for information about my son," he said. "Apparently you were the last person to see his aircraft."

I told the father what I knew, which wasn't much. But he kept pressing me for details. "I don't understand," he said. "Surely they would have radioed a distress call."

"Not necessarily," I said. "There was a lot of flak in the area. When he disappeared in the cloud, he could have taken a direct hit in a fuel tank. There would be no call."

He acted like I was holding back, but I had no more details. If his son's plane had exploded and spun earthward engulfed in flames, there would be no remains to bury. An official letter, some personal belongings, and an article in the hometown paper were all the families of MIA airmen could expect. Maybe there would be a medal awarded posthumously, but that could take many more months of paperwork.

I felt sorry for him, but like the rest of us, he'd have to find his own way of dealing with the death of someone close. I could understand his reluctance to leave my office, but I was beginning to lose patience. "There is always the possibility he's a POW," I said. "However, it could take months to find out."

I said the POW thing to make him feel better. Finally, I stood up and shook the father's hand. "I'm sorry," I said. "Good luck in your search."

Shortly after this interview, another father, Amon Carter, Sr., a legendary publisher from Fort Worth, Texas, was in France hoping for news of his son. Amon Carter, Jr., and I were field artillery cadets at Culver, and like me, he graduated as a second lieutenant. The last time I saw both Carters was over dinner in Fort Worth while I was in primary flight school at nearby Hicks Field. At the time, Carter Jr. had one more year at the University of Texas. After graduation, he joined the Army as an officer in the field artillery. By December 1942, he was stationed in England, not far from where our Culver classmate Gardner Johnson was serving with the 93rd Bombardment Group. Johnson wrote that he and Carter Jr. were in contact with one another, and the two were going to get together. Not long after, while Carter

Jr. was on duty in Tunisia as a forward observer, the Germans captured him and shipped him off to a POW camp near Szubin, Poland, Oflag 64.

When Carter Sr. finally heard that his son was imprisoned, his newspaper, the *Star-Telegram*, ran detailed stories about the efforts to free his son and to send blankets, warm clothing and food to others in the camp. He probably figured that if the world knew about his son, the Germans would keep him alive.

However, during these last months of the war, he had lost track of Carter Jr. What he could not know is that the Germans, fearing the advance of the Russian Army into Poland, had moved the prisoners from Oflag 64 to a camp near Berlin.

Gen. Eisenhower, knowing that the end of the war was near, invited several American publishers to inspect the German war zones. Carter Sr. was among them, and he was using the opportunity to search for his son. After the war, the Carters were reunited at an Army base in central Germany. Carter Jr. spent his life as a publisher and philanthropist. But like many prisoners of war, the physical hardships such as malnutrition and frostbite took their toll. He ended up with an enlarged heart and at age 62, died suddenly of a heart attack.

Officially, I completed my required missions on April 3, which was also Searle's final mission. Flight leaders accumulated extra points, so I only needed 57 missions instead of 60. But as squadron commander, I felt it was important to keep flying, to show leadership to my men. Having 60 or more missions wouldn't hurt my chances for promotion either.

April 4, the day following the Holzmenden mission, the group lost another Marauder. The target was a marshalling yard in Crailsheim, located between Stuttgart and Nuremburg. Allied intelligence had convinced Gen. Eisenhower that Hitler and his most fanatical followers were going to reorganize in the formidable Bavarian Alps surrounding Hitler's retreat at Berchtesgaden. The fear was that within mountain caverns, they would be able to manufacture armaments and protect vast amounts of supplies while waging guerrilla warfare against the occupying forces. The whole notion of such a national redoubt turned out to be a myth, which was probably fueled by German propaganda. But Gen. Eisenhower was taking no chances with any plan that might prolong the war. We began bombing marshalling yards, ordnance depots and flak positions farther south.

As the group approached the Crailsheim target, eyewitnesses saw a twin engine plane behind and closing quickly on a low flight of six aircraft. Before any of the gunners could respond, the Me-262 jet fired on the lead Marauder. Flames swept through and over the bomber, which rolled on its back and disappeared through the clouds. That day, the 323rd was not the only allied group under attack by the jets. Allied formations lost at least seven bombers and two fighters. Our fighters and gunners claimed eight Me-262s and five German pilots during the encounters. We airmen were facing one of our greatest challenges of this war.

One evening just before Searle left to go home, I joined some senior pilots in my squadron who were celebrating the end of his tour. They'd set up a bar in the barracks with plenty of whiskey. We all drank too much and talked too loudly as we swapped flying stories and speculated about how and when the Germans would give up.

At some point in the evening, an enthusiastic replacement pilot, a second lieu-tenant, entered the room. He'd come to discuss his most recent mission with me. Apparently, he'd led a flight of six and scored a direct hit on a marshalling yard. All the kid wanted was some recognition from his commander. I could not ignore him.

"Sir, I thought you'd like to see this picture of my most recent mission," he said. I looked at the bombing photo but had no interest in focusing on the details.

"We hit the rails dead center," he said pointing to the billowing smoke in the photo. OK, I believed him. He'd done an outstanding job of hitting the target. And if he'd come to my office during the day, I would have given him some joy. But this was my time off. Why was he bothering me?

What I should have done was invite him to have a drink with us—ask him to join the circle of camaraderie. But at the moment, I viewed him as an intruder. "Look, can't you see this is not the right time," I said. Embarrassed, he looked around the room. Fortunately, I had enough presence of mind to give him a graceful exit. "Come to my office tomorrow at 10:00," I said. "Bring the photo with you."

"Thank you, sir," he said, then quickly exited the barracks.

After he left, I said good-bye to Searle. He was heading to England the next day, hoping to catch the next troop ship to New York. We promised to see each other again when all this was over. "Thanks for everything Lou," he said as I headed off to bed.

The following day, the lieutenant with the photo showed up at my office. "I am very interested in your photo," I said and meant it. He'd done a beautiful job of precision bombing as he crossed directly over the center of the rails. His bombs must have stopped everything going on down there. "I am very proud of you," I said. "I like your spirit. We need more men like you."

"Thank you, Major," he said and left.

Not long after, Womeldorff paid me a visit.

"Lou, you haven't had a break in months," he said. "Pack your bags. You're headed for the Riviera." Then he handed me a pass for seven days in the Martinez Hotel in Cannes, an official U.S. military recreational area. Womeldorff, like the flight surgeons who often shared a drink with us after missions, was alert to signs of fatigue. Years later, I realized that the average group or box lead pilot flew between four and six missions for a 50-mission segment. There were several of us, however, who far exceeded that number. Col. Wood had flown 29, and three others had exceeded 30. My total came to 23 out of 57 missions. "Relax and enjoy yourself, Lou," Womeldorff said. "I'll see you when you get back."

April 10, I boarded a C-47 cargo plane headed for Cannes. On board were four other junior officers including Lt. Jim Siegling, who had flown copilot on several missions with me. Two nurses from the Women's Army Corps or WACs also rode along, but they kept their distance. They seemed afraid even to talk to us. It didn't matter. All of us were leaving the smoke and rubble behind as snow capped moun-tains, an alpine Shangri-La, slipped past our wings.

We checked into the Martinez, with its wrought iron balconies overlooking the azure Mediterranean. In my room, French doors opened to a view of a cove sur-rounded by a white sand beach lined with small palms.

In 1945, Cannes, France, became a U.S. military recreational rest area. In April 1945, I spent a week at the Martinez Hotel overlooking the Mediterranean, my first leave since November. These officers await transportation back to their bases and the war, which continued for another three weeks.

For a whole week, I had a chance to be a real tourist—enjoy drinks and dinner in the hotel, visit the casino, and walk the beach and shop. I hung out with the four other pilots from my group. When I made friends with a Frenchman who owned a small motor boat, he invited us to join him for a joy ride around the Mediterranean.

Two days after our arrival, President Franklin D. Roosevelt died. Out of respect, the French banned all music and dancing for three days. Vice President Harry S Truman was now the commander-in-chief, which meant that back at the base, the ground crews were wasting no time painting over the nose of one of our Marauders named *Truman's Folly*. This worthy ship, which had survived 171 missions, portrayed a cartoon character

Ration card for my weeklong visit to Cannes, France, in April 1945.

The patio at the Martinez was a favorite gathering place for airmen on leave. Siegling *(right)* **and I** *(second from right)* **join an unnamed airman for morning coffee.**

with a dunce cap. Marauder men never thought much of Senator Truman, whose Truman Committee attempted to stop production of their beloved aircraft.

The hotel patio, with its frost-heaved bricks, was a favorite gathering place, where officers kicked back and enjoyed the strong April sun. One morning while several of us pilots sipped coffee there, I saw something I will never forget. Above the water was a tiny dot that grew larger and larger. It was a Marauder skimming the water and aiming right for us. He was low and moving fast as hell. Directly in front of us, he pulled up and roared over our heads, barely clearing the hotel. Then everything was silent. He must have stayed low as he departed inland. We never saw him again. I thought it was wonderful, the perfect buzz job.

Seeking the company of women did not enter into my plans on what turned out to be a very quiet week. On the return flight to Denain-Prouvy, the WACs, who were stationed at Liège, Belgium, finally decided to warm up to us. There was one from Connecticut who was particularly friendly. I asked her how she was getting back to her base, which would have been a long drive from Valenciennes, but only a 45-minute flight in the Marauder.

"I'll find a ride," she said.

"How about having something to eat at our base, and I'll fly you back," I said.

She agreed. As we stepped out of the C-47, I noticed two broken Marauders, one on each end of the runway. Nothing unusual for a Marauder base. I directed a crew chief to warm up a plane and find me an engineer while we got some food. We were the only ones in the mess hall, but somebody there fixed us a couple of peanut butter sandwiches.

After we climbed into the cockpit, I let her sit in the copilot's seat. She was so excited. Nobody ever made her such an offer before. By the time we reached her base, it was dark. I pulled over to a lighted building to let her off. While I kept the engines running, the engineer helped her down through the hatch. Maybe she expected more, but I only wanted to do something for her she would never forget. Mission complete, the engineer and I took off into the night and headed back to France.

That break in Cannes was just what I needed. As I settled into the barracks, somebody told me Jake had completed his missions and was heading home. He had served with extraordinary courage and dedication and survived. For him, the war was over. It would be nearly 45 years before we saw each again.

11

The Last of the Jet Boys and Our Marauders, Denain-Prouvy Airdrome, Valenciennes, France

April–May 1945

When I returned from Cannes on April 17, the war should have been over. The Germans were finished. Everybody knew it, including them. But while Hitler lived, there would be no surrender. Allied commanders had no choice but to continue risking the lives of our airmen in raids on marshalling yards, oil and ordnance depots, barracks, and airfields. Destroy anything that could prolong the war. Both sides were caught in an absurd situation that bordered on madness. There was little to be gained and much to lose.

In April, the primary threat to our Marauder crews was Jagdverband 44 (JV 44), a small group of German aces flying the Messerschmidt Me-262. Under the leadership of legendary ace Gen. Adolf Galland, they conducted their own private war against our bombers and fighters. In January 1945, Galland defied Hitler and his Reichsmarshal Hermann Göring over their decision to use the Me-262 jet as a high speed bomber rather than a defensive fighter. Shortly after, Hitler acquiesced and gave Galland his own fighter group. Liberated from the madness and decay surrounding the Berlin leadership, Galland recruited some of Germany's most experienced fighter pilots. They were veterans and survivors. They had distinguished themselves with hundreds of victories over enemy aircraft. All had been wounded in battle. With the Allies overrunning Germany so rapidly, JV 44 set up operations in southern Germany at the Munich-Reim Airdrome.

Galland and his men accepted the inevitable defeat of Germany. Their main goal was to show the world that the Luftwaffe had the most advanced weapon in the aerial war. Honor, pride and their legacies were powerful motivators. Years later Galland wrote in his autobiography, *The First and the Last*, "They wanted to be known as the first jet boys of the last fighter pilots of the Luftwaffe. For this, they were ready, once more, to chance sacrificing their lives." Unfortunately, securing their place in history meant sacrificing the lives of dozens of Marauder men.

April 20 was Hitler's 56th birthday. His most trusted advisors and generals joined him in the Berlin bunker. At ground level, 50 feet above, chaos reigned as 800 Eighth Air Force bombers pounded nearby rail targets. The Russians, who were now only 10 miles outside, continually shelled the city. Those who joined Hitler urged him to abandon Berlin immediately before the enemy sealed all escape routes.

That morning, three Marauder groups, the 323rd, 394th and 397th, were scheduled to bomb the Memmingen marshalling yards south of Munich. No one expected trouble. During the last 10 missions, the 323rd had no casualties. Four days earlier, during a bombing raid in the same area, our group's Marauders returned with no flak damage. The mood among the crews who gathered that morning was light-hearted. There was cause for optimism. Just the day before, the newspaper *Stars and Stripes* had declared Allied victory in the air war.

A week off hadn't dampened my desire to keep flying. I did not need the missions, and I was willing to let others fly in the lead position. What mattered most was demonstrating my spirit for the group and completing the job of defeating Germany. Call it esprit de corps, honor, pride—and my own touch of madness. The airmen's superstition surrounding "the ones you volunteer for" never entered my mind.

During the briefing, the intelligence officer announced that we would encounter the usual flak positions protecting the target. But he assured us that the Germans were no longer capable of mounting any significant resistance to our air strikes. The weather with its blue skies and scattered clouds favored bombing altitudes of between 12,000–13,000 feet. We were to approach the target in a stream, single groups of six aircraft in trail, rather than in boxes of 18 aircraft flying in formations.

As we left the briefing and headed to the aircraft around 0800, the squadron photographer, 1st Lt. George Wolfe, asked me if he could ride along. He carried a camera with him and stationed himself in the rear so he could shoot photos through the open waist. Sgts. Alexander and Allen, my radioman and the tail gunner, had been with me since our days at Barksdale. I don't recall why Sgt. James Knight from Utah replaced my original engineer, Sgt. Bailey, but he'd been with me since Beaulieu. We got along as well as any enlisted men and their commanding officer could, given the fact that we slept, ate and socialized in separate areas. We always managed a few laughs together on the ground before and after a mission. It wasn't often that Alexander and Knight had to leave their seats behind the cockpit to man the waist and top turret. I'm sure they had plenty of their own stories to tell about close calls with ack-ack. But we were all lucky. Throughout our tour together, we'd had few encounters with German fighters.

Maj. Alfred E. Smith, the squadron commander for the 454th, led the formation of 48 Marauders. I was slotted behind him in the second group of six aircraft, the high flight to his right. The target was over two hours away. Just as we crossed the Rhine, southwest of Stuttgart, heavy ack-ack surrounded our formation. We evaded, but I wondered why in the briefing there was no mention of this hot pocket of resistance.

The only known picture of Marauders *(white arrows)* under attack by the German jet the Me-262 *(black arrow)*. Lt. George Wolfe, photographer for the 456th, took this photograph on April 20, 1945, from the waist of my Marauder. The jet is diving behind the low flight of six Marauders and prepares for another attack. Seven men and three Marauders from the group were lost in the aerial battle. Another seven men were wounded.

The Messerschmitt Me-262, flown by Gen. Adolf Galland's "jet boys"—the Jagdverband 44—during the last months of the war in Europe, was a formidable weapon against Allied aircraft. During the disarmament duties in Germany, I had orders to destroy the jets. That was before the military realized the value of studying this new technology. Several were shipped to the United States (National Archives photograph 342-FH-3B-34800-166315).

Our initial point was a town called Kempten, south of Memmingen. Here we tightened up our individual groups of six for a four-minute bomb run. We opened the bomb bays and held steady. Arcs of light flak, probably from positions in the higher terrain, crossed our path. Fifteen more seconds until the drop.

Suddenly, an aircraft ripped the skies directly overhead. Instantly, all hell broke loose. Within seconds, flames billowed from the left engine of a Marauder flying directly behind box leader Smith. Pieces of wing and fuselage blew past. The Marauder behind the damaged bomber barely avoided a mid-air collision. Then the ill-fated plane rolled over and dropped beneath the formation. Calls from other pilots to bail out went unheeded.

Simultaneously, the Me-262 pulled straight up as it passed over the formation. Then he abruptly reversed direction and came at us head on. What a hell of a mess. He dove underneath preparing for another strike. For an instant, I wanted to break formation, chase him, knock him out of the sky with my forward firing guns. Somebody had to do something.

Stick to the rules. Stay tight. Concentrate the firepower. Follow the leader. Now, bombs away!

A couple of P-51s flew past with their guns blasting. Two more jets zoomed up

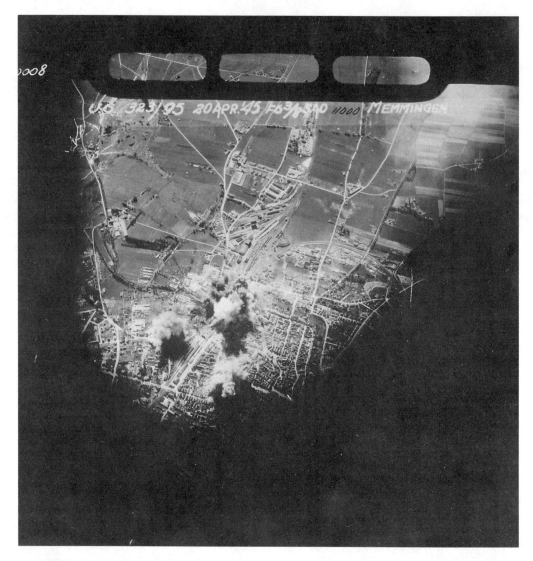

The 323rd Bomb Group successfully bombed the Memmingen, Germany, marshalling yards on April 20, 1945, despite coming under attack by Me-262 jets close to the target.

from beneath passing 100 yards to my right. Gunners and P-51s diverted them from taking aim at Smith.

Their sport did not end with the attack at the front of the formation. As the last six Marauders passed over the IP, a swarm of jets struck. Three jets following one another in 10-second intervals zoomed up from the six o'clock position, then dove on the formation. The first and second jets barely cleared the lead Marauder flown by 1st. Lt. James Hansen. The third jet would have collided with Hanson's bomber, but at the last second, the German dove his jet under the Marauder's right propeller. Half the jet's rudder flew off, and the aircraft fell away. Hanson was lucky. He managed to keep both engines running. But every other Marauder that followed was in trouble.

The last Marauder in his group of six took a hit and lost both engines. Then the right engine burst into flames, and the bomber dropped through the clouds. Fortunately, its crew managed to bail out over friendly territory.

Guns from another jet sent an explosion into the cockpit of the number 5 Marauder. The pilot, 1st Lt. James Vining, bled profusely from his lower right leg, where the blast had nearly severed his foot from his ankle. The jet's guns also knocked out his right engine. His copilot managed to crashland the plane, but it ran into a camouflaged tank trap. The aircraft broke into three pieces, killing the turret gunner and seriously injuring the others. The number 3 Marauder lost part of a propeller and continued flying on single engine. Numbers 2 and 4 had damage, but kept going. P-51s arrived on the scene, but they were too little, too late.

We ended the day with one of the highest casualty lists in the history of the 323rd. 1st Lt. Dale Sanders and his entire crew perished in the Marauder that blew up in front of me. In all, we lost seven men and three aircraft. Another seven men were wounded and seven aircraft damaged. From the waist of my bomber, Wolfe shot what may be the only photo of Marauders under attack by Me-262s. It is not easy to see the jets, which have dived well beneath us preparing for their treacherous climbs. Given the surprise and the speed of these attacks, it is a miracle there is any photo. Several of our gunners claimed hits on the jets, but at the end of the day, it was difficult to reconstruct those seconds of confusion and response.

That day, however, the Germans lost no men. Eduard Schallmoser, the Me-262 pilot with the severed rudder, managed to parachute to safety. Several gunners fired on Schallmoser's jet, as did pilot Vining, who used his forward guns. Vining later admitted that as he took aim, he loosened his position in the formation. This made him an easy target for the German aces. Schallmoser claims that he dropped into his mother's garden with an injured knee. Before heading back to the base and then a hospital, he enjoyed a plateful of her pancakes.

Gen. Galland was somewhere in the skies that day. Using the R4M rockets, he claimed two hits when one bomber caught fire and exploded and another lost part of its right tail and wing and plunged to earth. Perhaps he fired on another group. Or perhaps he confused this mission with others in the days that followed when his jets blew apart several more Marauders from other groups, senselessly annihilating their crews.

The 323rd would not fly again until April 25. This mission was another long one to southern Germany. The target was the Erding Aerodrome, where at least four Me-262's and 42 single engine fighters sat parked on the runway. Orders were to "post hole the area." Although other groups participated in this raid, we maxed out the loading with 308 men in 48 aircraft. Missions flown meant more points—85 and a man could go home. This war in Europe might be ending, but we were still battling Japan in the Pacific.

I did not need the points. I just wanted the 60th mission. On what turned out to be the group's last mission, I rode as an instructor pilot on the number 2 aircraft directly behind the group lead aircraft. With a pilot and copilot seated up front, I was really just an observer. I settled into the waist as I had done nearly a year ago on my second mission. The flight to the target was close to 2½ hours. We'd be lucky if everybody made it back without running out of fuel. Fortunately, the air was smooth, enabling the formation to stay together without constant throttle adjustments.

Approaching the bomb run, the Marauders tightened. Suddenly, a lone Me-262 was all over our lead box—diving, climbing, circling to get into position to fire a long, narrow cannon protruding from the nose. We'd not seen anything like this before. From both sides of the waist, I caught glimpses of him, then he'd disappear from view. Short, deafening bursts from our tail and turret vibrated the fuselage. Empty shells clattered onto metal. I tightened my parachute straps.

The Me-262 never fired. More than likely his cannon jammed. As it turned out, this unique design was still experimental, and problems with the cannon occurred more often than not. But if he had fired, a single 50mm shell was capable of blowing apart two Marauders at once.

The jet disappeared, and we completed the mission. We managed to "post hole" the airfield and destroy hangars and aircraft. All 48 Marauders arrived safely back at Denain-Prouvy.

The following day, Galland was injured when gunners from the 17th Bomb Group and a P-47 pilot shot down his jet. He would not fly combat missions again. But he succeeded in winning a unique place in history for himself and his pilots. I've read his autobiography. And his illegible signature is scrawled across the bottom of a Robert Taylor print that hangs among my aviation art. This dramatic painting depicts Marauders under attack by Me-262s. The scene represents an extraordinary part of my history while serving in World War II, and I am pleased to explain its significance to those who ask.

But a few years before his death in 1996, I chose not to attend a talk Galland gave somewhere near Washington, D.C. Nearly 50 years after the war, I was still not ready to accept him as an equal. Despite his heroics in aerial combat, I held no romantic notions about his gallantry as a fellow pilot, a man who like me wanted nothing more than to serve his country with honor. I believed he should have quit playing with Germany's shameful history and stayed home. I've mellowed somewhat now, convinced of the importance of telling our personal histories. But if he were alive today, I still would be uncomfortable listening to this former enemy talk about his "jet boys" and their legacies.

After that mission on April 25, our group stood by in restless anticipation. Day to day, the scene changed as word of Mussolini's execution and Hitler's suicide signaled the final chapter in this war. On May 4 and 6, we briefed for a mission to the Neumünster marshalling yards near Hamburg. The goal was to stop hordes of Nazis from fleeing into Holland. But weather and the dubious wisdom of such a raid kept us grounded. Finally on May 6, the loading list was scratched from the bulletin board. Combat flying for the 323rd had ended.

May 7, in the early morning hours, Womeldorff shared the news of the surrender with a few of us in his Butler hut, and we celebrated privately. Harlan wasn't there because he'd left Denain-Prouvy two weeks earlier with an advance echelon. Their orders were to prepare a primitive airstrip outside of Julich, Germany, for the seventh move of the squadron and group. I sent a plane over to get him. Harlan has vivid memories of that day. "One of our planes landed on the steel plank runway, and the pilot hunted me up to tell me to get my stuff and get in the plane," he said. "Major Rehr wanted me back at Denain-Prouvy that afternoon. The war would be over the next day, and he needed me back there to organize the ground echelon for a move into Germany."

The following day, May 8, the rest of the base and the world knew. Womeldorff sounded the siren setting off a non-stop party with plenty of booze, guns and flares that punctuated the celebrations that lasted well into the night. I preferred to spend VE Day quietly. Harlan and I played checkers. Then, I drove my jeep to the runway to spend a little time with the Marauders. With the celebrations back at the barracks, I had them all to myself. I loved these battered heroes, these survivors of historic combat missions in Normandy, Northern France, Ardennes, Rhineland and Central Europe. Some had over 100 missions to their credit, and their scarred and dented skins looked it. Since February 1943, I'd logged nearly 1,300 hours in Marauders. I caressed the props of a couple and admired their sleek lines. Lined up and ready to taxi, they still looked fast and mean. But taxi and launch to where? As it turned out, their destiny was a scrapheap in Germany.

By late fall, these and nearly every other Marauder flown in the ETO ended up at a huge disposal site near Landsberg, Germany. After the Air Force stripped them of engines, radios, and anything else of value, demolition teams exploded TNT

Moving day at Denain-Prouvy. After VE Day, only a third of my squadron followed me into southern Germany for disarmament duty. Others were transferred to the 397th, 322nd and eventually the 387th Bomb Groups.

packs under the wing roots, breaking their fuselages in half. There are a few photos of these crippled, disgraced Marauders, but for those of us who flew them, these are painful to look at.

The scrap aluminum was then melted down for use in the rebuilding of Germany. At Walnut Ridge Army Air Field in Arkansas, nearly 1,000 more Marauders along with trainers, fighters, cargo aircraft and bombers—11,000 in all—met a similar fate. These ended up as pots and pans. Such ironies are consequences of war.

Standing near my Marauders on VE Day, I did not know their fate. I just knew that from now on, things were going to be different. The following day, May 9, orders arrived for the squadrons. We were breaking up. I gathered my men in our mess— nearly 450—and gave them the news. Only 150 would follow me into southern Germany for disarmament duty. These included the squadron bombardier, navigator, the operations and assistant operations officers, Harlan and all ground officers and many enlisted men. Exactly what "disarmament duty" meant, nobody had bothered to explain. We'd have more specific orders after we arrived at Gablingen Aerodrome in Augsburg, northwest of Munich. The rest of the men were assigned to the 397th and 322nd Bomb Groups. Some men reacted with groans and bitching. Many thought they would be headed home. Others who sat in silence hid the turmoil of conflicting emotions. The intensity of our experiences bonded us, and it was difficult to face an uncertain future. I would miss them and told them so. At the end, men embraced and shook hands and snapped lots of photos so we would remember one

After VE Day, I am "grounded" and now pilot an open cockpit jeep into Germany.

Top: En route to Augsberg, Germany, immediately after VE Day, Maj. Ross Harlan *(pictured)* and I detour to Bastogne, Belgium, site of fierce fighting during the Battle of the Bulge, and stop for lunch. *Bottom:* Approaching the Rhine River near Mainz, Maj. Harlan poses with the jeep and trailer.

another. I thanked as many as I could individually for their service to the squadron, the group, their country.

Very early the following morning, Harlan and I left Denain-Prouvy headed for Germany. This time, we traveled in a jeep towing a trailer loaded with our duffel bags, food, fuel and repair equipment. Around our hips hung our holsters with loaded pistols. We didn't know what to expect in the immediate aftermath of this war. As it turned out, we were embarking on a postwar odyssey filled with unforgettable images.

I drove the jeep along the poorly marked, partially destroyed roads as Harlan attempted to navigate. There were few signs and no border crossings. We both wanted to detour to Bastogne, Belgium. The Battle of the Bulge had become an unforgettable part of our histories too. As we motored along, we had this part of the world to ourselves. No other vehicles crossed our path. Not a living soul had returned to the shelled farmhouses and clusters of gutted, burned out houses we passed along the way.

Nearing Bastogne, the roads improved dramatically—probably rebuilt by our engineers for the transport of troops and supplies. They led us through forests thick with growth and past open, sunny fields where no crops grew. Just west of Bastogne, we slowed to study the scene. Unlike Normandy, no dead soldiers, bloated animals or landmines littered the landscape. But what remained was bizarre. A C-47 lay on its back in a ditch like the carcass of a dead animal. On the other side of the road in an open field stood dozens of undamaged WACO gliders, which were perfectly lined up as if waiting for another mission.

Driving through town, we passed windowless, rubble filled buildings, some several stories high. Again there were no signs of life. After leaving the town behind, we pulled over near the remains of burned out German Tiger tank. Here, surrounded by the eerie silence of these fields and woods, we broke out some K rations.

Leaving Bastogne, we headed southeast through Luxembourg. We crossed into Germany somewhere near Trier and followed roads to a bridge that would enable us to cross the Rhine River at Mainz. On the other side, we climbed a steep road surrounded by vineyards, and enjoyed a magnificent view of the Rhine. Suddenly a deafening roar overhead scared the shit out of us. Before we even had a chance to duck, a P-47 Thunderbolt buzzed our jeep probably going 400 mph before he pulled up into a steep climb. No wonder the German infantry feared this aircraft more than any other. The pilot must have been patrolling the sector when he decided to have some fun with our jeep and trailer, which were clearly marked with large white stars. After his salute, he disappeared beyond our view.

By the time we stopped for the evening, we had reached a town southeast of Frankfurt called Aschaffenburg.

Part III

GERMANY

Frankfurt

Mainz

Aschaffenburg

Wurzburg

Trier

Augsburg

Munich

Kempten

Berchtesgaden

Germany and disarmament duty, May–June 1945.

12

Disarmament Duty, Kempten, Germany

May–June 1945

Every building in Aschaffenburg showed signs of heavy fighting. Although the German citizens had fled, white surrender sheets still hung from what was left of windows—something we saw in every German town we passed through. We unrolled our sleeping bags and broke out the K rations in a busted up building that still had a second floor. Sleeping at ground level would put us too close to the convoys of American military supply trucks that rumbled non stop through the streets. The place must have been a makeshift hospital because medical supplies, surgical equipment and bloodstained bandages lay among the debris.

The following day, we drove south passing through Wurzburg on the way to Augsburg. Walking along the sides of the roads were thousands upon thousands of people. Streams of them moved inexorably south. I remember only men with nothing but the tattered and soiled clothes they wore layered on their bodies. A few drove unfamiliar looking military trucks and carried weapons. But they presented no threat to us. They kept to the side of the road and did not seem to take notice as we passed them. These were DPs, displaced persons, headed homeward, wherever that was. Forced laborers in fields and factories, political prisoners—Hitler had rounded up over 10 million from all over Europe. These were the survivors. For the rest of the day and the next, we passed them. A couple of men who spoke English called to us asking for a ride. But we could not be burdened with the unknown.

When we arrived at the outskirts of Augsberg in the early evening, several American infantrymen halted our jeep and asked to see our orders. A couple of them escorted us to some barracks located on the perimeter of Gablingen Aerodrome. Greeting us was some pompous ass with enough rank that we had to listen to him. He let us know that here in Germany he could do what he wanted including kill more Germans. I wondered if our orders to disarm German aircraft included this kind of lawlessness. If so, I did not want any part of it.

Driving through Germany immediately after VE Day, Harlan and I passed through many towns like this one, which was lying in ruins.

The following day, sanity prevailed as Harlan and I joined Womeldorff in the officers' quarters. He and others had flown in the day before. He told me I'd be in charge of things down at Kempten, just south of Augsberg. But we'd all have to wait for more specific orders. Apparently nobody had figured out how this occupation and disarmament stuff was supposed to work.

Harlan and I toured the airdrome, which bordered a beautiful grass strip. Smashed equipment and furniture lay among piles and piles of paper. We joked that with so much paperwork, it was no wonder the Germans lost the war. Our airmen and some captured German prisoners, who were held in a former labor camp adjacent to the airfield, were cleaning out the basements and barracks filled with wired aircraft bombs and ammunition.

The following day, Harlan and I headed for Munich. I wanted to go back to a couple of places I'd visited before the war. From Augsburg, I drove the jeep southeast on secondary roads. Oddly we shared the highway with cars carrying German officers and truckloads of disarmed German troops. I guess there were just too many around to take as prisoners.

Along the route lay Dachau, the massive concentration camp. Word of the camp's liberation on April 29 spread quickly. Eisenhower wanted the world to bear

Arriving in Augsberg, Germany, I relax with friends and some brews as we await orders for aircraft disarmament. *Left to right:* Unknown, an English officer (see piping on right sleeve), Lt. Col. James Womeldorff, Capt. Frank Teachout (456th B.S.), and me.

witness to the starving and beaten prisoners, the emaciated bodies spilling out of railroad cars and trucks and piled high in corners. He encouraged all American military to visit the place to insure that future generations could not question its existence and the atrocities committed there.

Long before we approached the western end of the compound, the smell of inhumanity filled our nostrils. The first thing we saw was a railroad track with a string of cattle cars. The bodies had been removed but the sickening stench of decaying corpses haunted our senses.

We parked the jeep and headed toward some gates that stood wide open. Around the entrance, men gathered and moved about aimlessly. These must have been the ones who escaped the typhus epidemic that kept most of the prisoners isolated for treatment. It had been only two weeks since the camp's liberation, and I sensed these men could not comprehend their freedom. They were at liberty to go, but where? They lived, but for what? As we approached them, they asked for cigarettes with courteous gestures. Harlan and I gave them what we had.

Their eyes followed us as we focused our attention on several nearby buildings. The doors were wide open. We entered one with a large, blackened chimney. Inside, four brick ovens, narrow and deep spilled ash from their openings. "Ashes to ashes...."

Rays of sunlight through the open doorway illuminated a fine dust floating in the air. "Dust thou art and unto dust thou shalt return." No rites of passing had been uttered here, unless the prisoners who manned these ovens were willing to risk revealing their humanity. It was an efficient way to dispose of bodies while it lasted. But apparently these ovens had stood cold for the past few months. The Germans no longer had coal to keep them fired. We looked inside a gas chamber, one that was apparently used to delouse prisoners' clothes, not for mass murders. We'd seen enough and headed back to the jeep.

Although I had a camera in the jeep, I took no photographs of these men seeking to regain their dignity or of the shameful place where bodies were incinerated like trash. Leave that to the military photographers and the reporters who now swarmed over Germany in search of some truths. But the place left its mark on me. Dachau is part of why I avoided paying tribute to Galland, who launched his jets from Munich-Reim Airdrome, not far away.

What I did photograph was the Hofbrauhaus in Munich. It still stood despite damage from shelling. On its façade was printed "CP 157 Inf 45." The 157th Infantry Regiment of the 45th Thunderbird Division, Seventh Army were the first soldiers to enter Dachau. Shocked and distraught at seeing the boxcars filled with bodies, some of these soldiers summarily lined up the Waffen SS in the camp and shot them. What irony there was in scrawling CP, command post, here because the old beer hall was where Hitler founded the Nazi party in 1920.

The only other place I wanted to see was an elaborate shrine called the Feldherrnhalle built by Hitler in 1935 in honor of 16 followers who were killed in the "Beerhall Putsch" of 1923. This was a failed attempt to seize power. But when Hitler was firmly in control, he enshrined them in 16 iron coffins that he placed in an open-air mausoleum constructed of columns and marble.

In 1938, Gardner Johnson thought we ought to see the place. At the time, we were the only Americans among the Germans who stood reverently viewing the black coffins emblazoned with the German eagle. Fresh wreaths surrounded this resting place. Guarding the scene was a young German soldier, who was standing rigidly on a wooden platform and gripping a rifle. No one objected when I took a couple of photographs.

When Harlan and I found the place, the monument had become another symbol of the complete collapse of Hitler's dreams. The coffins were gone. Tangled vines grew up and around the columns. I stood on the same wooden platform, where the once proud German soldier kept watch and had Harlan snap my picture. Cocky with victory, I stood with open jacket and hands on my hips. This photo was the only souvenir I wanted to bring home from Germany. I was not interested in booty like guns and Nazi flags and never claimed that kind of memorabilia. The contrasting photos taken seven years apart are how I like to remember our defeat of Germany.

Opposite: **Immediately after the war, I returned to Munich's Hofbrauhaus, which I had visited in 1938. The 157th Infantry Regiment of the 45th Thunderbird Division, the men who liberated Dachau, have claimed this birthplace of the Nazi party.**

I took these photos in 1938 at Munich's Feldherrnhalle, where Hitler enshrined his 16 followers killed in the Beerhall Putsch in 1923. A German guard stands watch.

"You men want to go to Venice with me tomorrow?" Womeldorff asked Harlan and me that evening over a couple of beers. "Down to Italy, just overnight. I've written some orders to get us through the Austrian border." Any guy with the rank of lieutenant colonel could really take advantage of the confusion.

The following day, the three of us piled into a jeep that towed our equipment and headed south to the Austrian border. I don't know what our orders we supposed to be, but when Womeldorff presented papers to a couple of American infantrymen stationed at the border, they waved us through. There was absolutely nobody on the roads as the jeep struggled up the steep inclines then coasted down the other side. Occasionally we stopped to take photos of each other standing in the melting snowfields at the mountaintops. At one place, Womeldorff and Harlan gingerly

Cocky with victory, I stand on the same platform. Seven years later, the shrine is overgrown with vines, and the coffins have been removed.

walked across flimsy wooden slats suspended over a swollen river. It didn't look safe to me. "You guys are gonna kill yourselves," I shouted over the rushing waters as they wobbled precariously with nothing to hold onto but a rope on one side. I had no intention of surviving a war only to be swept away by turbulent waters somewhere in the Austrian Alps.

Safely back on firm ground, they joined me for a picnic of K rations, which we spread out on the hood of the jeep. That's when Womeldorff told me something I wasn't expecting. "Lou, all promotions are on hold indefinitely," he said.

"What you are telling me," I said, "is that I'm not going home as a lieutenant colonel."

"That's right, but you have more than enough points to head home," he said. "You have the freedom to leave when you choose."

I was surprised, then disappointed, but not devastated. I wanted to blame Commander Winingham for holding up the paperwork. But as we rolled down the curving mountains headed for Venice, I suddenly felt liberated by the realization that I didn't *have* to pursue a military career. I'd be free from the regimens and protocols I'd lived with since I was a teenager. I left college to become an Army Air Corps pilot, a dream I'd had since I was a kid. When war broke out, I wanted nothing more than to prove myself in combat. I'd done that and was proud of my record. And I survived. What more was I looking for? Why was it so important to have the rank of lieutenant colonel? What I really loved was being around airplanes and flying. I didn't need to stay in the military to do that. I could go back to Washington and Lee and finish my last year.

Having the choice when to leave Germany was a privilege few enjoyed. Word was that this disarmament work could take six months. If so, most men would be stuck here. Maybe that was better than shipping out to the Pacific. Then there was my operations officer and second in command, Maj. Calvin Gibson. He couldn't wait to take over as squadron commander for the 456th. I'd think about it.

As we neared Venice, we honked at the only traffic we'd seen all day—an old guy with a donkey headed in the same direction. The city of canals appeared untouched by the war. We checked into a hotel overlooking St. Mark's Square, where a few Italians threw crumbs to thousands of pigeons. Otherwise, we seemed to have the place to ourselves. Like tourists, we took photographs and rode in a gondola with a singing boatman. That evening over drinks, I told Womeldorff I wasn't ready to head home just yet. I still had a job to do in Kempten.

Lt. Col. James Womeldorff served as ground executive officer for the 323rd B.G. from October 1944 until the group returned home in September 1945. I took this photograph of him riding in a gondola in Venice. He invited Maj. Ross Harland and me to make an unauthorized trip over the Austrian Alps before disarmament duties began in earnest. Womeldorff was a respected leader and mentor to the airmen who served with him.

A few days later, the squadron and I set up operations in that scenic Bavarian town. "Heraus! Sie haben 15 minuten," I said to a German frau who stared sullenly at me after I ordered her out of her house. She lived in one of the more beautiful homes in Kempten. I gave her and her neighbor 15 minutes to gather up a few possessions and get out. My staff and I needed housing. Armed sergeants surrounded both places.

The house in which I stood was relatively new, a large three storied structure adorned with wooden shutters. From one of the second floor bedrooms, French doors opened onto a balcony overlooking a garden. The other bedrooms were spacious and furnished with quality furniture and bed linens. Here we'd even be able to enjoy the luxury of private bathrooms—that is after we removed the towels the housefrau flushed down the toilets. When she complained about her treatment to our new friend the burgermeister, one of the few male civilians around, he locked her up for a night.

The entire town of Kempten, located in the foothills of the Alps northeast of Lake Constance, had weathered the war very nicely. There was no bomb damage. No rubble to sift through. By the time I arrived, my enlisted men had already taken over a hotel adorned with turrets, chimneys and elaborate carvings. Good for them. These guys were going to be putting in some long days in the effort to "render impotent the Nazi aeronautical industry," as our orders read. They deserved a comfortable place to settle into each night.

I ordered the German occupants out of these houses in Kempten when my squadron arrived to conduct our aircraft disarmament duties. As the victors, American military personnel had their choice of living quarters.

The day before I arrived in Kempten, the 2nd Disarmament Wing finally showed up at Augsberg to brief the squadron commanders on how to handle the disarmament and occupation duties in our four assigned sectors: the 453rd would remain in Augsberg, the group headquarters; the 455th was assigned to Leipheim Airdrome, located west of Augsberg; my squadron, the 456th was in charge of Kempten; and the 454th settled into scenic Innsbruck, Austria.

Orders were to set up operations in the best houses and hotels. Figure the occupants were probably Nazis. Strictly enforce the non-fraternization rules, which were going to be in effect for the next 60 years. Liaisons between military and the local fräuleins were strictly forbidden. (By the middle of July, American, British and Canadian soldiers were allowed to speak with adults in the street and in public places.) Germans walked in the streets, not on the sidewalks. The way the planners of this postwar period figured it, the Germans were people who innately believed in their superiority. They might appear compliant. But underneath, they were filled with bitter resentment and could resort to subterfuge.

Our objective was to destroy anything aircraft-related that looked like it had military significance. This included the artificial silk factory in Kempten that manufactured parachutes and camouflage nets. Of primary importance was the destruction of the Me-262s. We didn't find these at Kempten's small airdrome, but in fields and woods a few miles outside of town. For several days, my enlisted men really enjoyed setting off a charge in the cockpit, which broke the aircraft in half.

Then someone urgently called a halt to blowing up the jets. Apparently U.S. engineers wanted them sent back to the states so they could study the technology. There must have been a lot of haggling among those who oversaw this disarmament. One day, there'd be an order to destroy everything in sight, including Nazi paperwork, then somebody would reverse the orders. Confusion reigned. The order to preserve the jets probably came about the time some of our men who were clearing out the Munich-Reim Airdrome discovered an Me-262 equipped with the 50mm cannon. Speculation was that this was the same jet that attempted to attack our group on April 25, our last mission.

Each day, my men left Kempten to search barns, haystacks, churches, and warehouses not just for aircraft but aircraft engines, tires, spark plugs, salvage dumps, and fuel. They burned what they could and buried the rest. However, one of their discoveries was so startling that the intelligence personnel ordered the equipment packed up immediately for shipment to Wright Patterson Air Base in Dayton, Ohio. In a warehouse near Munich, the enlisted men found a cache of Luftwaffe developed automatic engine control units, which may have been the guidance system for the V-1 robot bombs.

On the outskirts of Kempten was a large grass field with a single aircraft hangar. Inside, we discovered several small planes. One was a primary glider. After World War I, the Treaty of Versailles forbid Germany to create an air force. Cleverly, Germans continued teaching each other to fly using these open cockpit gliders. There were also three Klemm KL-35s, military trainers similar to the open cockpit PT-19 I'd flown in primary flight school. I could see no strategic importance to destroying them. Far better to make use of them for our own sport.

Above: Disarmament duty in Kempten, Germany. Four enlisted men and I pose with captured automatic control units, which were developed by the Luftwaffe for use in robot planes. The find was so startling, intelligence ordered them packed up immediately for shipment to Wright-Paterson AFB. *Left to right:* Maj. Rehr, T/Sgt. Ralph Felice, Sgt. Denman Pence, Sgt. George Schmidt, T/Sgt. Jack Reeves (courtesy Ross E. Harlan). *Right:* Captured automatic control unit (courtesy Ross E. Harlan).

Me-262 with the 50mm nose cannon found at Munich-Reim Airdrome by 323rd disarmament crews, who believed this was the jet that attacked the group on its last mission on April 25, 1945 (courtesy Ross E. Harlan).

The windscreens to the Klemm were missing, no doubt hidden in somebody's basement or barn. I asked the enlisted men to look for some as they scoured the countryside, but the Germans were unwilling to help. So I flew the Klemm by keeping my head low as I soared over the rolling terrain and buzzed a nearby lake where the local girls sunned themselves. We launched the primary glider by towing it behind a car with a very long rope. Strapped in an open cockpit, a pilot had everything he needed to control the glider: a stick for aileron and elevator control, rudder pedals and some basic instruments. I'd release somewhere near 1,000 feet, make a couple of turns and land. I knew nothing about the art of using thermals to stay aloft. In 30 minutes, I logged five take-off and landings. This was my first experience with an activity that eventually became a lifelong passion.

This hangar at Kempten, Germany, housed a Klemm KL-35, an open cockpit German trainer and a primary glider. Since they posed no threat, I and others flew these aircraft rather than destroy them.

One morning, my men found a Fieseler Storch parked in front of the Kempten hangar. Overnight, an elusive stranger landed it, then disappeared. He or she left behind this beautiful German scout plane that had been used for low level reconnaissance. Its slow take-off and landing speeds made it ideal for short field operations. It was the type of plane that Hanna Reitsch, a renowned German test pilot, and another high-ranking official named General Robert Ritter von Greim used during the last days of the war to meet with Hitler in Berlin. Flying at treetop level through Russian defenses, they landed the Storch at the Brandenburg Gate and rushed off for the final visit before Hitler committed suicide.

After our mechanics checked this model over, a couple of us flew it around. Unfortunately, my squadron didn't get to keep our Storch for long. Somebody back at headquarters in Augsberg ordered it flown there, where it may have been disassembled for shipment to the U.S. It was hard to resist flying this German equipment. In those first few weeks, there were no restrictions on playing with the aircraft. Group Commander Winingham even had a German pilot check him out in the Me-262, and he may have been the first American to fly the jet. But flying unknown aircraft led to several deaths and injuries and eventually a ban.

At Kempten, we had no incidents, despite the efforts of a local farmer. He was in charge of mowing the grass runway, a job he'd had for years. On the pretense of reminding himself of where he'd left off the day before, he pounded a stake or two in the field. I guess he just couldn't adjust to Americans occupying his turf. His attempts at sabotage ended after I reminded him that runways needed to be free of obstacles.

After nearly three weeks at Kempten, I became restless. My enlisted men knew exactly what they were doing. Operations officer Gibson was supervising the activities. Harlan carried on his responsibilities as executive officer. There wasn't much reason for me to hang around. But before I packed up and shipped out, I still had one more place I wanted to visit—Berchtesgaden, the location of Hitler's alpine retreat, the Eagle's Nest. I didn't know what to expect once I got there. I just didn't want to leave Germany without having a look around there.

Berchtesgaden was several hours drive from Kempten. On the outskirts of town, I saw something that my squadron could really use. Lined up in a field were several Ju-52s, a German transport plane. These tri-motor aircraft were the workhorses of the German military delivering supplies and paratroopers, much like our C-47s. Hitler even used one as his private transport. I figured my men could use one for day trips to anywhere they wanted to go. I was also thinking about my own transportation to Paris, the first leg of my trip home. The Ju-52 was perfect. As the victors, we had the feeling we could take what we wanted. Lugers and Nazi memorabilia meant nothing to me. But I was interested in this transport plane.

I needed to find the commanding officer of this sector to get his permission to fly one of these planes out of here. I stopped the jeep at the base of Hitler's Eagle's Nest, where a soldier easily discouraged me from climbing to the top of the 8,000-foot mountain. He let me know there was nothing up there to see but a red phone and a view. I believed him. It had been several weeks since our ground troops had "liberated" the place.

"Where can I find the commanding officer for the area?" I asked.

"You want Colonel Sink," he said and gave me directions to where I'd find him. Col. Robert L. Sink was the regimental commander of the 101st Airborne's 506th Parachute Infantry Regiment. Finding his headquarters was not easy, and I had to ask several times before arriving at a house somewhere outside of Berchtesgaden.

It was the cocktail hour by the time I arrived at a comfortable town home that served as Col. Sink's headquarters. The colonel greeted me warmly as if he had expected a visitor. He was a tall, slender man around 40 years old with a polished southern accent. On his right hand, he wore a West Point ring. "Join us for a drink, Major," he said. With him was Col. Robert Strayer, regimental executive officer for the 101st.

"I'd be honored to have a drink with the airborne," I said. I was hoping the cordial reception would last so they'd get wound up and tell me something about their war. We airmen had almost no contact with ground troops except for the time our bomb group participated in an "exchange program." Some budding public relations type thought it might be a good idea to send our airmen to the front for a few days. In return a few infantrymen had the opportunity to sit through a mission in a Marauder. If the goal were to scare the hell out of everybody, it worked. I never visited the front lines, but a couple of GIs rode with me and my crew. The response was, "Never again. Give me some place where I can take cover. A foxhole, tank, a wall. But don't leave my ass hanging out there at 10,000 feet."

Our aircrews had a similar response. "You get out there in a tank, and you just sit there with bullets rattling off the armor. Give me an aircraft any day."

What I'd stumbled into here were two commanding officers who had participated in every major campaign since D-Day. I was in awe. Suddenly requesting the Ju-52 didn't seem so important anymore. But I had to ask anyway. I told them what my squadron was doing at Kempten, and why I wanted the plane.

"Flying is your business, Major," Sink said. "It's up to you what you do with it." He didn't care, but I also had the feeling he didn't want the responsibility for what was clearly a matter for the Army Air Corps. "It might be wise to round up a German engineer to take along if you are going to fly it out of here," he said. I agreed.

Then he offered me another drink. "Tell us about what it was like flying those Marauders," he said. "I hear it was a tricky son-of-a-bitch." He was genuinely interested. I knew I was in for an evening of drinking and swapping war stories.

For the next several hours the colonels held me spellbound as they recalled their campaigns in Normandy, Holland, Belgium and Germany. These men had been partners since they trained their paratroopers in Georgia and North Carolina. Together they commanded these same men during some of the worst ground fighting of the war, with no small loss to their ranks. With humor and humility they recalled some of their triumphs and defeats.

Sink was a real balls-a-fire guy, a hands-on leader, who had jumped along with his three battalions behind Utah Beach in the early morning hours of June 6. His men were ordered to secure two causeways behind the beachhead and to seize two wooden bridges leading over the Douve River. The drop didn't go as planned, and his troops became separated. "Bob here was in charge of the 2nd Battalion," said Sink. "He rounded up about 200 of our men, and killed a few Germans trying to reach a causeway." They both smiled at the understatement.

"But the hostile boys wiped out my 3rd Battalion," he said much more seriously. "Lost a good commander there and 20 men. But at the time, I didn't know it." The "hostile boys" were the German gunners who had the 3rd's drop zone surrounded. As the airborne troops floated toward the field, the Germans lit a few barns soaked with oil to illuminate the sky and easily picked them off.

When Sink couldn't make radio contact with the 3rd, he frantically set out in a jeep to find his troops. Accompanied by another officer, a driver, and two enlisted men with tommy guns, Sink charged inland, right through the German infantry. "Kraut soldiers didn't know what to think," he said. "They hit the ditches when we fired on them. Surprised everybody, including me."

"Damn lucky you didn't get killed," said Strayer laughing.

They spoke of the failed Market Garden operation during the fall of 1944 and their retreat from Eindhoven, Holland. The 506th was supposed to cross the Wilhelmina Canal at the Zon Bridge, but it blew up just as Sink got there. Undaunted, he and his men grabbed boats and ferried across to get to Eindhoven, which was the first large city in Holland to be liberated. While waiting for the British to arrive, his men captured four other bridges. "Holland's where I learned when to keep my head down," Sink said.

Sink and Strayer really did want to hear about our Marauders. Already, I was feeling nostalgic about those rugged bombers and our dedicated crews. "We never set out on a mission without thinking about what you men on the ground were going through," I said. "It was hell waiting for the weather to break back in December. That was the closest we came to feeling like ground troops preparing for retreat."

"We lost too many good men in Belgium," said Strayer.

Sink asked me about the Me-262 because he'd seen a few here in southern Germany. "The engineers back home want to study the technology," I said. "The days of flying piston aircraft in war are numbered."

And so the conversation and bourbon sipping continued until well past midnight. He graciously offered me a room in the house next door. As we parted, Col. Sink told me he was looking forward to a homecoming in a New York City. "I think we should have a helluva big dance in Madison Square Garden," he said, "and invite about 5,000 women."

Only recently have I learned that Sink, a 1927 West Point grad, and Strayer had trained some of the most physically fit combat troops in the Army—men who were able to march great distances in record time. Their rigorous training in the rugged mountains of Georgia and the heroism of their men from one company, Easy, are the subject of the Stephen Ambrose book and the HBO film *Band of Brothers.*

The following morning, I awoke to a cold, gray fog that enveloped the area. Taking a Ju-52 no longer seemed like such a good idea. I'd lost the desire to hang around Berchtesgaden looking for a suitable engineer and waiting for the fog to lift. I just wanted to return to Kempten and make plans to head home.

My conversation with Sink and Strayer only confirmed what I already knew. I could never have survived the war as a ground soldier. It wasn't the fear of dying or being wounded or ending up as a prisoner of war. In the air or on the ground, we all faced those dangers. No, it was all about my body's ability to endure rain-soaked clothes and boots and having to sleep in frigid foxholes with no warmth other than the guy next to me. If frostbite or trench foot didn't get me, it would have been pneumonia. We didn't have it easy at Laon-Athies, but it was luxury compared to what Sink's men and tens of thousands of others endured. How many under-equipped soldiers died during that terrible winter simply because they no longer had the physical stamina to duck or run or even hold a rifle?

Arriving back at Kempten, I called Womeldorff and told him I was ready to head home. "Give me a couple of days, Lou," he said. "I'll have your orders ready." Then I got hold of Gist, who was also at Augsberg serving as the operations officer for the 453rd. "Spike, I need transportation to Paris," I said. "Can you fly me there?"

"Get yourself up here," he said. "I'll get us an airplane."

"See you in two days," I said. "I've got a few loose ends to tie up here."

Major Gibson could barely hide his joy at the news that he was going to move into the position as squadron commander for the 456th. He was another career military type who remained in Germany for some time after the war. When Col. Winingham assumed command of the Frankfurt Airdrome in August, he kept Gibson on his staff

Before leaving Kempten I wanted to show my appreciation to the enlisted men who were unceasingly faithful in their support of the squadron. I had a lot of respect for these men who endured blizzards, freezing rain, bitter cold and mud to keep us flying. These were the men who stood alongside the taxiway as I led the group on a mission and saluted me with a wave before I roared down the runway. They were there when I landed to go over the damage with me then patch things up for the next mission. God knows, they'd given every bit of talent and stamina to the cause. And they would remain behind doing whatever they were ordered to do, while I had the privilege of heading home whenever I chose.

I met with them for the last time in a large meeting room at the hotel that they had converted to an enlisted men's club. I don't remember exactly what I told them other than to thank them and to wish them good luck. As I was leaving, I spoke privately to the club president, Tech Sgt. Bedford M. McKenzie. "I want the men to have this," I said as I handed him an envelope. In it was a couple of month's pay I wanted donated to the club. Several weeks later I received this letter dated July 11, 1945.

> Lacking precedent, we, as representatives of the enlisted men of this squadron find a shortage of words to express the various thoughts that came to light as a result of the announcement telling of your fine gesture. No commanding officer that we have ever known has taken such a deep interest in us, and needless to add, you received a unanimous ovation in return. Therefore, the following named representatives take this opportunity of expressing, on behalf of the enlisted personnel of this squadron, a short but emphatic "thanks" and a wholesome wish for the best of luck in any and all of your future enterprises.
>
> T/Sgt. Bedford M. McKenzie, President
> T/Sgt. Vernon E. Brant, Vice President
> T/Sgt. Homer L. Vise, Secretary-Treasurer
> M/Sgt. Walter I. Werness, Board Member
> 1st Sgt. Joseph H. Elston, Honorary Board Member and Advisor

Their letter, neatly typed and signed, has remained among my treasured wartime artifacts.

Before I drove a jeep to Augsberg on the first leg of my journey home, Harlan and I said our farewells and thanks. He'd been overseas for more than two years, and had more points than any other ground personnel in the Ninth Air Force. He could have gone home, but his continued dedication to the group and his men motivated him to remain. When I arrived in Augsberg, Womeldorff and I shared a farewell drink together. The three of us—Harlan, Womeldorff and I—promised to stay in touch and get together back in the states. I can't recall if that really happened, but their legacy is what really matters. Both always put the interest of the group and its airmen ahead of any personal ambitions. I have never forgotten their support and friendship.

Gist was there to meet me with a beautiful Noorduyn Norseman C-64, not a woman, but a single engine Canadian built plane that could carry 10. This was the same type of plane in which Glenn Miller rode the night he was killed. Gist was his usual good-natured self. He introduced me to a young lieutenant, who wanted to check out in the Norseman. "You're riding in the back, Lou," said Gist. "I'm training." The day was beautiful. Perfect for arriving in Paris. They set up for a landing at Le Bourget northeast of the city. The problem was that the trainee was not ready

This Ju-52, a German transport plane, sat on the ramp at Le Bourget Airport when I arrived in Paris on the first leg of my trip home. The markings, including the Lorraine Cross, indicate that DeGaulle's Free French Air Force commandeered it. While visiting Berchtesgaden, I had been eager to take one for use by my squadron but changed my mind.

for the significant crosswind. We touched down, bounced, then dropped on the runway and swung violently to the left. We almost made a complete circle on one wheel which brought the wing dangerously close to the surface. "Christ, doesn't anybody know how to land in a crosswind," I hollered to my crew.

"Don't worry, Lou," Gist yelled over the engine. "This Cubbie just lost control."

"Yeah, but did you forget how to instruct?" I said half seriously. "I didn't survive the war only to be killed in the back of a plane flown by a junior birdman."

We taxied to a ramp where he and I got out and shook hands. "Hey, buddy," I shouted over the idling engine, "I really appreciate the ride. Take care of yourself. See you stateside." Unspoken was the recognition that four of us had begun the journey together from Dodge City. He and I were the lucky ones. Gist climbed aboard the Norseman, then saluted me from the right seat as they taxied to the runway for the flight back to Germany.

Maj. Chester "Spike" Gist became the squadron commander of the 453rd on August 16, 1945, when his predecessor, Maj. Robert Adams, was killed flying a German Gotha. When his duties ended sometime that fall, Gist headed home to Manhattan, Kansas. Nearly there, he hitched a ride on a B-25 headed to New Orleans. But the weather was bad, and the pilot crashed in Lake Pontchartrain, killing all onboard. Echoes of "Nothing but a Cubbie, Lou" still haunt me.

Fate took Gist, Farrell, Browning and my two good Washington and Lee classmates, Dabney and Boyce. That's the way it was. They were friends who served bravely and with honor. Their photos remind me of our youth and high-spirited antics. But as any soldier who has survived war knows, the sense of loss never goes away. I miss them and think of them often. That's the way it is.

I lay on the bottom of a bunk bed in one of the partitioned sections of what may have been a hall for sporting events. For a week, I was either unconscious or semiconscious. In between long periods of sleep, I must have nourished my body and cleaned myself, but I have no recollection of these things. At times, I was only vaguely aware of echoing voices and laughter. Then sleep once again overwhelmed my senses and drew me into a womb of unconsciousness.

After saying my farewell to Gist, I arrived in Paris only to discover that next troop ship back to New York wouldn't leave the port at Le Havre for nearly three weeks. In the meantime, I was housed at an Army Air Corps facility located in a beautiful park, a short ride from the Arc de Triomphe. Perhaps it was the Bois de Bologne, but I can't remember anymore. Knowing that I had an extended stay in Paris, I yielded to the luxury of sleep—the long rest my body and spirit craved.

Awakening after at least a week of rest, I had the feeling that I was starting life over again. The enthusiasms for drink and women that defined my previous visits to Paris were gone. I had no desire to sit in the bars of Montmartre. I couldn't walk the streets of the Left Bank. Instead, I preferred the safe places of my mother's

Paris, July 1945. I spent three weeks here while awaiting transport home. American military personnel were a common sight in the streets of Paris.

youth. Stepping off a military transport at the Arc de Triomphe, I made my way along the Champs-Élysées and settled into an outdoor café for coffee or an occasional drink with a couple of other officers. Except for the ubiquitous presence of American military, life in Paris was back to normal. The war was over, and the French went about the business of living.

I had a lot of time to think about my future. Once I arrived home in Ohio, I'd spend a month's leave with my family. I was eager to get out on the golf links with my sister Judy, who'd been playing since she was four. I wouldn't be able to beat her. But I might be there in time to celebrate her 17th birthday. She'd probably like me to bring her something from Paris.

After that, I didn't know what my orders would be. The war in the Pacific was still on. I was willing to serve there, if that's what was needed to bring the final end to the battles on islands with names I couldn't pronounce. When it was over, I could say that I served my country proudly and honorably. But the passion to prove myself as a combat pilot was spent.

I'd find a way to return to Washington and Lee and finish my senior year. I wondered how many of my classmates there and at Culver had been sacrificed to this war. It could take years to learn about all the casualties.

Right on schedule, the U.S.S. *West Point* steamed into Le Havre to pick up hundreds of us who were lucky enough to be heading back home. I was packing my things when a young airman who was staying at our makeshift barracks approached me and introduced himself.

"Major Rehr, I want to thank you for saving my life," he said.

Puzzled, I tried to recall his face.

"I'm the one who made you go around back there at Denain-Prouvy. I was lost, and all I wanted to do was land," he said. "Everybody could have been killed. I just want to say I'm sorry."

I remembered the incident, but the memory felt like something that happened a long time ago.

"We're both lucky. It's over, and we're going home."

Afterword: Remembrance and Reflection, October 2002

by Carleton Rockefeller Rehr

FRANCE: LAON-ATHIES AIRDROME

Grass sprouts wherever it finds cracks in what had been one of the main runways of the Laon-Athies airbase. It has been over 40 years since any military planes have flown in and out of here. But several thousand feet of wide concrete make this an ideal place for the obstacle course that a trucking school has set up to train its drivers. Ribbons of tire tread mar the surface. Dragsters, too, find this deserted airstrip useful for their sport.

"I taught my children to drive here," said our friend Jac Evrard, a retired veterinarian, whose family has lived in the town of Laon since the early 1900s. This day, he risks destroying the shocks in his Citroen as he navigates in and around large ruts that threaten to overwhelm the narrow perimeter road bordering the woods known as the Forêt de Samoussy.

This is our second visit to the abandoned Laon-Athies airbase from which the 323rd Bombardment Group flew missions during that difficult winter of 1944-45. The first time was 14 years ago in 1988. That's when we met Jac, who at the time helped us locate the site by giving us an aerial tour in his Cherokee Six aircraft, which was based at a nearby airport. We've been good friends ever since.

Jac, who was a teenager during the war, recalls that "flights of approaching bombers meant we were driving toward freedom." But there was a price to pay. Bombs destroyed the house built in 1919 by his father, a World War I calvaryman. After World War II, Jac's family rebuilt on the same spot. Today, he and his wife Jacline continue to live in this home.

Jac parks his car in this wooded area on the southernmost end of the base so we can survey the scene and make sense of what remains. "When the Germans occupied here, they hid their planes and ammunition throughout this forest," he said.

In October 1944, after Allied ground troops and bombers forced the Germans to retreat, the men of the 323rd Bombardment Group set up a tent city in these woods. As Lou's memoir shows, they fought not only a war, but also Europe's coldest winter in 100 years.

Of the six bases occupied by the 323rd during the last year of the war in Europe, this place holds the most poignant memories for Lou. There is no single event that defines his relationship with this place—just memories of a way of life that demanded an enormous expenditure of youthful spirit. With protracted autumn rains delaying the advance of the ground troops, the men of the 323rd no longer harbored any optimism for an early surrender by a retreating enemy. As Lou's memoir reveals, day to day life on this busted-up airfield was challenging, and the missions were dangerous—especially after the Germans mounted their offensive known as the Battle of the Bulge. Yet the resolve of these crews to support the ground forces in the Ardennes never faltered, even during the darkest days when it looked like the Germans would overrun this base and once again claim it as their own.

Today, the dense undergrowth and forest make it impossible to locate the elevated concrete slab that served as the floor for the Rehr crew's tent. In 1988, we discovered it in a sunny clearing surrounded by young trees. At that time, we even stood on the foundation of what was probably the squadron's mess hall.

Fourteen years later, nothing here is recognizable.

Jac drives the car along a taxiway where the potholes are not as treacherous. But it won't be long before neglect and nature render impassible all the hard surfaces of this World War II relic.

Several miles to the west, the ancient town of Laon rises abruptly out of the flat landscape. Atop the plateau, the five towers of the Cathedral of Notre Dame stretch heavenward as they have for nearly 800 years. At their highest point, the towers reach nearly 1,000 feet above the surrounding area. Lou mentions to Jac how much he depended on that landmark to predict changes in the weather when he led bombing missions from this runway.

"It's the same today," he said. Pilots flying in and out of the Laon-Chambry airfield, located northwest of town, still use these towers to help determine sky conditions.

We head back to Laon to admire its historic heart: the narrow cobblestoned streets, the 13th century cathedral with its oxen carvings adorning the towers—a tribute to the beasts that hauled the stone up steep paths—the courtyards and abbeys, and the view from the ramparts encircling the oldest part of town. Let the forest and grass reclaim the old airbase built by the Germans to launch their night fighters. What matters is that those who followed them, the young airmen of the 323rd Bombardment Group, played a role in restoring a way of life that has endured for centuries.

With the help of Jac and others who want to show their deep appreciation to the airmen of the 323rd Bomb Group, a permanent monument of remembrance will be erected in the nearby town of Samoussy.

THANKS, GIS

Keeping alive the memory of the Americans who fought for the liberation of France is not just the work of Jac and his generation who endured the occupation and rejoiced at the sight of the first GIs.

Lou and I were passengers on the train between Paris and Kaiserslautern, Germany. It stops at Metz, France, the ancient and heavily fortified city where Gen. George S. Patton's Third Army stalled out during the fall of 1944. German resistance was stiff, and unrelenting rains and dense clouds scrubbed mission after mission to targets in this area.

Just before our train stopped in Metz, a young Frenchman named Alain Gozzo began a conversation with us. He lives in Corny, a town on the Moselle River just southwest of Metz. When he heard that Lou was a B-26 Marauder pilot, he was overcome with joy. "You are our dear liberators. You are our heroes," he told Lou as he held his hand. "And we will never forget you."

Thanking World War II veterans for the liberation of France is more than a gesture for Alain. In 1998, his wife Elisabeth established an association called Thanks, GIs. One hundred members strong, this organization's mission is to perpetuate the memory of all the Americans who helped liberate France. Elisabeth's parents never forgot December 1944, when Gen. Patton's troops routed the last Germans from their defenses. They instilled in Elisabeth a deep appreciation for the sacrifices of the Americans. Alain's passion comes from his father's liberation from a concentration camp.

Among the association's activities is working with veterans' groups whose members wish to return to the battle sites. They have also renamed streets after the infantry divisions that liberated this part of France and erected commemorative markers. Every two years, the members organize an exhibition dedicated to the veterans, including fighter pilots and bomber crews. Presently, they are planning the development of a museum commemorating the liberation.

On March 2, 2002, Elisabeth, who is president of the association, was honored by the American Embassy in France for another significant project: the group's efforts to recover the remains of World War II soldiers and airmen declared missing in action and return them to their families. In her speech that day she said,

> There was a price to pay in terms of suffering and the spilling of blood which often ended in the loss of their lives. And among those who made the supreme sacrifice, there are still some who rest unknown in our soil where their lives were torn from them. Those soldiers who were reported as missing have not been forgotten, neither by their families, nor by their nation, nor, humbly, by us. We shall continue to offer them our homage by doing everything in our means to ensure that these brave heroes be returned to their country to rest in American soil close to those who remember them. That is the least we can do for them, who did so much for us.
>
> Today we are happy to be free and French. Never forget the terrible price paid for our freedom. Never forget those who made it possible.

Receipt from Flobert shop dated July 13, 1938.

3 BOULEVARD ST. MICHEL

Curiosity draws us to 3 Boulevard St. Michel in the Latin Quarter of Paris. We know this is the address of the gun shop that Lou visited before the war because he still has the receipt dated July 13, 1938, for the dueling pistols he bought from Monsieur and Madame Flobert.

We exit the St. Michel underground station and cross the street where a beautiful stone building, number 3, sits at the corner of a busy intersection near the banks of the Seine. Where their shop once stood, there is now a toney café called Saint Séverin, which on this day is offering specials like chicken caesar salad, grilled salmon and French onion soup. A yellow awning stretches over the outdoor tables and seats that are bolted to the sidewalk. Above, French windows open onto ornately carved balconies. After nearly 60 years, there is little that Lou recognizes.

That's OK. What remains are memories that we cherish. At this address, there once lived a couple who extended a welcome to two American teenagers. Those were the halcyon years, the late 1930s, before Hitler ordered his troops into Paris—before a young airman on leave from the war discovered the fate of the Floberts.

Appendix One:
Tributes to the Marauder

by Carleton Rockefeller Rehr

These endured all and gave all that justice among nations might prevail and that mankind might enjoy freedom and inherit peace.
United States Military Cemetery,
Colleville-sur-Mer, France

A steady rain falling throughout the night has left a cool, gray, mist hanging over the grounds of the American Military Cemetery at Omaha Beach. Few visitors wander the expansive grounds where the crosses and Stars of David face westward to the home country of the 9,387 soldiers who are remembered here—the men and a few women who "endured all and gave all" on this foreign soil. Paths lead to the historic beach below, where today the waves roll gently onto wide, sandy stretches.

This is a place where serenity and peace are perpetual. Even the gardeners and other workers do their jobs quietly and with respect for the sanctity of this ground. I notice several areas where they are digging, and ask a silly question. "Is it possible for others to be buried here?" The French gardener, who does not speak English, nevertheless, understands my question and shakes his head. However, from his words and gestures, I understand that sometimes families bring the ashes of a veteran here and scatter them in secret. I am not surprised. The bond that survivors have with those who died fighting alongside them seems to grow stronger as they reach the end of their lives.

What draws us here on this October morning is something else Lou wants to see again. On these sacred grounds is an image of the B-26 Marauder. It can be found inside a small chapel in the center of the cemetery. The circular ceiling is a complex mosaic, which according to the brochure depicts "America blessing her sons as they depart by sea and air to fight for freedom, and a grateful France bestowing a laurel wreath upon the American dead who gave their lives to liberate Europe's oppressed peoples." In the sky of this mosaic is a twin-engine bomber with that unmistakable cigar shape. Flying near the Marauder is a single-engine fighter, a P-47, the "little friends" who protected these bombers when German fighter aircraft threatened.

For several years, this photo of Lou Rehr and his crew standing in front of *Ole 33 Gal* was used by Sporty's Pilot Shop to advertise military flight jackets. The caption read: *Our good customer, Louis Rehr, was kind enough to send us this 1944 photo of his crew in their original military flight jackets. These brave men were group lead in the 323red medium bomb group, 456th squadron. From left to right they are: Victor Jacobs, Louis Rehr, Frank Burgmeier and James Siegling.*

Just across the channel from here, there is another artistic rendering of Marauders that recognizes the significant role they played in the war. The centerpiece of the D-Day Museum in Southsea, England, is "The Overlord Embroidery." This 272 feet long needlework depicts in remarkable detail scenes spanning the period from the London Blitz in 1940 to the retreat of the Germans from Normandy in late summer 1944. Panel 26 shows a flight of Marauders, the yellow tails from the 386th, sweeping over the Cotentin Peninsula shortly after D-Day. In the last panel, number 34, a British infantry platoon walks along a tree-lined road heading east to the front. They pass a mother and her family kneeling over the body of a dead son, someone the Germans suspected of working with the Resistance.

Overhead, woven into the sky, are a couple of Marauders, suggesting the ubiquitous presence of these bombers over France.

There is another place where the Marauders and their crews will always be remembered—Utah Beach, the westernmost landing beach. On June 6, 1944, the 323rd and five other Marauder groups hammered the German shore positions here minutes before the 4th Infantry Division, 23,000 strong, came ashore. To remember the role the Marauders played in minimizing the casualties here at Utah Beach on that historic day, this memoir includes the perspective of Lt. Frank Burgmeier, lead navigator for the 456th Bombardment Squadron, who would later become part of the Rehr crew.

This is our first visit to Utah Beach, where the natural beauty of this stretch of coastline lies undisturbed. We survey the flat expanse of sand and water from behind a barbed wire fence that protects the dunes grown thick with grass. It is low tide, and the waves lapping the shore are at least a quarter of a mile away. The scope of the landscape dwarfs a couple walking along this beach, which was once known by the beautiful name La Madeleine. That was before Adolf Hitler's armies built the antitank wall and the ugly network of pillboxes and bunkers. Before they laid tank traps and land mines to defend his right to occupy Europe. Before this place became immortalized as Utah Beach.

There is a small museum here, which is built around one of the bunkers. Charles de Vallavieille, a former mayor of the nearby village of Saint-Marie-du-Mont is responsible in large part for preserving the history of the D-Day landings here. His village was the first town liberated by seaborne troops.

Inside, a museum guide, Patrice Dallet, greets us. He does not ask if Lou is a World War II veteran. He just knows, and invites him to sign a book and tour the museum. Among the exhibits is a copy of Maj. Gen. John Moench's book *Marauder Men*, which is the history of the 323rd Bombardment Group—another valuable resource for the writing of this book.

The original Rehr crew missed participating in D-Day—or "the big one" as the fraternities of men who participated in the invasion like to call it—but only by a few days. Everyone understood the historic significance of the moment and the sacrifices that had to be made. "I would have liked to have been there," said Lou. "But there was so much more to come."

Appendix Two:
Biographies

by Carleton Rockefeller Rehr

For several years in the early 1990s, Sporty's Pilot Shop, which publishes catalogs for pilots, included the photograph of Lou and his crew standing in front of *Ole 33 Gal* (see page 200). The idea was Lou's. He sent the photo to Hal Shevers, the founder and chairman of the company, with the suggestion that if he were going to sell "authentic military flight jackets," he should use a picture of what guys really wore back in World War II. Shevers agreed—on one condition. Lou had to get model releases from the other three men. This is how bombardier Victor Jacobs, navigator Frank Burgmeier, and copilot Jim Siegling found each other again.

Capt. Victor E. Jacobs

Victor E. Jacobs—Jake—lived in San Francisco, where for nearly 50 years, he was in the court reporting business. We could never get him to travel east for the occasional reunion dinners we had with Frank and Jim—although we always phoned to say that we missed him. However, Lou and I made sure that on our yearly vacation to Hawaii, we switched planes at San Francisco International Airport. For several years, Jake caught a bus from his North Beach neighborhood so he could be there at the gate waving and greeting us with big hugs. He was handsome with white hair and mustache, and he always wore a black leather jacket. We'd sit in one of those airport bars and have a drink together and "talk story" for an hour or so before we boarded another plane for Honolulu.

One weekend, on a whim, we flew to San Francisco to have dinner with him. At the time, he was very involved with volunteer work, especially helping victims of the 1989 earthquake. Our last meeting was in December 1993. He looked tired, and it was clear that making this journey to the airport had sapped his strength. He died five months later of lung cancer. Once more, Lou and I flew to San Francisco, where Lou delivered an eloquent eulogy at his memorial service. His niece, Ann Hanson, displayed artifacts of his military service including his Distinguished Flying Cross for the Merzig mission. Over the years, he'd lost the original medal. Thanks to Lou's efforts, this was a replacement presented to him on June 21, 1989. Lou also read a moving tribute from

Frank Burgmeier: "Victor was the ultimate professional. None was steadier on a bomb run, and he was the best bombardier I had ever flown with."

Lt. Frank Burgmeier

Frank Burgmeier and Tedi were married in July 1943, just days before he left for his tour of duty as a navigator with the 323rd Bombardment Group. He kept a diary, which was invaluable in the writing of this memoir. As his entries show, he spent nearly every evening writing letters to her. But according to Tedi, she received only half of them. What did arrive was so censored that all she really knew was that he was alive when he wrote the letter.

When Frank shipped overseas during the late summer of 1943, Tedi returned to her home in Syracuse, New York. Working as a senior cost accountant at a factory and training her horse Copper King for hunts and dressage exhibitions kept her from dwelling on her fears. She rode every day, before and after work, even during the bitterest cold days of the Upstate New York winters.

When Frank arrived home after a year and a half of separation, they quickly discovered how the war had changed them both. "We had led separate lives that had to be put together again," said Tedi. "I had a very responsible job, and Copper was my life." She added that it did not take her long to realize that Frank "was not the same as when he left."

Frank remembers this time as "a period of withdrawal. My close tent buddies, my crew, and the entire squadron had been my family for over a year," he said. Instead of feeling great joy at the reunion with his wife, Frank notes that he "arrived here in a somewhat dulled and confused state."

Their separate lives came together again during a vacation spent at a beautiful military rest camp in the mountains near Asheville, North Carolina. This was a place where the officers who had been at war met daily with flight surgeons to help them adjust to civilian life. It was a vacation, military style. Tedi recalls this time as pleasant, except "I was not used to bed checks and lights shining in the window." Frank remembers "starting to feel human again thanks to my patient and understanding wife."

Today, the Burgmeiers still live in Upstate New York and are partners in a public relations firm that bears Frank's name. On November 27, 2002, New York Senator Charles Schumer presented Frank with the Distinguished Flying Cross for the November 19, 1944, mission to Merzig. After returning home from the war, he never received it. Moving forward with his life was more important than pursuing a medal from the past. But years after the reunion of the Rehr crew, he recalled a diary entry dated November 22, 1944, that said, "Heard today that Jake, Rehr and I are to be put in for DFC's for Sunday's mission."

As his commanding officer on the Merzig mission, Lou wrote a letter and submitted documentation in support of the award. The full story of Frank's role in this important mission is told in Chapter 7.

Fifty-eight years later, Tedi pinned the ribbon holding the bronze cross, engraved with a four-bladed propeller on his jacket as their three children, six grandchildren, Frank's brother and friends looked on with pride.

Of that day, Frank said, "When Senator Schumer asked me if I wanted to make comments, I thanked him and his staff for doggedly seeing this project through." But as he attempted to thank others, he choked up. "All I could do is end with a thumbs up gesture that my five year old grandson and I always exchange," he said. "And it was over."

Lt. Col. James Siegling

The last time, we saw Lt. Col. Jim Siegling was at Lou's retirement party June 5, 1999. He drove the three hours from his home in Pennsylvania to celebrate Lou's 60 years of flying.

The photos of Jim in Lou's wartime album show a guy who could have been a movie star. Thick, dark, wavy hair enhanced his handsomely chiseled face. Fifty-four years later, he still had a full head of silver hair. Age had softened the sharper features of his youth, but he was still a handsome man.

As a copilot in Lou's squadron, he flew 34 combat missions. After VE Day, he did not follow Lou into Germany for the disarmament. Instead, he was transferred to the 397th Bombardment Group and then to the 387th before arriving back in the states in early September 1945.

He remained in the service and eventually became an aircraft commander on a B-47. During the Korean War, he was stationed in Japan at Iwakuni Air Base near Hiroshima.

After the B-47 was phased out, he was sent to Travis AFB in California, where he became a C-124 Globemaster aircraft commander. He made frequent flights in the Globemaster to Vietnam until he received a yearlong assignment there for duty at Danang Air Base. Returning to the states, he continued to fly the Globemaster to Spain and Europe from Dover AFB in Delaware. After working at the headquarters for the USAF at the Pentagon, he retired in May 1, 1970.

Jim is modest when speaking about his military career, which spanned three wars. Although he lives in Pennsylvania, he often spoke about moving to New Mexico, where he was born. On vacations, he and his wife Olga would look for houses there, but they never followed through. Now Jim's failing health is keeping both of them close to home.

"You can't look back," he said.

The crew photo in Sporty's also brought letters from men who had flown with Lou. Lt. George Wolfe, photographer for the 456th, who shot the only known photo of Marauders under attack by ME-262s from the back of Lou's plane, wrote to remind him of that Memmingen mission. He wanted Lou to know, "I have not forgotten the good things you did for me. Thanks for picking me up at that airfield somewhere in Belgium after that episode at Wesel. You may have forgotten all about that, but it still sticks with me. The memories are hard to erase." Lou remembers picking him up but not the details of the incident.

Maj. Ken Brown, another pilot who flew in Lou's squadron, wrote Sporty's asking that they forward a note and some World War II photos to Lou. Most of the photos were taken while setting up tents and digging slit trenches at Lessay. He noted that they depict the "not so glamorous side of combat flying." He also included a photo of himself in a flying jacket "so he may remember me."

Lt. Col. Joseph Searle

Much to Lou's regret, he lost touch with Joe Searle, his copilot and close friend during the war. Recently, thanks to the Internet, we found him living happily in Albany, Georgia.

Joe was recalled to active duty in 1948 and continued to serve as an Air Force pilot until his retirement from the military in 1966

with the rank of lieutenant colonel. Toward the end of his career, he flew 40 B-52 missions over Vietnam. Launched from Guam, these missions lasted 12 hours and required aerial refueling over the Philippines. Twenty-one years after World War II, he was still flying dangerous and difficult missions.

When he retired in late 1966, he returned to school to earn both bachelor's and master's degrees. He taught high school history until his second retirement in 1982. Then he and his wife Vera, whom he married before he joined the Rehr crew, traveled throughout the U.S. in their Airstream travel trailer. With pride, he notes that they have "three wonderful grown children," four grandchildren and one great-grandchild.

Recalling what it was like to fly with Lou, he said, "Lou created a spirit among the crew that made us really want to fly the mission and feel disappointed if we had to abort. He was the best there was."

Lt. Col. John Guldemond

John Guldemond's wife Edythe, whom he married in May 1943, is one of those people who reads every inch of a newspaper including the transfers of property. In 1984 she saw a name that she'd heard John mention when he recalled his war years: Louis Rehr. A year later, she saw an article about a glider business Lou and I had at Somerset Airport in Bedminster, New Jersey. That's when the two of them showed up at the airport to surprise Lou. At the time, they lived only 10 minutes from our New Jersey home.

John shipped overseas shortly after he and Edythe married. On D-Day, he flew as a copilot for the 456th. Shortly after, he moved into the left seat. His tour overseas ended in January 1945, but because of the difficulty of finding transport home, he remained in England until March.

John served in the Air Force Reserves and retired as a lieutenant colonel. He also had a successful career as the chief electrical engineer at a New Jersey company, Research Cotrell. But his heart was always with the Marauders. For over 20 years, he attended squadron and class (43D) reunions. A couple of these were held at Earls Colne, at the site of the old airbase, now occupied by an estate, a business park and a flight school. He and Edythe also organized a couple of local reunions, that included navigator Joe Lazar, who was the Gee navigator on the memorable February 14, 1945, mission, and pilot Charles Rothschild, who was in Lou's squadron. On Memorial Day, we often invited John and Edythe for dinner. Lou would stand next to the American flag that hung outside out home and greet John with a scotch.

Age has limited John's mobility these days, but throughout his life he has kept alive the spirit of the Marauder and the men who flew this bomber.

Lt. Col. Ross E. Harlan

By the time Major Ross Harlan headed home in September 1945, he had been overseas for 2½ years, longer than any other airman in the Ninth Air Force. "I did not want to leave until it was all over," he said.

Today he lives in Oklahoma City, Oklahoma, where throughout his life, he has distinguished himself as a businessman, writer, and speaker.

In January 1985, he retired as a senior vice president of Oklahoma Gas and Electric Company. In addition to the five years he served on active duty during World War II, he spent 35 years in the Air Force Reserves and National Guard 45th Infantry Division.

Shortly after the war, he published *Strikes*, a short text and photographic history of the 323rd Bombardment Group, which was also a valuable resource for the writing of this book. Following his retirement, he was a contributing writer to a *Readers Digest* publication entitled *Off the Beaten Path*, with articles about tourist destinations in Oklahoma, Arkansas and Kansas. He continues to be in demand as a public speaker. Twice, the Freedoms Foundation of Valley Forge has awarded him the George Washington Honor Medal—first in 1970 for his speech "What's Right with America" and again in 2002 for the hundreds of patriotic speeches and other efforts of behalf of his church, community, country, and especially for the disabled. In 1985, Toastmasters International presented him with the annual Leadership and Communication Award for the State of Oklahoma.

Throughout his life, he has served as president and trustee on numerous councils and boards. Presently, he is a board member with the Center of Family Love, a residential and vocational services provider for developmentally disabled adults. For 53 years, he has been an active member of the Putnam City United Methodist Church, where he teaches adult Sunday school classes.

Fifty-nine years ago, he married a Shreveport, Louisiana, woman named Margaret Burns. They have three sons and a daughter, 14 grandchildren and four great-grandchildren.

His achievements come as no surprise to Lou, who has never forgotten how Ross's organizational and managerial skills enabled him to focus on flying missions.

"We also enjoyed some good times together," said Lou.

Ross adds that during his tenure as ground executive officer for the 456th, he delegated the administrative paperwork to a very capable 1st Sgt. Joseph Elston. Joe's name appears on the letter of thanks Lou received after the war from his enlisted men in Kempten. Ross tells us they have remained friends and that Joe is living an active life in Louisiana.

It also comes as no surprise that after all these years, Ross has preserved an extraordinary collection of photographs and memorabilia from his extended tenure with the 323rd Bomb Group. Some of his photos that appear here have not been published before.

In a recent conversation with Lou he said, "It was a pleasure and great honor to serve with you. You were a great pilot and splendid commander."

Lt. Col. James E. Womeldorff

Lou's wartime album has several pictures of Lt. Col. James Womeldorff, the group's executive officer. In his late 30s when he served, "Chief" looked out for his men, like a father. Photos taken right after VE Day show the camaraderie as he poses with his arms around the shoulders of friends from the 456th. Others show him and Harlan—friends from the time they shared a Nissen hut back at Earls Colne—standing on a deserted road somewhere in the snow covered Austrian Alps, crossing a flimsy suspension bridge spanning a racing river, and standing in St. Marks Square in Venice. The war was over, and it was time to enjoy life.

As the 323rd's executive officer, he was always sensitive to the needs of his men, especially during the disarmament duty. After Lou headed home, the airmen of the 323rd

who were left behind faced at least six more months of disarmament duty. To keep up the morale, Chief instituted a newsletter, *The 323rd Observer*, aimed at keeping families and friends informed about the postwar life of loved ones in Germany. Headlines like "Buddies Greet Ex POW," and "Group Ends ETO Combat Operations with Outstanding Record" were typical. The newsletter also ran a column called "What Do You Think?" in which the men spoke mainly of what they wanted to do when their duty ended.

In September 1945, when it looked like going home would happen sooner than later, he once again found a way to return to Venice, not for an overnight but an extended trip of 10 days. In postwar comments printed in *Marauder Men*, he notes that Venice had become a "rest and return" place for the British, but he carried some intelligence credentials that enabled him to talk his way into the city. Once again he stayed in a hotel overlooking St. Marks Square and rode the canals with a singing gondolier. He returned to Germany via the Brenner Pass so he could visit his men from the 454th, who were on duty at Innsbruck, Austria.

After his wartime duties, Jim Womeldorff came home to Little Rock, Arkansas, where he was a successful investment banker underwriting and selling municipal bonds. Occasionally, when Ross Harlan was in town, they'd get together and talk about the war years.

For a while, Lou corresponded with his good friend and mentor and then lost touch. According to Ross, Jim "Chief" Womeldorff died in the early 1990s.

2nd Lt. William A.M. Dabney

Located on the grounds of Duxford Airport at Duxford, England, is the American Air Museum in Britain, a magnificent structure built in the shape of an aircraft hanger. Part of its purpose is to honor the aircraft and crews that flew missions from England during World War II. Etched in glass panels outside are figures of aircraft representing every U.S. military plane lost while flying from English bases: 6,346 from the Eighth Air Force; 692 from the Ninth Air Force; 24 from the U.S. Navy.

Inside, beyond the impressive displays of aircraft, is the Georgia Frontiere Gallery listing the names of the 30,000 American airmen who were killed flying from England. When we first visited the museum in 1998, the name of Lou's good friend from cadet training, William A. M. Dabney, was missing from the Roll of Honour. He was an American Spitfire pilot, who was killed on August 19, 1942, during the air battle over Dieppe.

Once again using the power of the Internet, we contacted Graham Thompson, who at the time was the museum's Exhibitions Assistant for the Department of Interpretation. We also sent him Bill's obituary and a copy of the letter Bill wrote Lou one month before he died.

Shortly after, we received information assuring us that his name would be added to the replacement panels to be installed by the end of the year 2000. Mr. Thompson also provided the following information:

Name:	William Alexander Miller Dabney
Rank:	2nd Lt.
Hometown:	Lynchburg, VA
Unit:	308th Fighter Squadron, 31st Fighter Group
Aircraft:	Spitfire Mk V (serial unknown)
Date:	19 August 1942
Fate:	KIA
Awards:	Air Medal, Purple Heart Medal
Memorial:	Ardennes American Cemetery, Neuville-en-Condroz, Belgium

Knowing how important it would be for any of his family still living in the Lynchburg area to know that his name is among the honored, we contacted an ABC television affiliate there, and they ran the story on the evening news. Shortly after, his widow, Kitty, called us to say thanks. She had remarried Bolling Hobbs, a friend whom she and Bill knew in high school. The Hobbs still live in Lynchburg.

In a recent letter, she mentioned the death of Lt. Robert Boyce, Lou's other close friend from cadet training, who was killed in a training accident shortly after graduation from Kelly Field.

"Will and I were in Orlando when Bob was killed," she wrote. "We both loved him very much. We escorted his body home [to

Ohio] to his lovely, lovely parents—they were heartbroken to lose their beautiful son but became very good friends to us."

Four months later, they must have been heartbroken again over the loss of Kitty's "Will," whom she calls "a wonderful, wonderful, fun person." Lou agrees.

Lt. Col. Louis S. Rehr

When Lou returned home from the war, he finished his senior year at Washington and Lee University. Although his diploma is dated June 1, 1946, the university considers him a graduate of the Class of 1942.

Lou spent his life flying, although his Marauder experiences made him something of a maverick. He chose not to sign on with a major airline like Eastern or Pan Am. Instead he took up farming 400 acres in South Florida, and he flew everything he could get his hands on. He used the GI Bill to add ratings to his civilian license, including helicopter and seaplane.

In early 1946, he bought a Seversky P-35, the forerunner to the P-47, and flew it around south Florida until maintenance problems took the fun out of it. Somebody he knew owned a Marauder that had escaped the meltdown. According to Owen Gassaway, the fixed base operator at Palm Beach County Park Airport since 1945, it sat for a long time on a short grass strip called Sunny South, which was located within the city limits of Miami. One day, Lou flew that Marauder out of there, and nobody could figure out how he did it. Lou recalls nothing remarkable about taking off in the Marauder. What he does remember were the federal agents waiting to impound the bomber after he landed so it could not be delivered to Central America.

His desire for high adventure led him to a business partnership with a Brazilian pilot and banker named Renato Arens. From 1946 to 1963, Lou periodically ferried single and twin-engine aircraft to Brazil for sale to industrialists and plantation owners—classic models like the Beech Staggerwing, Howard DGA, Stearman, AT-6, Stinson Reliant, Bamboo Bomber, Pawnee and various models of Beech Bonanzas and Piper twins. The 5,000-mile journey over open water and jungles usually began at Gassaway's airport at Lantana, Florida, and ended at Congonas Airport in São Paulo, Brazil.

To reach Brazil, Lou navigated along the same southern route that he and other World War II pilots followed. But there were no navigational aids or dependable weather forecasting services. He relied on recognizing landmarks, following a compass and occasionally picking up signals from outposts north of the Amazon, often with a hand held low frequency Zenith radio. In between these ferry flights, he flew for a "variety of outfits," including the Air Force Reserves.

Throughout his 60 years of flying, he has been an air transport pilot for the Flying Tiger Line and Modern Air Transport, a corporate pilot, charter pilot, tow pilot for gliders and crop dusting pilot. When he retired at age 80, he was still a flight instructor and designated examiner for the Federal Aviation Administration giving private, commercial, multi-engine and instrument tests.

As he points out in his memoir, he flew his first glider shortly after VE Day while on disarmament duty in Germany. He took up the sport of sailplane flying in earnest in the late 1950s and won two national championships—one as part of a three man team in Bishop, California, in 1958, and the other in 1968 as the standard class champion at Elmira, New York. He holds one of the first international Gold Badges in soaring, number 62. While living in Florida, he raised the bar for sailplane pilots in that state with a number of "first" flights, for example flying from one coast of Florida to the other. In August 1965, he completed a diamond goal flight (300 km), and in May 1970, he flew a diamond distance flight (500 km) which was actually 420 miles from south Florida to Tifton, Georgia.

Still adventurous at age 79, he accepted an invitation from a New Jersey pilot he had trained, Clifford Evans, to fly across the North Atlantic from Morristown, New Jersey, to Cardiff, Wales, in a single-engine Mooney Bravo. He couldn't have been happier squeezing into the cockpit of the Mooney while wearing a bulky suit meant for surviving in the frigid waters of the North Atlantic in case they had to ditch. Within two days of his return to New Jersey, he hopped into an AT-6, the advanced World War II trainer, belonging to his good friend Dan Dameo, and flew it to the Wings of Eagles Airshow in Elmira, New York.

Like many of his generation, Lou has always been reluctant to speak of his wartime experiences, even to one of his aviation heroes, Gen. Jimmy Doolittle. Once in the early 1980s at a luncheon at the Wings Club in New York, Lou had the opportunity to shake hands with the general, who was responsible for convincing the Army Air Corps commanders that the Marauder was a formidable weapon if flown by experienced pilots and maintained by trained mechanics.

"Did you fly with me?" asked Gen. Doolittle as he studied Lou's face.

"No sir," said Lou. "But in 1932, I saw you fly the Gee Bee racer at Cleveland."

That was true. A wide-eyed 13 year old named Lou Rehr was in the audience when Gen. Doolittle won the Thompson Trophy flying the highly unstable 800 hp Gee Bee R-1 racer, which mastered the course at speeds close to 300 mph. Perhaps a combination of awe and modesty kept Lou from mentioning their connection with the Marauder.

Over the years, most people who flew with Lou had only a vague idea that he was a World War II pilot. Now his memoir brings clarity to his role as a Marauder man. One thing for certain, however, is that anybody who flew with him—students, aircrews, passengers, flight test applicants—knew there was something extraordinary about this cool headed, speak-only-when-necessary man, who still loves the sky and all the challenges that it presents.

The Marauder

Between 1940 and 1945, the Martin Company produced 5,266 Marauders. Today, only six airframes survive, and only one of these still flies. It belongs to collector Kermit Weeks and is on display at his Fantasy of Flight museum in Polk City, Florida. It is one of three recovered many years after several Marauders crash-landed in British Columbia in January 1942. One of these is under restoration at the Empire State Aerosciences Museum at the Schenectady County Airport in New York. The other is undergoing restoration at the Military Aircraft Preservation Society at Akron-Canton Airport, Ohio. These projects will require several more years to complete.

A beautifully restored Marauder stands in the Concorde Hall of the Air and Space Museum outside Paris at Le Bourget Airport. It is the only one in Europe.

The most exciting news is that sometime between 2005 and 2007, the U.S. National Air and Space Museum will complete the restoration of its venerable *Flak Bait* and put it on display in the new Steven F. Udvar-Hazy facility at Dulles Airport, Chantilly, Virginia. The front section of this Marauder has sat for years in the National Air and Space Museum in Washington, D.C. During the war, it belonged to the 322nd Bombardment Group's 449th Squadron and is the survivor of 202 missions, more than any other bomber in World War II.

Another survivor can be seen at the Air Force Museum in Dayton, Ohio. Although it belonged to the Free French Air Force at the end of the war, its restoration with its striped tail looks like a model flown by the 387th Bomb Group.

These restorations stand as permanent tributes to the heroism, sacrifices and spirit of all Marauder men and their beloved aircraft.

Appendix Three: Citations Received

Distinguished Flying Cross (19 November 1944)

For extraordinary achievement in aerial flight on 19 November 1944. Capt. Rehr served as pilot and box leader of a B-26 type aircraft in an attack upon a heavily defended target in Germany. When accurate visual bombing was rendered impossible because of poor visibility, Capt. Rehr, despite intense antiaircraft fire, led his box in two complete turns at the completion of which he was six thousand feet below the briefed altitude. Fully cognizant of the danger involved Capt. Rehr nevertheless made a forty-five second bombing run to allow the bombardier to make necessary corrections and led his box to bomb the objective with unusual precision.

Distinguished Flying Cross (14 February 1945)

Louis S. Rehr, Maj. Air Corps, 323rd Bombardment Group. For extraordinary achievement while participating as pilot and box leader of a B-26 type aircraft in aerial flight against the enemy. On 14 February 1945, when heavy clouds totally obscured the target at the briefed altitude, Maj. Rehr elected to descend to 3000 feet in withering antiaircraft fire, and although his right engine was knocked out shortly before bombs away, bombed visually and with such precision that a vital enemy supply concentration was greatly damaged and destroyed. His outstanding airmanship in keeping his formation tightly together despite the existing hazards, and his devotion to duty are in keeping with the highest traditions of the Army Air Forces.

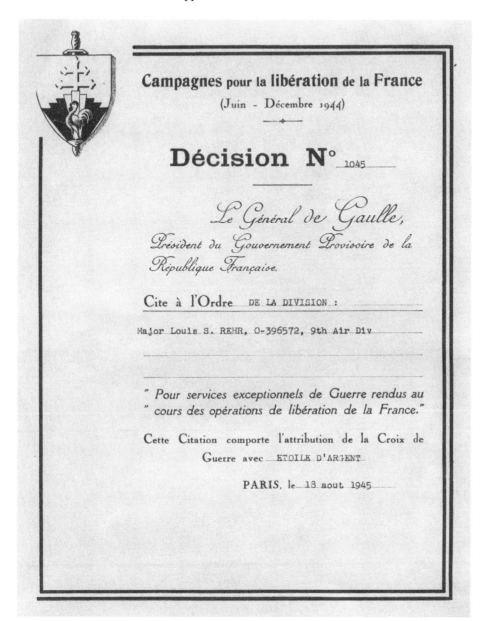

Croix de Guerre

Campagnes pour la libération de la France (Juin–Décembre 1944)

Décision No 1045

Le Général de Gaulle, Président du Gouvernement Provisoire de la République Française, cite à l'Ordre de la Division:

Major Louis S. Rehr, 9th Air Div

"Pour services exceptionnels de Guerre rendus au cours des opérations de libération de la France."

Cette Citation comporte l'attribution de la Croix de Guerre avec Etoile d'Argent

Paris, le 18 août 1945

Military History of Louis S. Rehr

Louis S. Rehr began his military life at 14 when he entered Indiana's Culver Military Academy, known as the "West Point of secondary schools." Even during the Depression, Culver maintained its long tradition of preparing young men for college while training them to be dedicated soldiers and patriotic citizens.

Before he graduated in 1938, Rehr distinguished himself as a cadet in the mounted Field Artillery unit by earning a position in its honor organization known as the Four Gun Drill Team. In 1936, he also won the national rifle championship for military schools. With additional summer training at Fort Knox, Kentucky, he graduated as a second lieutenant.

Although Rehr held a commission in the Field Artillery, his dream was to become an Army Air Corps pilot. During the summer of 1940, he was accepted into the government initiated Civilian Pilot Training Program, which was established in response to the growing threat of war abroad. He trained at Ohio's Cleveland Airport, where the year before, he soloed his first aircraft. By summer's end he earned his private license.

During Rehr's junior year at Washington and Lee University, Army Air Corps recruiters visited the campus, and he jumped at the opportunity to sign up. He was inducted into the Corps in July 1941, five months before the bombing of Pearl Harbor.

The Culver experience with its emphasis on dedication to duty and responsible leadership guided Rehr throughout his military service. At his graduation from primary flight school at Hicks Field, Fort Worth, Texas, he was awarded the Military Achievement Award given by the World War I Flyers of Fort Worth. After completing his basic training at Goodfellow Field, San Angelo, Texas, and advanced training at Kelly Field, San Antonio, Texas, he earned his wings on February 13, 1942—the Class of 42B.

Following graduation, he remained at Kelly as an advanced instructor. Six months later he transferred to Waco, Texas, to train advanced students in twin-engine aircraft. Motivated by a desire to be assigned to a combat unit, he volunteered to instruct in the Martin B-26 Marauder, despite this bomber's reputation as a "winged coffin."

"Sure the Marauder was faster, heavier and noisier than anything I'd flown before," he said. "But I was convinced that flying it for the first time would not be a terrifying event."

Beginning in February 1943, he spent nearly a year as a Marauder instructor at Del Rio, Texas, and Dodge City, Kansas. Finally, in January 1944, his commanders approved his repeated requests for transfer to a combat unit. His orders were to report for transitional training at Barksdale Field, Shreveport, Louisiana. By the time he arrived in England in May 1944, Capt. Rehr had over 2,000 hours of flight time, half of those in the Marauder.

He served overseas from June 1944 to July 1945 with the 323rd Bombardment Group, also known as the "White Tailed Marauders." Assigned to the 456th Bombardment Squadron, Rehr became its assistant operations officer in December 1944, then operations officer the following month. From February to July 1945, Major Rehr held the position of squadron commander.

During his combat duty, he flew 60 missions, 23 of which were group or box leads. Rehr earned 12 air medals and five battle stars for campaigns in Normandy, Northern France, Rhineland, Ardennes-Alsace, and Central Europe. He was awarded two Distinguished Flying Crosses for bombing missions flown over Germany on November 19, 1944, and again on February 14, 1945. He is also the recipient of the French Croix de Guerre with Silver Star. His bomb group earned a Distinguished Unit Citation for its extraordinary bombing successes from December 24 to 27 during the Battle of the Bulge. After VE Day, he directed the aircraft disarmament activities at Kempten, Germany, until his return home in July 1945.

Rehr served with the Air Force Reserves until 1958 when he was discharged with the rank of lieutenant colonel.

Index